A Text Book Of

LABOUR LAWS III

For
MPM Semester - III

SHARAD D. GEET
M.A. (Eco.), M.Com., LL.B., D.C.L.
NASHIK.

AMIT DESHPANDE
B.E. (Production), M.B.A.
Director, Sai Associates
SATARA.

ASMITA A. DESHPANDE
B.Com., M.B.A.,
Manager (Finance), Akur Industries
PUNE.

N2115

LABOUR LAWS III : MPM (Part - II, Semester - II) (Course 305)   ISBN 978-93-5164-056-1
First Edition : July 2014
© : **Authors**

The text of this publication, or any part thereof, should not be reproduced or transmitted in any form or stored in any computer storage system or device for distribution including photocopy, recording, taping or information retrieval system or reproduced on any disc, tape, perforated media or other information storage device etc., without the written permission of Authors with whom the rights are reserved. Breach of this condition is liable for legal action.

Every effort has been made to avoid errors or omissions in this publication. In spite of this, errors may have crept in. Any mistake, error or discrepancy so noted and shall be brought to our notice shall be taken care of in the next edition. It is notified that neither the publisher nor the authors or seller shall be responsible for any damage or loss of action to any one, of any kind, in any manner, therefrom.

Published By :
NIRALI PRAKASHAN
Abhyudaya Pragati, 1312, Shivaji Nagar,
Off J.M. Road, PUNE – 411005
Tel - (020) 25512336/37/39, Fax - (020) 25511379
Email : niralipune@pragationline.com

Printed By :
Repro Knowledgecast Limited,
Thane

DISTRIBUTION CENTRES
PUNE

Nirali Prakashan
119, Budhwar Peth, Jogeshwari Mandir Lane
Pune 411002, Maharashtra
Tel : (020) 2445 2044, 66022708, Fax : (020) 2445 1538
Email : nirallocal@pragationline.com

Nirali Prakashan
S. No. 28/27, Dhyari,
Near Pari Company, Pune 411041
Tel : (020) 24690204, Fax : (020) 24690316
Email : bookorder@pragationline.com

MUMBAI
Nirali Prakashan
385, S.V.P. Road, Rasdhara Co-op. Hsg. Society Ltd.,
Girgaum, Mumbai 400004, Maharashtra
Tel : (022) 2385 6339 / 2386 9976, Fax : (022) 2386 9976
Email : niralimumbai@pragationline.com

DISTRIBUTION BRANCHES

NAGPUR
Pratibha Book Distributors
Above Maratha Mandir, Shop No. 3, First Floor,
Rani Jhanshi Square, Sitabuldi, Nagpur 440012,
Maharashtra, Tel : (0712) 254 7129

JALGAON
Nirali Prakashan
34, V. V. Golani Market, Navi Peth, Jalgaon 425001,
Maharashtra, Tel : (0257) 222 0395
Mob : 94234 91860

BENGALURU
Pragati Book House
House No. 1, Sanjeevappa Lane, Avenue Road Cross,
Opp. Rice Church, Bengaluru – 560002.
Tel : (080) 64513344, 64513355,
Mob : 9880582331, 9845021552
Email: bharatsavla@yahoo.com

KOLHAPUR
Nirali Prakashan
New Mahadvar Road,
Kedar Plaza, 1st Floor Opp. IDBI Bank
Kolhapur 416 012, Maharashtra. Mob : 9855046155

CHENNAI
Pragati Books
9/1, Montieth Road, Behind Taas Mahal, Egmore,
Chennai 600008 Tamil Nadu, Tel : (044) 6518 3535,
Mob : 94440 01782 / 98450 21552 / 98805 82331, Email : bharatsavla@yahoo.com

RETAIL OUTLETS
PUNE

Pragati Book Centre
157, Budhwar Peth, Opp. Ratan Talkies,
Pune 411002, Maharashtra
Tel : (020) 2445 8887 / 6602 2707, Fax : (020) 2445 8887

Pragati Book Centre
Amber Chamber, 28/A, Budhwar Peth,
Appa Balwant Chowk, Pune : 411002, Maharashtra,
Tel : (020) 20240335 / 66281669
Email : pbcpune@pragationline.com

Pragati Book Centre
676/B, Budhwar Peth, Opp. Jogeshwari Mandir,
Pune 411002, Maharashtra
Tel : (020) 6601 7784 / 6602 0855

PBC Book Sellers & Stationers
152, Budhwar Peth, Pune 411002, Maharashtra
Tel : (020) 2445 2254 / 6609 2463

MUMBAI
Pragati Book Corner
Indira Niwas, 111 - A, Bhavani Shankar Road, Dadar (W), Mumbai 400028, Maharashtra
Tel : (022) 2422 3526 / 6662 5254, Email : pbcmumbai@pragationline.com

www.pragationline.com   info@pragationline.com

Preface ...

We feel highly delighted in presenting this book of "Labour Laws - III" to the M.P.M. students preparing for their examination. This book is primarily intended as a text-book for the students. This book has been written as per the Syllabus prescribed for M.P.M. Part II, Semester III Course by the University of Pune and made effective from July, 2014.

The main object of this book is to state and explain the provisions of the Acts prescribed for the examination, so that the students may find it convenient to refer to them. From this point of view, all efforts have been made to state and explain various provisions of the Acts prescribed for the examination in simple and concise language. Each chapter contains adequate text and illustrations. Questions and Practical Problems are also given at the end of each chapter.

Our books on Labour Laws for M.P.M. Part - I and Semester - II have been well received by the student and teacher community alike. We hope that they will receive this book also with the same enthusiasm.

We are sure that this book will be of immense use to the students from the view point of their examination and will help them to enhance the knowledge of the Acts prescribed for their examination.

In spite of sincere efforts, printing errors might have crept in the book at some places. We hope that we will be excused for the same.

We would like to express our gratitude to Shri. Dineshbhai Furia, Shri. Jignesh Furia, Mr. Malik Shaikh, Mr. Nirja Sharma, Mr. Prasad Chintakindi, Mr. Parag Ghamandi and the entire staff of Nirali Prakashan, Pune without whose untiring efforts, wholehearted co-operation and sincerity, this edition of the book would never have come out in time.

We shall consider our labour amply rewarded if this book is appreciated by those for whom it is meant.

Pune
July, 2014

Prof. Sharad D. Geet
Mrs. Asmita A. Deshpande

Syllabus ...

1. Minimum Wages Act – 1948: (Wage Legislation)
(Number of Sessions 11 + 2)

Objects, Scope and Application of the Act, Important Definitions - Appropriate Government, Competent Authority, Cost of Living Index Number, Employees, Employer, Scheduled Employment, Wages, Fixing of Minimum Rate of Wages, Minimum Rate of Wages, Procedure for Fixing and Revising Minimum Wages, Advisory Board, Central Advisory Board - Composition of Committees.

Wages in Kind Overtime, Payment of Minimum Rate of Wages, Validation of Fixation of Certain Minimum Rates of Wages, Fixing Hours for a Normal working day, Wages of Worker who works for less than Normal Working Day, Wages for two or more Classes of Work, Minimum Time Rate Wages for Piece Work, Maintenance of Registers and Records. Appointment, Powers and Functions of Inspectors. Claims - Single Application in respect of a Number of Employees, Bar of Suits – Contracting Out Payment of Undisbursed Amounts due to Employees, Exemption of Employer from Liability in Certain Cases, Exemptions and Exceptions, Penalties for Certain Offences, General Provision for Punishment and other Offences, Cognizance Of Offences, Offences by companies.

2. The Maharashtra Recognition of Trade Unions and Prevention of Unfair Labour Practices Act, 1971.
(Number of Sessions 11 + 2)

3. Payment of Gratuity Act, 1972 (Social Security Legislation)
(Number of Sessions 5 + 2)

Entire act and Rules thereunder

4. The Apprentice Act, 1961
(Number of Sessions 10 + 2)

Objects, Applicability, Definitions Apprentice, Apprenticeship Training, Apprenticeship, Advisor, Apprenticeship Council. Board or State Council of Technical Education, Designated Trade, Employer, Establishment, Establishment in Private and Public Sector. Graduate or Technician Apprentice, Industry, National Council, prescribed, Regional Board, State, State Council, State Government Technician Vocational, Trade Apprentice, Worker, All India Council, Qualifications for being engaged as an Apprentice, Novation of Contract of Apprenticeship, Period of Apprentice Training, Termination of Apprenticeship Contract, Practical and Basic Training of Apprenticeship, Obligations of the Employers, Obligation of Payment, Health Safety and Welfare of Apprentices, Hours of Work, Overtime, Leave, Settlement of Disputes, Grant of Certificates to the Apprentices, Offer and Acceptance of Employment, Administration of the Act, Offences and Penalties, Protection of Action in Good Faith.

***

Contents ...

1. The Minimum Wages Act, 1948 (Wage Legislation)   1.1 – 1.32

2. The Maharashtra Recognition of Trade Unions and Prevention of Unfair Labour Practices Act, 1971 (M.R.T.U. and P.U.L.P.)   2.1 – 2.64

3. The Payment of Gratuity Act, 1972 (Social Security Legislation)   3.1 – 3.54

4. The Apprentices Act, 1961   4.1 – 4.42

Publisher's Note

In spite of the best efforts, care and caution, errors might have crept in for which the students, readers, and the like are requested to bear with us. The publication is being sold on the condition and understanding that the information given in this book is merely for guidance and reference. It must not be taken as having authority of, or binding in any way on the author, publisher, sellers etc. who do not owe any responsibility for any damage or loss to any person, who may or may not be a purchaser of this publication on account of any action taken on the basis of this publication. However, if any discrepancies, omissions, errors and the like are noticed, kindly bring the same to our notice, so that we can take necessary steps to correct them in the next edition.

***

Chapter 1...

The Minimum Wages Act, 1948 : (Wage Legislation)

Contents ...

1.1 Introduction
1.2 Objects, Scope and Application of the Act
    1.2.1 Important Features of the Act
1.3 Meaning of the term "Minimum Wages"
1.4 Definitions of Words, Terms etc. as are given in Section 2 of the Act
1.5 Fixing of Minimum Rates of Wages
1.6 Minimum Rate of Wages
1.7 Procedure for Fixing and Revising Minimum Wages
1.8 Advisory Board and Committees
1.9 Wages in Kind
1.10 Provisions related to "Overtime"
1.11 Payment of Minimum Rates of Wages
1.12 Validation of Fixation of Certain Minimum Rates of Wages
1.13 Fixing the Hours for a Normal Working Day
1.14 Wages of Workers who Work for Less than Normal Working Day
1.15 Wages for Two or More Classes of Work
1.16 Minimum Time Rate Wages for Piece Rate Work
1.17 Maintenance of Registers and Records
1.18 Appointments of Inspectors and their Powers
1.19 Claims
    1.19.1 Which Claims can be Heard and Decided for any Specified Area by the Authority under this Act
    1.19.2 Who can be Appointed as an Authority to Hear and to Decide any Claims under this Act
    1.19.3 Who can Apply where an Employee has any Claim?
    1.19.4 When the Application for Claims is to be Presented
    1.19.5 Procedure for Deciding the Claims
    1.19.6 Recovery of the Amount under the Order of the Authority
    1.19.7 Finality of Directions given in Section 20 and Power of the Authority for Certain Purposes

1.20 Single Application in respect of a Number of Employees [Section 21]
1.21 Bar of Suits [Section 24]
1.22 Contracting Out [Section 25]
1.23 Payment of Undisbursed Amounts Due to Employees
1.24 Exemption of Employer from Liability in Certain Cases [Section 23]
1.25 Exemptions and Exceptions
1.26 Penalties for Certain Offences
1.27 General Provisions for Punishment of Other Offences
1.28 Cognizance of Offences
1.29 Offences by Companies
- Points to Remember
- Questions for Discussion
- Practical Problems

Learning Objectives...

After going through this chapter, you will be able to know:
- The objects, scope and applications of this Act
- Procedure for fixing and revising minimum wages
- Composition of the Advisory Board and Central Advisory Board
- Provisions of the Act relating to wages in kind, payment of minimum rates of wages
- Provisions relating to fixing hours for a normal working day, wages of workers who work for less than a normal working day, wages for two or more classes of work etc.
- Provisions of the Act relating to maintenance of registers and records
- Powers and functions of inspectors appointed under this Act
- Provisions relating to claims, single application in respect of a number of employees etc.
- Penalties for certain offences
- Offences by companies

1.1 Introduction

Any discussion on the different methods of fixing wages has to take into consideration the concepts of a minimum wage, a living wage, and a fair wage. It is very important to consider these concepts while fixing wage rates in a developing country like India.

The government and the agencies connected with wage fixation have constantly been concerned with this problem. In India, various methods are employed while fixing wages. Different bodies such as pay commissions, wage boards, industrial tribunals, labour courts, high courts, the Supreme Court play a very important role in the process of wage fixation. Wages are also fixed through collective bargaining.

However, it is very essential to create conditions that make it possible for employees to enjoy a minimum standard of life. For that purpose, certain efforts must be carried out and fixation of the minimum rates of wages is one of the efforts in that direction. Of course, a minimum wage rate must ensure not merely physical needs of an employee which would keep him just above starvation but it must ensure for him not only his subsistence and that of his family but also preserve his efficiency as a workman.

Prima facie, it seems that the Minimum Wages Act of 1948 *ultra vires* Article 19 (1) (g) of the Constitution of India gives the right to all Indian citizens to practice any profession, or to carry on any occupation, trade or business, they desire.

While Article 19 (h) of the Indian Constitution assures that nothing in Article 19 (1) (g) shall affect the operation of any of the existing laws in so far as they impose or prevent the State from any law imposing, in the interest of the public, reasonable restrictions on the exercise of the right conferred by the sub-clause of the Article 19 of the Indian Constitution.

Further, the Article 43 of the Indian Constitution makes it clear that, "the State shall endeavour to secure by suitable legislation a living wage, a decent standard of life to the workers".

From this point of view, basically to protect the interest of the workers, to prevent their exploitation and to guarantee the workers working in industries, trade or business in respect of working conditions, payment of wages, compensation, various labour laws have been enacted. The Minimum Wages Act of 1948 is one such Act.

The Minimum Wages Act of 1948,

- Empowers the Government for fixing the minimum wages for employment mentioned in the Schedule of the Act.
- It provides that the appropriate Government shall fix or revise the minimum rates of wages by appointing committees or publishing its proposal by notification for the fixation or revision of wages.
- The provisions have been made in the Act for the fixation of minimum wages especially in those industries where there are inevitable chances of exploiting the workers and where there exists sweated labour.

Today, in India, it is found that workers are organised to a certain extent in some industries. But in the past, they were not organised and as their bargaining capacity was weak, they were exploited to a great extent. Therefore, there was a great need to take steps to fix minimum wages. But in spite of various efforts, no steps could be taken up to 1945.

It was only on 11th April 1946, that the Minimum Wages Bill was introduced in the Parliament. However, because of constitutional changes, it could not be passed immediately. *The Minimum Wages Act was ultimately passed in 1948 and came into operation on 15th March 1948.*

1.2 Objects, Scope and Application of the Act

The Minimum Wages Act, 1948 was basically passed to provide for fixing minimum rates of Wages in certain employments and it extends to the whole of India. The Minimum Wages Act of 1948 in totality states that *a minimum wage rate must ensure for an employee not only his subsistence and that of his family but also preserve his efficiency as a workman.*

- The Act enables the Central or the State Government, as the case may be, to fix the minimum rates of wages payable to employees in certain selected industries and trades. These industries and trades are those in which sweated labour exists and labour is exploited.
- The industries and trades to which this Act is made applicable are listed in the schedule appended to the Act and an Appropriate Government is authorised to extend the same to any employment in respect of which it is of the opinion that the minimum rates of wages should be fixed under this Act.
- The Appropriate Government is empowered to review the minimum rates of wages fixed under this Act at such intervals as it may think proper, but such intervals shall not exceed five years and the Government is also authorised to revise the same, if necessary.
- The Appropriate Government may refrain from fixing minimum rates of wages in respect of any of the scheduled employments in which there are in the whole state less than one thousand employees engaged in such employment. However, if it finds, at any time, that the number of employees in any scheduled employment has arisen to one thousand or more, it shall fix minimum rates of wages payable to employees in that employment immediately.

Thus, the scope of the Act seems to be narrow. It has excluded many regulated and un-regulated industries and trades where wages are extremely low and where sweating is common, e.g. coir, coir-mat manufacture, furniture making, potteries, bangle manufacture and so on.

The main object of the Act is to provide machinery and procedure for fixing the minimum rates of wages in certain employments. The other objects are given below:

(a) To prevent sweating in industry. This means that care must be taken so that the payments are not so low as to put the workers working in certain employments at a disadvantage.

(b) The wages must correspond to the toils the workers put in and they should not be exploited.

(c) To see that lock-outs, strikes etc. are rooted out by satisfying the workers through fair payments.

(d) To see that the unorganised workers do not suffer from unfair bargaining and their rights are protected.

(e) The Act also provides for the fixation of a minimum piece-rate, a guaranteed time-rate, an overtime-rate appropriate to different occupations, minimum time-rates etc.

(f) The Act does not only intend to protect male workers, but also women, children and adolescent workers and apprentices too.

It is quite possible that the employers may find it very difficult to bear the restrictions imposed on them by this Act in view of the economic conditions. Some people may charge the Act as unreasonable. But in Cotton Mills V/s Ajmer State, it has been held that the Act is not repugnant to Article 19 (1) (9) of the Indian Constitution. The restrictions imposed by the Act are neither unreasonable nor unrealistic within the meaning of Article 19 (6) of the Constitution.

The Minimum Wages Act does not cast any statutory obligation on the State Government to fix or revise the rates of minimum wages strictly according to the cost of living index. If the cost of living index in any particular locality is not strictly followed while either fixing or revising minimum wages rates, there is no breach committed of a statutory duty.

1.2.1 Important Features of the Act

The important features of the Act are as follows:

(a) The Act provides for the fixation of minimum rates of wages in certain employments and it extends to the whole of India. It contemplates that a minimum wage rate must ensure for an employee not merely his subsistence and that of his family but also preserve his efficiency as a workman. It attempts to prevent sweating in industry.

(b) While making the provisions, necessary care has been taken to see that the wages fixed correspond to the toils the workers put in and they are not exploited.

(c) The Act provides for the fixation of a minimum time rate of wages, a minimum piece-rate, a guaranteed time rate and overtime rate appropriate for different occupations, localities or classes of work.

(d) The Act does not only intend to protect male workers, but also women, children and adolescent workers and apprentices too.

(e) The Act makes it clear that the minimum rate of wages may consist of : (i) a basic rate of wages and a cost of living allowance; or (ii) a basic rate of wages with or without the cost of living allowance and the cash value of the concessions in respect of essential commodities supplied at concessional rates.

(f) The Act provides that wages are to be paid in cash. It also empowers the appropriate government to authorise the payment of minimum wages either wholly or partly in kind in particular cases.

(g) The provisions have been made in the Act for fixation and revision of minimum rates of wages in a particular manner. Different minimum rates of wages can be fixed for different scheduled employed, for different classes of work in the same employment according to the provisions of the Act. The Act also empowers the appropriate government to fix the number of hours of work per day, to provide for a weekly holiday and the payment of overtime wages of which minimum rates of wages have been fixed under the Act.

(h) The Act empowers the Government to appoint Inspectors and other authorities to hear and decide claims arising out of payment of wages at less than the minimum rates of wages or remuneration for days of rest or of work done on such days or of overtime wages. Powers of the Inspectors are also made clear in Section 19 of the Act.

(i) The establishments to which the Act is applied are required to maintain the registers and records in the prescribed manner.

(j) There are provisions in the Act to impose penalty for certain offences. The Act also provides the procedure for dealing with complaints which arise out of the violation of the provisions of the Act.

1.3 Meaning of the term 'Minimum Wages'

Industrial unrest immediately prior to and after independence led to the evolution of a policy on 'Minimum Wages' in India.

Various factors contributed to the enactment of the Minimum Wages Act of 1948 and to regulate industrial wages. The important factors among them were,

- the emergence of the I.L.O. which set standards in respect of labour, and
- the increasing power and militancy of the trade union movement.

The Minimum Wages Act of 1948 emphasised that if exploitation of labour through meager or low payment of wages was to be prevented, wages had to be regulated and they should not be determined by the market forces.

The terms which have acquired urgency in discussing various wage problems since 1948 are :

(i) Statutory minimum wage;
(ii) Bare or basic minimum wage;
(iii) Minimum wage;
(iv) Fair wage;
(v) Living wage; and
(vi) Need-based minimum wage.

The term *Statutory Minimum Wage* owes its origin to the provisions of the Minimum Wages Act of 1948.

The term *Bare or Basic Minimum Wage* is used in awards and judicial pronouncements, while the terms Minimum wage, Fair wage and Living wage have been introduced in the resolution of the 15th session of the Indian Labour Conference in July 1957.

The *basic or bare minimum wage* is that wage which provides bare subsistence and it is at poverty line level. A little above is the fair wage and the living wage comes at comfort level. However, it is very difficult to demarcate these levels of wage structure with any precision.

It must be noted that the term *'Minimum Wage'* is not defined in the Minimum Wages Act of 1948. It is so because it is not possible to lay down a uniform minimum wages for all industries throughout India on account of nature of industries and conditions prevailing in different industries and industries located in different parts of India. However, it is understood that a minimum wage must provide not merely for the bare subsistence of life which would keep him just above starvation but must ensure for him not only for his subsistence and that of his family but also preserve his efficiency as a workman. Hence, it must also provide for some measure of education, medical requirements and amenities.

The Tripartite Committee of the Indian Labour Conference (1957) accepted the following five norms for fixing of 'Minimum Wages'.

(a) The standard working class family (Three consumption units for one earner).
(b) Minimum food requirements.
(c) Clothing requirements estimated at per capita consumption of Eighteen Yards × Average four family members = Seventy Two Yards.
(d) Housing (the rent corresponding to the minimum area provided for under Government Industrial Housing Scheme).
(e) Fuel, lighting and other miscellaneous items of expenditure constituting 20% of the total minimum wages.

Besides the above mentioned items, considering the socio-economic aspect of the wage structure, minimum wage should include the other components such as children education, medical requirements, provision for old age, marriages etc. and further constitute 25% of total minimum wages.

1.4 Definitions of Words, Terms etc. as are given in Section 2 of the Act

The definitions of eleven words, terms and so on are given in this Act. Unless there is anything repugnant in the context or subject, the meanings, definitions of words, terms etc. given in Section 2 of the Act are as follows:

(1) Adolescent [Section 2 (a)]

'Adolescent' means a person who has completed his fourteenth year of age but not completed his eighteenth year.

(2) Adult [Section 2 (aa)]

'Adult' means a person who has completed his eighteenth year of age.

(3) Appropriate Government [Section 2 (b)]

'Appropriate Government' means

(i) in relation to any scheduled employment carried on by or under the authority of the Central Government or Railway Administration or in relation to a mine, oil-field or major port, or any corporation established by any Central Act, the Central Government; and

(ii) in relation to any other scheduled employment, the State Government.

(4) Child [Section 2 (bb)]

'Child' means a person who has not completed his fourteenth year of age.

(5) Competent Authority [Section 2 (c)]

'Competent authority' means the authority appointed by the Appropriate Government by notification in the Official Gazette to ascertain from time to time the cost of living index number applicable to the employees employed in the scheduled employments specified in such notification.

(6) Cost of Living Index Number [Section 2 (d)]

'Cost of living index number', in relation to employees in any scheduled employment in respect of which minimum rates of wages have been fixed, means 'the index number ascertained and declared by the competent authority by notification in the Official Gazette to be the cost of living index number applicable to employees in such employment.

(7) Employer [Section 2 (e)]

'Employer' means any person who employs, either directly or through another person, or whether on behalf of himself or any other person, one or more employees in any scheduled employment in respect of which minimum rates of wages have been fixed under this Act, and includes, except in sub-section 3 of Section 26.

(i) in a factory where there is carried on any scheduled employment in respect of which minimum rates of wages have been fixed under this Act, any person named under clause (f) of sub-section (1) of Section 7 of the Factories Act, 1948, as a manager of the factory.

(ii) in any scheduled employment under the control of any Government in India in respect of which minimum rates of wages have been fixed under this Act, a person or an authority appointed by such Government for the supervision and control of employees or where no person or authority is so appointed, the head of the department;

(iii) in any scheduled employment under any local authority in respect of which minimum rates of wages have been fixed under this Act, the person appointed by such authority for the supervision and control of employees or where no person is so appointed, the chief executive officer of the local authority,

(iv) in any other case where there is carried on any scheduled employment in respect of which minimum rates of wages have been fixed under this Act, any person responsible to the owner for the supervision and control of the employees or for the payment of wages.

(8) Prescribed [Section 2 (f)]

'Prescribed' means prescribed by rules made under this Act.

(9) Scheduled Employment [Section 2 (g)]

'Scheduled employment means, an employment specified in the schedule, or any process or branch of work forming part of such employment.

Section 27 empowers the State Governments to add to the Schedule appended to the Act. Section 27 lays down that, *"The appropriate Government, after giving by notification in the Official Gazette not less than three month's notice of its intention to do so, may, by like notification, add to either part of the Schedule any employment in respect of which it is of the opinion that minimum rates of wages should be fixed under this Act, and thereupon the Schedule shall in its application to the State, be deemed to be amended accordingly."* Thus, the appropriate Government, according to the provisions of Section 27, can add to the Schedule appended to this Act.

The Schedule appended to this Act is given below:

	The Schedule – Part I
1.	Employment is any wollen carpet making or shawl weaving establishment.
2.	Employment in any rice mill, flour mill or dal mill.
3.	Employment in any tobacco (including bidi making) manufactory.
4.	Employment in any plantation, that is to say, any estate which is maintained for the purpose of growing cinchona, rubber, tea or coffee.
5.	Employment in any oil mill.
6.	Employment under any local authority.
7.	Employment on the construction or maintenance of roads or in building operations.
8.	Employment in stone breaking or stone crushing.
9.	Employment in any lac manufactory.
10.	Employment in any mica works.
11.	Employment in public motor transport.
12.	Employment in tanneries and leather manufactory.
13.	Employment in gypsum mines.
14.	Employment in barytes mines.
15.	Employment in bauxite mines.
16.	Employment in manganese mines.
17.	Employment in the maintenance of building and construction and maintenance of runway.
18.	Employment in China clay mines.
19.	Employment in kyanite mines.
20.	Employment in copper mines.
21.	Employment in clay mines covered under the Mines Act, 1952.
22.	Employment in magnesite mines covered under the Mines Act, 1952.
23.	Employment in white clay mines.
24.	Employment in stone mines.
25.	Employment in steatite (including the mines producing seapstone and talc)
26.	Employment in ocher mines

27.	Employment in asbestos mines.
28.	Employment in fire clay mines.
29.	Employment in chromite mines.
30.	Employment in quartzite mines.
31.	Employment in silica mines.
32.	Employment in graphite mines.
33.	Employment in feldspar mines.
34.	Employment in laterite mines.
35.	Employment in dolomite mines.
36.	Employment in red-oxide mines.
37.	Employment in wolfarm mines.
38.	Employment in iron ore mines.
39.	Employment in granite mines.
40.	Employment in rock phosphate mines.
41.	Employment in haematite mines.
42.	Employment in loading and unloading in: (i) Railways, goods shed – (ii) Docks and ports.
43.	Employment in marble and calcite mines.
44.	Employment in uranium mines.

The Schedule – Part II

Employment in agriculture, that is to say, in any form of farming, including the cultivation, growing and harvesting of any agricultural or horticultural commodity, the raising of live stock, bees or poultry, and any practice performed by a farmer or on a farm as incidental to or in conjunction with farm operations including any forestry or timbering operations and the preparations for market and delivery to storage or to market or the carriage for transportation to market of farm produce.

(10) Wages [Section 2 (h)]

'Wages' means all remuneration, capable of being expressed in terms of money, which would, if the terms of the contract of employment, express or implied, were fulfilled, be payable to a person employed in respect of his employment or of work done in such employment, and includes house rent allowance, but does not include:

- (i) the value of:
    - (a) any house accommodation, supply of light, water, medical attendance, or
    - (b) any other amenity or any service excluded by general or special order of the Appropriate Government.
- (ii) any contribution paid by the employer to any Pension Fund or Provident Fund or under any scheme of social insurance;
- (iii) any travelling allowance or the value of any travelling concession;
- (iv) any sum paid to the person employed to defray special expenses entailed to him by the nature of his employment; or
- (v) any gratuity payable on discharge.

(11) Employee [Section 2 (i)]

'Employee' means any person who is employed for hire or reward to do any work, skilled or unskilled, manual or clerical, in a scheduled employment in respect of which minimum rates of wages have been fixed; and includes an out-worker to whom any articles or materials are given out by another person to be made up, cleaned, washed, altered, ornamented, finished, repaired, adapted or otherwise processed for sale for the purposes of the trade or business of that other person where the process is to be carried out either in the home of the out-worker or in some other premises not being premises under the control and management of that other person; and also includes an employee declared to be an employee by the Appropriate Government; but does not include any member of the Armed Forces of the Union.

If the minimum wages have not been fixed for any branch of work of any scheduled employment, the person employing workers in such branch is not an employer within the meaning of this Act.

If an out-worker produces goods at his place and thereafter supplies the same to his employer, he is treated as an employee for the purpose of this Act.

1.5 Fixing of Minimum Rates of Wages

Sections 3, 4 and 5 pertain to fixing of minimum rates of wages, minimum rates of wages and procedure for fixing and revising minimum wages respectively. Let us now consider the provisions of these three Sections i.e. Section 3, Section 4 and Section 5.

Section 3 of the Act states the basic principles and procedure to be observed in fixing the minimum rates of wages payable to employees in an employment specified in Part I and Part II of the schedule. For the benefit of the students, Section 3 of the Act is reproduced as follows:

The Appropriate Government shall, in the manner hereinafter provided:

(a) fix the minimum rates of wages payable to employees employed in an employment specified in Part I or Part II of the schedule and in employment added to either part by notification under Section 27.

Provided that the appropriate government may in respect of employees employed in an employment specified in part II of the schedule, instead of fixing of minimum rates of wages under this clause for the whole state, such rates for a part of the State or for any specified class or classes of such employment in the whole State or part thereof;

(b) review at such intervals as it may think fit, such intervals not exceeding five years, the minimum rates of wages so fixed and revise the minimum rates, if necessary.

Provided that where for any reason the appropriate government has not reviewed the minimum rates of wages fixed by it in respect of any scheduled employment within any interval of five years, nothing contained in this clause shall be deemed to prevent it from reviewing the minimum rates after the expiry of the said period of five years and revising them, if necessary, and until they are so revised the minimum rates in force immediately before the expiry of the said period of five years shall continue in force [Section 3 (1)].

Notwithstanding anything contained in such-section (1) of Section 3 mentioned above, the Appropriate Government may refrain from fixing minimum rates of wages in respect of any scheduled employment in which there are in the whole State less than one thousand employees engaged in such employment, but if at any time; the Appropriate Government comes to a finding after such inquiry as it may make or cause to be made in this behalf that the number of employees in any scheduled employment in respect of which it has refrained from fixing minimum rates of wages, has risen to one thousand or more, it shall fix minimum rates of wages payable to employees in such employment as soon as may be after such finding [Section 3 (1-A)].

The Appropriate Government may fix:

(a) a minimum rate of wages for time work (Minimum time-rate).

(b) a minimum rate of wages for piece work (Minimum piece-rate).

(c) a minimum rate of remuneration to apply in the case of employees employed on piece work for the purpose of securing to such employees a minimum rates of wages on a time-rate basis (A guaranteed time-rate).

(d) a minimum rate (whether a time-rate or a piece-rate) to apply in substitution for the minimum rate which would otherwise be applicable, in respect of overtime work done by employees [Overtime rate] [Section 3 (2)].

Where in respect of an industrial dispute relating to the rates of wages payable to any of the employees employed in a scheduled employment, any proceeding is pending before a Tribunal or National Tribunal under Industrial Disputes Act, 1947 or before any like authority under any other law for the time being in force, or an award made by any Tribunal or

National Tribunal or such authority is in operation, and a notification fixing or revising the minimum rates of wages in respect of the scheduled employment is issued during the pendency of such proceeding or the operation of the award, then, notwithstanding anything contained in this Act, the minimum rates of wages so fixed or so revised shall not apply to those employees during the period in which the proceeding is pending and the award made therein is in operation or, as the case may be, where the notification is issued during the period of operation of an award, during that period, and where such proceeding or award relates to the rates of wages payable to all the employees in the scheduled employment, no minimum rates of wages shall be fixed or revised in respect of that employment during the said period [Section 3 (2-A)].

In fixing or revising the minimum rates of wages under this section:
(a) different minimum rates of wages may be fixed for:
  (i) different scheduled employments;
  (ii) different classes of work in the same scheduled employment;
  (iii) adults, adolescents, children and apprentices;
  (iv) different localities.
(b) minimum rates of wages may be fixed by any one or more of the following wage periods, namely:
  (i) by the hour,
  (ii) by the day;
  (iii) by the month; or
  (iv) by such other larger wage-period as may be prescribed.

and where such rates are fixed by the day or by the month, the manner of calculating wages for a month or for a day, as the case may be, may be indicated.

Provided that where any wage-periods have been fixed under Section 4 of the Payment of Wages Act, 1936, minimum wages shall be fixed in accordance therewith [Section 3 (3)].

1.6 Minimum Rate of Wages

Any minimum rate of wages fixed or revised by the Appropriate Government in respect of any of the scheduled employments under Section 3 of this Act may consist of :
(i) a basic rate of wages and a special allowance at a rate to be adjusted at such intervals and in such manner as the Appropriate Government may direct, to accord as nearly as practicable with the variation in the cost of living index number applicable to such workers (hereinafter referred to as the cost of living allowance); or
(ii) a basic rate of wages with or without the cost of living allowance, and the cash value of the concessions in respect of supplies of essential commodities at concessional rates, where so authorised; or
(iii) an all inclusive rate allowing for the basic rate, the cost of living allowance and the cash value of the concessions, if any [Section 4 (1)].

The cost of living allowance and also the cash value of the concessions in respect of supplies of essential commodities at concessional rates shall be computed by the competent authority at such intervals and in accordance with such directions as may be specified or given by the Appropriate Government [Section 4 (2)].

It must be remembered here that the basic wage is an integral part of the minimum wage. The question of dearness allowance arises only if the basic wage falls short of the minimum wage (State of Karnataka V/s. Karnataka Film Chambers, 1986). *Bhatta* is an extra payment over and above pay. The only extras that can be added to the pay under this Minimum Wages Act, 1948 are allowance and concessions contemplated in Section 4 (1) (i) and (ii).

1.7 Procedure for Fixing and Revising Minimum Wages

Section 5 of the Act lays down the procedure for fixing and revising the minimum rates of wages and according to it, the Appropriate Government shall adopt any of the following procedures while fixing minimum rates of wages in respect of scheduled employment for the first time under this Act or in revising minimum rates of wages so fixed:

(a) The Appropriate Government may appoint as many committees and sub-committees as it considers necessary to hold enquiries and advice it in respect of such fixation or revision, as the case may be [Section 5 (a)], or

(b) It may publish its proposals by notification in the Official Gazette for the information of persons likely to be affected thereby and specify a date, not less than two months from the date of the notification, on which the proposals will be taken into consideration [Section 5 (b)].

After considering the advice of the committees appointed and all representations received by it before the date specified in the Official Gazette; the Appropriate Government shall, by notification in the Official Gazette, fix or revise, as the case may be, revise the minimum rates of wages in respect of each scheduled employment, and unless such notification otherwise provides, it shall come into force on the expiry of three months from the date of its issue [Section 5 (2)].

It is further provided that where the Appropriate Government proposes to receive the minimum rates of wages by the mode specified in Section 5 (1) (b), the Appropriate Government shall also consult the Advisory Board.

It must be remembered that any committee or sub-committee appointed under Section 5 (1) (a) is only an advisory body and the advice of such committee or sub-committee is not binding on the Government. If no advice is given or if the inadequate advice is given by such committee, the Government has power to fix or revise the minimum rates of wages.

The provision has been made in Section 10 of this Act to correct the errors, if any. The Appropriate Government may, at any time, by the notification in the Official Gazette, correct clerical or arithmetical errors or mistakes in any order fixing or revising minimum rates of wages under this Act or arising therein from any accidental slip or omission and every such notification shall, as soon as may be, after it is issued, be placed before the Advisory Board for its information.

1.8 Advisory Board and Committees

It has already been made clear that for fixing minimum rates of wages in respect of any scheduled employment for the first time under this Act, or in revising minimum rates of wages so fixed under Section 5 of this Act, the appropriate Government shall either –

(a) appoint as many committees and sub-committees as it considers necessary to hold enquiries and advise it in respect of such fixation or revision, as the case may be, or

(b) by notification in the Official Gazette, publish its proposal for the information of persons likely to be affected thereby and specify a date, not less than two months from the date of notification, on which the proposals will be taken into consideration.

After considering the advice of the committee or committees thus appointed and all representations received by it before the date specified in the notification, the Appropriate Government shall, by notification in the Official Gazette, fix, or, as the case may be, revise the minimum rates of wages in respect of each Scheduled employment, and unless such notification otherwise provides, it shall come into force on the expiry of three months from the date of its issue.

The appropriate Government is empowered under this Act to appoint an Advisory Board for coordinating the work of committees and sub-committees appointed under Section 5 and also to advice the appropriate Government in respect of fixing and revising the minimum rates of wages. Further, the Central Government is also empowered under this Act to appoint the Central Advisory Board in order to advice the Central as well as State Governments in respect of the fixation and revision of the minimum rates of wages, other matters under this Act and also for coordinating the work of the Advisory Boards. The provisions relating to appointments, composition etc. of the Advisory Boards and Central Advisory Boards have been made in Sections 7th, 8th and 9th of this Act. Besides these provisions, there are rules from 3 to 17 incorporated in Chapter II of the Minimum Wages (Central) Rules of 1950. These provisions and rules are given below.

1.8.1 Advisory Board

For the purpose of coordinating the work of committees and sub-committees appointed under Section 5 of this Act and advising the Appropriate Government, generally in the matter of fixing and revising the minimum rates of wages, the Appropriate Government shall appoint an Advisory Board [Section 7].

(A) Composition of the Advisory Board

Each of the committees, sub-committees and the Advisory Board shall consist of persons to be nominated by the Appropriate Government representing employers and employees in the schedule employments, who shall be equal in number; and independent persons not exceeding one-third of its total number of members; one of such independent persons shall be appointed as the chairman by the Appropriate Government [Section 9].

It is not necessary that the employers of every item in the Schedule must be given representation on the Minimum Wages Advisory Board.

(B) The Central Advisory Board

The Central Advisory Board is appointed by the Central Government for the purpose of advising the Central as well as the State Governments in the matters of fixing and revising minimum rates of wages and other matters under this Act and also for coordinating the work of the Advisory Boards [Section 8 (1)].

(C) Composition of the Central Advisory Board

The Central Advisory Board consists of persons who are nominated by the Central Government and they represent employers and employees in the scheduled employments. They are equal in number. Independent persons are also nominated by the Central Government and their number does not exceed one-third of the total number of members of the Central Advisory Board. One of such independent persons is appointed as the chairman of the Board by the Central Government [Section 8 (2)].

Here, independent persons are those persons who do not belong to the category of employers neither that of employees.

1.9 Wages in Kind

Section 11 (1) of the Act states *that the Minimum Wages payable under this Act shall be paid in cash.*

However, where it has been the custom to pay wages wholly or partly in kind, the Appropriate Government being of the opinion that it is necessary in the circumstances of the case may, by notification in the Official Gazette, authorise the payment of minimum wages either wholly or partly in Kind [Section 11 (2)].

If the Appropriate Government is of the opinion that the provision should be made for supplying the essential commodities at concessional rates, the Appropriate Government may, by notification in the Official Gazette, authorise the provision of such supplies at concessional rates [Section 11 (3)].

The cash value of wages in kind and of concessions in respect of supplies of essential commodities at concessional rates authorised under sub-section (2) and (3) of Section 11 shall be estimated in the manner prescribed for this purpose.

From these provisions of Section 11, it becomes clear that the minimum wages payable under this Act must be paid in cash. However, where it is a custom to pay wages wholly or partly in kind, it is permissible under this Act, subject to the following conditions.

(a) The Appropriate Government should be of the opinion that it is necessary in the specific circumstances to pay the wages in kind.

(b) It should, by notification in the Official Gazette, authorise the payment of minimum wage either wholly or partly in kind.

(c) If the Government is of the opinion that provision should be made for supply of essential commodities at concessional rates, it should do so by notification in the Official Gazette authorising such supplies.

(d) The cash value of wages in kind and of concessions in respect of supplies of essential commodities should be estimated in the prescribed manner.

1.10 Provisions related to Overtime

Where an employee, whose minimum rate of wages is fixed under this Act by the hour, by the day or by such a longer wage-period as may be prescribed, works on any day in excess of the number of hours constituting a normal working day, the employer shall pay him for every hour or for part of an hour so worked in excess at the overtime rate fixed under this Act or under any law of the Appropriate Government for the time being in force, whichever is higher [Section 14 (1)].

And nothing in this Act shall prejudice the operation of the provisions of the Factories Act of 1948 in any case where those provisions are applicable.

It must be remembered that the minimum rate of wages for overtime work need not be confined to double the minimum rates of wages but they may be fixed at double the wages ordinarily received by the employees [Mamarde V/s. Authority under Minimum Wages Act case (1972) 2 Sec. 108].

Thus, over-time, in short, means wages for the work done in excess as prescribed 'under normal working day'. The rates of overtime are fixed under this Act or under any Law for the time being in force whichever are higher.

1.11 Payment of Minimum Rates of Wages

The Minimum Wages Act, 1948 provides for the payment of minimum wages to all those employees who are covered by the Act. If the contract rate of payment of wages is higher than the minimum rate, the statutory rights and obligations do not come in the way. Thus, except the liability of paying the minimum, the contract between employer and his employees is left intact. Of course, payment of wages less than the minimum on the ground of less performance or output is not legal.

The employer can fix any reasonable norm specifying the quantity of work which he expects from his workmen during the day; but if any of the workmen or many of them do not produce in conformity with the norms fixed, the employer cannot pay anything less than the minimum wages. The employer may take any other disciplinary action for doing less work other than paying his workers less than the minimum wages.

Section 12 (1) of the Act states that, *"where in respect of any scheduled employment a notification under Section 5 of the Act is in force, the employer shall pay to every employee engaged in a scheduled employment under him, wages at a rate not less than the minimum rate of wages fixed by such notification for that class of employees in that employment, without any deductions except as may be authorised within such time and subject to such conditions as may be prescribed"*, while; Section 12 (2) lays down that, *"Nothing contained in this section shall affect the provisions of the Payment of Wages Act of 1936".*

Thus, the provisions of Section 12 make it clear that when the minimum rates of wages are made enforceable by the notification vide Section 5 of the Act, the employer has to pay to every employee engaged in a scheduled employment under him, the wages at a rate not less than the minimum rate of wages fixed by such notification under this Act and such payments must be made without any deductions except as may be authorised within such time and subject to such conditions as has been prescribed. These provisions do not affect the provisions of the Payment of Wages Act of 1936.

1.12 Validation of Fixation of Certain Minimum Rate of Wages

Where during the period –

(a) commencing on the 1st day of April 1952 and ending with the date of the commencement of the Minimum Wages (Amendment) Act, 1954 (26 of 1954); or

(b) commencing on the 31st day of December, 1954 and ending with the date of the commencement of the Minimum Wages (Amendment) Act, 1957; or

(c) commencing on 31st day of December, 1959 and ending with the date of the commencement of the Minimum Wages (Amendment) Act, 1961 (31 of 1961).

Minimum rates of wages have been fixed by an Appropriate Government as being payable to employees employed in any employment specified in the Schedule in the belief or purported belief that such rates were being fixed under clause (a) of sub-section (1) of Section 3 as in force immediately before the commencement of the Minimum Wages (Amendment) Act, 1954 (26 of 1954), or the Minimum Wages (Amendment) Act, 1957 (31 of 1961), or the Minimum Wages (Amendment) Act, 1961, as the case may be, such rates shall be deemed to have been fixed in accordance with law and shall not be called in question in any Court on the ground merely that the relevant date specified for the purpose in that clause had expired at the time the rates were fixed.

Provided that, nothing contained in this section shall extend, or be construed to extend, to effect any person with any punishment or penalty whatsoever by reason of the payment by him by way of wages to any of the employees during any period specified in this section of an amount which is less than the minimum rates of wages referred to in this section or by reason of non-compliance during the period aforesaid with any order or rule issued under Section 13 [Section 31].

1.13 Fixing the Hours for a Normal Working Day

In regard to any scheduled employment, minimum rates of wages in respect of which have been fixed under this Act, the Appropriate Government may –

(a) fix the number of hours of work which shall constitute a normal working day, inclusive of one or more specified intervals;

(b) provide for a day of rest in every period of seven days which shall be allowed to all employees or to any specified class of employees and provide for the payment of remuneration in respect of such day of rest;

(c) provide for payment for work on a day of rest at a rate not less than the overtime rate [Section 13 (1)].

This Section 13 lays down the procedure for fixing the hours for a normal day working. The Appropriate Government, under this section, is authorised to take action or decision in respect of the number of hours of work as well as the classes of employees. So far as the number of hours of work is concerned, the Appropriate Government may –

(a) fix the number of hours of work which shall constitute a normal working day, inclusive of one or more specified intervals;

(b) provide for a day of rest in every period of seven days which shall be allowed to all employees or to any specified class of employees and provide for the payment of remuneration in respect of such days of rest;

(c) provide for payment for work on a day of rest at a rate not less than the overtime rate.

1.14 Wages of Workers who Work for Less than Normal Working Day

If any employee whose minimum rate of wages has been fixed under this Act by the day, works on any day on which he was employed for a period less than the requisite number of hours constituting a normal working day, he shall be entitled to receive wages in respect of work done by him on that day as if he had worked for a full normal working day [Section 15].

However, he shall not be entitled to receive wages for a full normal working day:

(i) in any case where his failure to work is caused by his unwillingness to work and not by the omission of the employer to provide him with work; and

(ii) in such other cases and circumstances as may be prescribed [Proviso to Section 15].

1.15 Wages for Two or More Classes of Work

Where an employee does two or more classes of work to each of which a different minimum rate of wages is applicable, the employer shall pay to such an employee in respect of the time respectively occupied in each such class of work, wages at not less than the minimum rate in force in respect of each such class [Section 16].

1.16 Minimum Time-rate Wages for Piece Rate Work

Where an employee is employed on piece work for which minimum time-rate and not a minimum piece-rate has been fixed under this Act, the employer shall pay to such employee wages at not less than the minimum time-rate [Section 17].

1.17 Maintenance of Registers and Records

The employer is responsible for maintaining the required registers, records and so on in the particular form according to the provisions of Section 18 of the Act and of rule 26 of the Minimum Wages (Central) Rules of 1950. These provisions and relating rules are as under:

(1) Every employer shall maintain such registers and records giving such particulars of employees employed by him, the work performed by them, the wages paid to them, the receipts given by them and such other particulars and in such forms as may be prescribed [Section 18 (1)].

(2) Every employer shall keep exhibited, in such manner, as may be prescribed in the factory, workshop or place where the employees in the scheduled employment may be employed, or in the case of out-workers, in such factory, workshop or place as may be used for giving out work to them, notices in the prescribed form containing prescribed particulars [Section 18 (2)].

(3) The Appropriate Government may, by rules made under this Act, provide for the issue of wage books or wage slips and attendance cards to employees employed in any scheduled employment in respect of which minimum rates of wages have been fixed and prescribed to manner in which entries shall be made and authenticated in such wage books or wage slips and attendance cards by the employer or his agent [Section 18 (3)].

1.18 Appointments of Inspectors and their Powers

Section 19 of the Act pertains to the appointments, powers etc. of the Inspectors. Section 19 is given below:

(1) The Appropriate Government may, by notification in the Official Gazette, appoint such persons as it thinks fit to be Inspectors for the purposes of this Act, and define the local limits within which they shall exercise their functions [Section 19 (1)].

(2) Subject to any rules made in this behalf, an Inspector may within the local limits for which he is appointed –

    (a) enter at all reasonable hours with such assistants (if any), being persons in the service of the Government or any local or other public authority, as he thinks fit, any premises or place where employees are employed or work is given out to out-workers in any scheduled employment in respect of which minimum rates of wages have been fixed under this Act, for the purposes of examining any register, record of wages or notices required to be kept or exhibited by or under this Act or rules made thereunder, and require the production thereof for inspection;

(b) examine any person whom he finds in any such premises or place and who, he has reasonable cause to believe is an employee employed therein or an employee to whom work is given out therein;

(c) require any person giving out-work and any out-workers, to give any information which is in his power to give, with respect to the names and addresses of the persons to, for and from whom the work is given out or received and with respect to the payments to be made for the work;

(d) seize or take copies of such register, record of wages or notices or portion thereof as he may consider relevant in respect of an offence under this Act which he has reason to believe has been committed by an employer; and

(e) exercise such other powers as may be prescribed [Section 19 (2)].

(3) Every Inspector shall be deemed to be a public servant within the meaning of the Indian Penal Code, 1860 (Act XLV of 1860) [Section 19 (3)].

(4) Any person required to produce any document or thing or to give any information by an Inspector under sub-section (2) shall be deemed to be legally bound to do so within the meaning of Section 175 and Section 176 of the Indian Penal Code, 1860 (Act XLV of 1860) [Section 19 (4)].

From these provisions of Section 19, we come to know that the Appropriate Government has the right to appoint inspectors for the purposes of this Act and it may define the local limits within which they shall exercise their rights and perform the duties entrusted to them. Every inspector is deemed to be a public servant within the meaning of the Indian Penal Code. These inspectors have to see that the provisions of this Act are complied with. The powers given to inspectors appointed under this Act are as follows:

(a) To enter at all reasonable hours any premises with his assistants or any place where employees are employed in respect of which the minimum rates of wages have been fixed. The inspectors are empowered to examine any register, record of wages or notices required to be kept or exhibited under this Act and require the production thereof for the purpose of inspection.

(b) To examine any person whom an inspector finds in any such premises or place and who, he has reasonable cause to believe, is an employee.

(c) To require any person giving out-work and any out-worker to give any information he wants, which is in his powers to give, with respect to other persons to, for and from whom the work is given out or received, and with respect to the payments to be made for the work.

(d) To seize or to take copies of such register, record of wages or notices as he considers relevant in respect of an offence under the Act which he has reason to believe has been committed by an employer.

(e) To exercise all such other powers as may be prescribed [Section 19].

These provisions of Section 19 also make clear the functions of the Inspectors appointed under this Act. For example, to enter any premises where employees are employed in any scheduled employment for examining the records, registers etc. along with the assistants authorised for this purpose, to examine any person in such premises who is an employee for the purposes of the Act, to seize or to take copies of such registers, record of wages, notices etc. which the Inspectors or his assistance have reasons to believe has been committed by an employer etc.

1.19 Claims

Provisions relating to claims under this Act have been made in Section 20 and 21. Besides these provisions, there are also rules from 27 to 31 relating to claims in Chapter V of the Minimum Wages (Central) Rules of 1950.

1.19.1 Which Claims can be Heard and Decided for any Specified Area by the Authority under this Act

Section 20 (1) throws light on the aspect of hearing and deciding for any specified area by the authority under this Act.

According to Section 20 (1), *"The appropriate government may, by notification in the Official Gazette, appoint any commissioner for workmen's compensation or any officer of the Central Government exercising functions as a Labour Commissioner for any region, or any officer of the State Government not below the rank of a Labour Commissioner or any other officer with experience as a Judge of a Civil Court, or a stipendiary Magistrate to be the authority to hear and decide for any specified area all claims arising out of the payment of less than the minimum rates of wages or in respect of the payment of remuneration for days of rest or for work done on such days under Clause (b) or Clause (c) of sub-section (1) of Section 13 or of wages at the overtime rate under Section 14 to employees employed or paid in that area."*

From the above mentioned provisions of Section 20 (1), we come to know that the Appropriate Government is empowered under Section 20 (1) to appoint an authority to hear and decide for any specified area the following claims:

(a) arising out of payment of less than the minimum rate of wages fixed for his class of work; or

(b) in respect of payment of remuneration for rest of the days or for work done on such days under Section 13 (1) (b and c); or

(c) in respect of wages at the overtime rate under Section 14 to employers employed or paid in that area.

In Anand Oil Industries V. Labour Court, Hyderabad (AIR 1979 AP 182) case, it was held that this Section 20 (1) does not cover all claims in respect of minimum wages. It covers only those cases in which there is a dispute relating to the rate which the minimum wages are payable. Where there is no dispute as to the rate of wages, but the dispute is about the quantum of wages to which a workman is entitled, it would not be a matter falling under this Section 20 (1) of the Minimum Wage Act, 1948 and consequently a petition under Section 33-C (2) of the Industrial Disputes Act could not be barred.

1.19.2 Who can be Appointed as an Authority to Hear and to Decide any Claims under this Act?

According to Section 20 (1), the following may be appointed as an Authority to hear and to decide any claim:

(a) Any commissioner for Workmen's Compensation; or

(b) Any officer of the Central Government exercising functions as a Labour Commissioner for any region, or

(c) Any officer of the State Government not below the rank of a Labour Commissioner; or

(d) Any other officer with the experience as a Judge of a Civil Count or as a Stipendiary Magistrate.

1.19.3 Who can Apply where an Employee has any Claim?

We find the answer to this question in the Provisions of Section 20 (2). These provisions are as under. "*Where an employee has any claim of the nature referred to in sub-section 1, the employee himself or any legal practitioner or any official of a registered trade union authorised in writing to act on his behalf, or any Inspector, or any person acting with permission of the Authority appointed under sub-section 1, may apply to such Authority for a direction under sub-section 3 i.e. Section 20 (3).*"

Thus, any of the following persons can apply to the Authority appointed under Section 20 (1) to hear and to decide for any specified area all claims for a direction:

(a) The employee himself.

(b) Any legal practitioner authorised in writing to act on behalf of the employee.

(c) Any official of a registered trade union authorised in writing to act on behalf of the employee.

(d) Any Inspector.

(e) Any person acting with the permission of the Authority.

1.19.4 When is the Application for Claims to be Presented?

It is made clear in proviso 1 to Section 20 (2) that "*every such application shall be presented within six months from the date on which the minimum wages or other amounts became payable. It is provided further that any application may be admitted after the said period of six months when the applicant satisfies the Authority that he had sufficient cause for not making the application within such period [Proviso 2 to Section 20 (2)].*"

Thus, proviso 2 to Section 20 (2) empowers the Authority to admit the application even after the said period of six months if the applicant satisfies the Authority that he had sufficient cause for not making the application within the prescribed period of six months. The exercise of power by the Authority for the condonation of delay is not controlled by the period of limitation prescribed by the Limitation Act for a suit and the Authority performing its function has in its discretionary power to condone the delay in that respect.

In Special Officer, Thanjavar Central Co-Operative Bank Employees Co-operative Thrift and Credit Society Ltd. V. Deputy Commissioner of Labour [(2003) I L.L.J. 1035 (Mad)] case, the employees made applications for the payment of minimum wages to the prescribed Authority. The prescribed Authority ordered the payment even though the applications were made after the expiry of six months from the date the wages became payable. That order was challenged on the ground that the orders were made as the applications submitted beyond the six months from the date on which the wages became payable. Dismissing the petition, the High Court held that the employees had shown more than sufficient cause for the delay in making the application which was duly considered and the Deputy Commissioner of Labour has rightly exercise his discretion in favour of the employees.

1.19.5 Procedure for Deciding the Claims

Provisions of Sections 20 (3) and 20 (4) make clear the procedure for deciding the claims under this Act. These provisions are as under :

1. When any application under Section 20 (2) is entertained the Authority shall hear the applicant and the employer, or give them an opportunity of being heard, and after such further inquiry, if any, as it may consider necessary, may, without prejudice to any other penalty to which the employer may be liable under this Act, direct :

   (i) in the case of a claim arising out of payment of less than the minimum rates of wages, the payment to the employee of the amount by which the minimum wages payable to him exceed the amount actually paid, together with the payment of such compensation as the Authority may think fit, not exceeding ten times the amount of such excess;

   (ii) in any other case; the payment of the amount due to the employee together with the payment of such compensation as the Authority may think fit, not exceeding ten rupees and the Authority may direct payment of such compensation in cases where the excess or the amount due is paid by the employer to the employee before the disposal of the application [Section 20 (3)]

2. If the Sauthority hearing any application under this section is satisfied that it was either malicious or vexatious, it may direct that a penalty not exceeding fifty rupees be paid to the employer by the person presenting the application [Section 20 (4)].

1.19.6 Recovery of the Amount under the Order of the Authority

It is stated in Section 20 (5) that, "Any amount directed to be paid under this Section 20 may be recovered:

(a) if the Authority is a Magistrate, by the Authority as if it were a fine imposed by the Authority as a Magistrate, or

(b) if the Authority is not a Magistrate, by any Magistrate, to whom the Authority makes an application in this behalf, as if it were a fine imposed by such Magistrate [Section 19 (5)]."

1.19.7 Finality of Directions given in Section 20 and Power of the Authority for Certain Purpose

According to Section 20 (6) of this Act, "*every direction of the Authority under this Section (i.e. Section 20) shall be final.*" *This implies that the decision of the Authority appointed under Section 20 cannot be questioned under any provision of this Act*".

Provisions of Section 20 (7) make it clear that the Authority appointed under Section 20 (1) shall have all the powers of a Civil Court under the Code of Civil Procedure of 1908 for the purpose of :

(a) taking evidence.

(b) enforcing the attendance of witnesses, and

(c) compelling the production of documents.

It is further stated in Section 20 (7) that every such Authority shall be deemed to be a Civil Court for all the purposes of Section 195 and the chapter XXXV of the Code of Criminal Procedure of 1898.

1.20 Single Application in Respect of a Number of Employees [Section 21]

The provisions have been made in Section 21 relating to a single application in respect of a number of employees and these provisions are as follows:

(1) Subject to such rules as may be prescribed; a single application may be presented under Section 20 on behalf or in respect of any number of employees employed in the scheduled employment in respect of which minimum rates of wages have been fixed and in such cases the maximum compensation which may be awarded under sub-section (3) of Section 20 shall not exceed ten times the aggregate amount of such excess or ten rupees per head, as the case may be [Section 21 (1)].

(2) The Authority may deal with any number of separate pending applications presented under Section 20 in respect of employees in the scheduled employments in respect of which minimum rates of wages have been fixed, as a single application presented under sub-section (1) of this section and the provisions of that sub-section shall apply accordingly [Section 21 (2)].

1.21 Bar of Suits [Section 24]

The provisions relating to bar of suits have been made in Section 24. It seems that the object of this Section 24 is to prevent the multiplicity of legal remedies. However, the provisions of Section 24 do not bar the jurisdiction of a tribunal to adjudicate upon a dispute relating to the fixation and payment of wages.

Section 24 bars the jurisdiction of the Civil Courts to entertain a suit, the subject-matter of which the application made to the Authority under Section 20 of the Act.

Section 24 says that, "No court shall entertain any suit for the recovery of wages in so far as the sum so claimed –

(a) forms the subject of an application under Section 20 which has been presented by or on behalf of the plaintiff, or

(b) has formed the subject of a direction under that section in favour of the plaintiff, or

(c) has been adjudged in any proceeding under that section not to be due to the plaintiff, or

(d) could have been recovered by an application under that Section".

1.22 Contracting Out [Section 25]

Any contract or agreement, whether made before or after the commencement of the Act, whereby an employee either relinquishes or reduces his right to a minimum rate of wages or any privilege or concession occurring to him under this Act shall be null and void and so far as it purports to reduce the minimum rate of wages fixed under this Act [Section 25].

Thus, any agreement which reduces the wages below minimum rate of wages fixed under this Act is void. Even apprentices are covered by this Act and minimum wages can be fixed for them.

1.23 Payment of Undisbursed Amounts Due to Employees

All amounts payable by an employer to an employee as the amount of the minimum wages of the employee under this Act or otherwise due to the employee under this Act or any rule or order made thereunder, if such amounts cannot or could not be paid to the employee on account of his death before the payment is made or on account of his whereabouts not being known, be deposited with the prescribed authority who shall deal with the money so deposited in such manner as may be prescribed [Section 22-D].

1.24 Exemption of Employer from Liability in Certain Cases [Section 23]

Where an employer is charged with an offence against this Act, he shall be entitled, upon complaint duly made by him, to have any other person whom he charges as the actual lender, brought before the court at the time of appointment for hearing the charges, and if, after the commission of the offence has been proved, the employer proves to the satisfaction of the court :

(a) that he has used due diligence to enforce the execution of this Act, and
(b) that the said other person committed the offence in question without his knowledge, consent or connivance that the other person shall be convicted of the offence and shall be liable to the like punishment as if he were the employer and the employer shall be discharged.

It is provided in this section that in seeking to prove as aforesaid, the employer may be examined on oath, and the evidence of the employer or his witness, if any, shall be subject to cross-examination by or on behalf of the person whom the employer charges as the actual offender and by the prosecution [Section 23].

1.25 Exemptions and Exceptions

Section 26 provides for the following exemptions:

(1) The Appropriate Government may, subject to such conditions, if any, as it may think fit to impose, direct that the provisions of this Act shall not apply in relation to the wages payable to disabled employees [Section 26 (1)].

(2) The Appropriate Government may, if for special reasons it thinks so fit by notification in the Official Gazette, direct that subject to such conditions and for such period as it may specify the provisions of this Act or any of them shall not apply to all or any class of employees employed in any scheduled employment or to any locality where there is carried on a scheduled employment [Section 26 (2)].

(3) The Appropriate Government may, if it is of opinion that, having regard to the terms and conditions of service applicable to any class of employees in a scheduled employment generally or in a scheduled employment in a local area, or to any establishment or a part of any establishment in a scheduled employment, it is not necessary to fix minimum wages in respect of such employees of that class or in respect of employees in such establishment or such part of any establishment as are in receipt of wages exceeding such limit as may be prescribed in this behalf, direct, by notification in the Official Gazette and subject to such conditions, if any, as it may think fit to impose, that the provisions of this Act or any of them shall not apply in relation to such employees [Section 26 (2-A)].

(4) Nothing in this Act shall apply to the wages payable by an employer to a member of his family who is living with him and is dependent on him [Section 26 (3)].

Explanation:

In this sub-section a member of the employer's family shall be deemed to include his or her spouse or child or parent or brother or sister. Thus, the explanation to Section 26 (3) implies that a member of the employers' family in this regard is deemed to include his or her spouse or child or parent or brother or sister.

1.26 Penalties for Certain Offences

Provisions have been made in Section 22 for imposing certain penalties for certain offences. These provisions of Section 22 are as under.

Any employer who:

(a) pays to any of his employees less than the minimum rates of wages for that class of employee's or less than the amount due to him under any of the provisions of this Act, or

(b) contravenes any rule or any order made under Section 13 of this Act i.e. fixing hours of normal working day etc. is punishable with the imprisonment for a term which may extend to six months or with a fine which may extend to five hundred rupees or both [Section 22].

It is also provided that in imposing any fine for an offence under this Section, the Court shall take into consideration the amount of any compensation already awarded against the accused in any proceedings under Section 20. Section 20 is related to 'Claims'.

1.27 General Provision for Punishment of other Offences

Any employer who contravenes any provision of this Act or of any rule or any order made thereunder, if no other penalty is provided for such contravention by this Act, is punishable with a fine which may extend to five hundred rupees [Section 22-A].

1.28 Cognizance of Offences

No court shall take cognizance of a complaint against any person for an offence;

under clause A of Section 22 unless an application in respect of the fact constituting such offence has been presented under Section 20 (claims) and has been granted wholly or partly and the Appropriate Government or an officer authorised by it in this behalf has sanctioned making of the complaint [Section 22-B (1)], and no court shall take cognizance of an offence under clause A or clause B of Section 22, unless the complaint thereof is made within the period of one month of the grant of sanction under this section and under Section 22-A unless the complaint thereof is made within the period of six months from the date on which the offence is alleged to have been committed [Section 22-B (2)].

1.29 Offences by Companies

If the person committing any offence under this Act is a company, every person, who at the time the offence was committed, was incharge of and was responsible to the company for the conduct of the business of the company as well as the company shall be deemed to be guilty of the offence and shall be liable to be prosecuted against and punished accordingly [Section-22C (1)].

It is provided further that nothing contained in this sub-section shall render any such person liable to any punishment provided in the Act if he proves that the offence was committed without his knowledge or that he exercised all due diligence to prevent the commission of such offence [Proviso to Section 22-C (1)].

Notwithstanding anything contained in the sub-section (1) mentioned above, where an offence under this Act has been committed by a company and it is proved that the offence has been committed with the consent or connivance of, or is attributable to any neglect on the part of any director, manager, secretary or other officer of the company, such director, manager, secretary or any other officer of the company shall also be deemed to be guilty of that offence and shall be liable to be prosecuted against and punished accordingly [Section 22-C (2)].

For the purpose of this Section 22-C, a Company means any body corporate and includes a firm or other association of individuals and a director in relation to a firm means a partner in the firm.

Points to Remember

- The Minimum Wages Act of 1948 is basically passed to provide for fixing minimum rates of wages in certain establishments and it extends to the whole of India.
- While making the provisions, necessary care has been taken to see that the wages fixed correspond to the work the workers put in and they are not exploited.
- The Act intends to protect not only male workers, but also women, children and adolescent workers and apprentices too.
- The procedure for fixing and revising minimum wages in laid down in Section 5 of the Act.
- There is the provision in this Act to appoint the Advisory Board to coordinate the working of committees appointed under this Act and also to advice the Appropriate Government in fixing and revising minimum rates of wages.
- The minimum wages payable under this Act must be paid in cash. However, where it is a custom to pay the wages wholly or partly in kind, it is a permissible subject to the provisions of Section 11 of the Act.
- There is a provision for making payments for overtime work. The work done in excess as prescribed under normal working day is overtime work.
- The provision is made in Section 13 of the Act for fixing the hours for a normal working day.
- The employees are required to maintain the registers and records as per the provisions of Section 18.
- There is a provision in this Act to appoint Inspectors for the purposes of this Act. They are given certain powers to perform their duties and functions under Section 19.
- There are provisions relating to claims, when an application for claims to be submitted, who can apply for the claims, which are the Authorities to decide the claims etc.
- Provisions have been made in the Act for punishment for offences in Section 22.

Questions for Discussion

1. Discuss fully the nature and the scope of the Minimum Wages Act, 1948. What are the objects and extent of the Minimum Wages Act, 1948?

2. Explain the objectives behind the enactment of the Minimum Wage Act, 1948. What is the scope of its application and coverage?

3. Definition of Wages is different in the Minimum Wages Act, 1948 as compared to the one under the Payment of Wages Act, 1936. Why so?

4. State the definitions of the following words and terms as given in the Minimum Wages Act of 1948.

    (a) Appropriate Government

    (b) Competent Authority

    (c) Cost of living Index

    (d) Employees

    (e) Employer

    (f) Scheduled Employment

5. Elaborate the basic principles and procedures to be observed in fixing and also in revising the minimum rate of wages in an industry.

6. State the composition of minimum rate of wages fixed or revised ay an Appropriate Government in respect of scheduled employment.

7. What are the constituents of minimum rate of wages fixed or revised by an Appropriate Government in respect of scheduled employment?

8. Explain the functions and the compositions of Advisory Boards and Central Advisory Board.

9. Write a detailed note on provisions as contained in Sections 18 to 23 with regard to the enforcement of the Act.

10. How does the Appropriate Government fix the hours for normal working day and charges in respect thereof?

11. What remedy is available to a workman who has been paid less than the minimum rate of wages?

12. Describe how the Inspectors are appointed for the purpose of this Act. What are their powers?

13. Explain the provisions relating to penalties and their cognizance under this Act.

14. When is the employer exempted from the liability of paying minimum rates of wages under this Act?

15. Write notes on the following:
    (a) Objects and the scope of the Act
    (b) Fixation and Revision of the Minimum Rates of Wages
    (c) Procedure for fixing and revising minimum wages
    (d) Functions and composition of the Advisory Board
    (e) Functions and composition of the Central Advisory Board
    (f) Wages in kind
    (g) Fixing hours for a normal working day
    (h) Provisions relating to overtime
    (i) Claims under the Minimum Wages Act, 1948
    (j) Penalties for offences under this Act
    (k) Meaning of 'Minimum Wages'

16. What are the provisions of the Act relating to:
    (i) a worker who works less than normal working day
    (ii) wages to an employee who does two or more classes of work

17. Explain the provisions of this Act relating claims arising out of payment of less than minimum rates of wages to employees.

18. Explain the provisions of this Act relating to:
    (a) Penalty for certain offences
    (b) Bar of suits
    (c) Payment of wages for overtime work

19. Which claims can be heard and decided for any specified area by the Authority under this Act?

20. Who can apply under this Act where an employee has any claim? When the application for claims is to be presented?

Practical Problems

1. Mr. X is working in a co-operative society which carries on the business of buying milk from its members and distributing it. Mr. X claims payment of minimum wages under the Minimum Wages Act. Can his claim be admitted?

   [**Hint** : No. This case is similar to that of "Secretary, Padippu K. S. Sangam Ltd. V. C. Varghese [2007 II L.L.J. 544 (S.C)] case. In that case, the Supreme Court observed that the question was whether the concerned dairy farming co-op. society was engaged in dairy farming so as to fall within the preview of the Minimum Wages Act; schedule II appended to the Act. The Supreme Court held that the concerned co-op. society was not so engaged. The mere activity of buying milk from its members and distributing it would not constitute 'Dairy farming". Where there was no rearing of milch cows and no farming activity was carried on by the said society.]

2. Mr. Y is working in XYZ Mica Mines Ltd. He has not been paid wages according to the M.W. Act. Hence, he files a suit for getting minimum wages as per the provisions of the Act. Can he became successful?

[**Hint:** No. In Chatturam Darsanram V. Union of India [(1980) II L.L.J. 465 (Pat)] case was similar to the case mentioned above. In that case, the question was whether workmen working in mine were working in the scheduled employment. It was held that the item No. 10 of the part I of the schedule relates to employment in any "Mica Works' and not 'Mica Mines'. The connotations of 'Mica Mines' and 'Mica Works' are different. It would not be reasonable to read 'Mica Mines' in the expression 'Mica Works', and 'Mica Mines' is not included in the said schedule.]

3. Mr. X is an outdoor worker and Mr. Y engages him for producing some goods at the residence of Mr. X or at some other place not controlled by Mr. Y. Mr. X supplied the goods so produced to Mr. Y. Is Mr. X covered under the M.W. Act?

[**Hint :** Yes]

4. Mr. X is an employee in the hospital run by the local authority. The minimum wages fixed for such employees by the notification is ₹ 900 as the basic pay and ₹ 400 as special allowance. But the hospital pays ₹ 650 as the basic pay and ₹ 850 as D.A. Mr. X applies for receiving ₹ 900 as a basic pay and lodges his complaint. Can he become successful?

[**Hint :** No. Both the components of wages should be taken into consideration together and what is paid to Mr. X i.e. ₹ 650 + ₹ 850 = ₹ 1500 is more than the minimum wages fixed by the notification i.e. ₹ 900 + ₹ 400 = ₹ 1300. This case is similar to that of Hari Lal Doshi Hindu Sabha Hospital V. Maharashtra General Kamgar Union [(1999) II CLR 799 (Bom. H.C.) case.]

Chapter 2...

The Maharashtra Recognition of Trade Unions and Prevention of Unfair Labour Practices Act, 1971 [M.R.T.U. & P.U.L.P.]

Contents ...

2.1 Introduction
2.2 Objects of the M.R.T.U. and P.U.L.P. Act of 1971
2.3 Extent, Commencement and Application of the Act
2.4 Definitions
2.5 Authorities Under this Act
2.6 Industrial Court - Its Constitution, Duties and Powers
    2.6.1 Constitution of the Industrial Court and Qualification of the Members of the Industrial Court
    2.6.2 Duties of the Industrial Court
    2.6.3 Powers of the Industrial Court
2.7 Labour Court - Its Constitution, Duties and Powers
    2.7.1 Constitution of Labour Court
    2.7.2 Duties of Labour Court
    2.7.3 Powers of Labour Court
2.8 Investigating Officers - Their Appointment, Duties and Powers
    2.8.1 Appointment of the Investigating Officers
    2.8.2 Duties of the Investigating Officers
    2.8.3 Powers of the Investigating Officers
2.9 Recognition of Unions
    2.9.1 Application for Recognition of an Union [Section 11]
    2.9.2 Recognition of an Unions [Section 12]
    2.9.3 Cancellation of Recognition and Suspension of Rights [Section 13]
    2.9.4 Recognition of other Union [Section 14]
    2.9.5 Application for Re-recognition [Section 15]
    2.9.6 Liability of Union or Members not Relieved by Cancellation [Section 16]
    2.9.7 Publication or Order [Section 17]
    2.9.8 Recognition of Union for more than One Undertaking

2.10 Obligations and Rights of Recognised and Other Unions
  2.10.1 Obligations of Recognised Unions [Section 19]
  2.10.2 Rights of Recognised Unions [Section 20]
  2.10.3 Rights of Unrecognised Unions [Section 22]
  2.10.4 Employees Authorised by Recognised Union to Appear or Act in Certain Proceedings to be considered as on Duty [Section 23]
2.11 Illegal Strikes and Lock-outs
  2.11.1 Illegal Strikes
  2.11.2 Illegal Lock-outs
  2.11.3 Reference to the Labour Court for Declaration whether the Strike or Lock-out is Illegal [Section 25]
2.12 Unfair Labour Practices
  2.12.1 Meaning of Unfair Labour Practices and Various Unfair Labour Practices [Section 26]
  2.12.2 Provisions Relating to Modification of Schedules
  2.12.3 The Procedure to be followed for Dealing with Complaints Relating to Unfair Labour Practices [Section 28]
  2.12.4 Parties on whom an Order of the Court is Binding
2.13 Penalties
  2.13.1 Penalty for Disclosure of Confidential Information
  2.13.2 Penalty for Contempts of the Industrial or Labour Courts [Section 48]
  2.13.3 Penalty for Obstructing Officers from carrying out their Duties and for Failure to Produce Documents or to Comply with Requisition or Order [Section 49]
2.14 Recovery of Money due from Employer and Recovery of Fines
  2.14.1 Recovery of Money Due from Employer
  2.14.2 Recovery of Fines
- Points to Remember
- Questions for Discussion
- Practical Problems

Learning Objectives...

After going through this chapter, you will be able to know:

- The objects of the M.R.T.U. and P.U.L.P. Act
- Various authorities appointed under this Act and their duties and powers
- Provisions of this Act relating to recognition of unions
- Obligations and rights to recognition of unions
- Provisions relating to Strikes and Lock-outs under this Act
- Unfair labour practices on the part of employers, trade unions and employees
- Penalties for offences under this Act
- Provisions of recovery of money due from the employer and recovery of fines

2.1 Introduction

One of the major and important pre-requisites for industrial progress is the prevalence of industrial peace i.e. a suitable climate in which the industries can thrive. Industrial peace broadly implies the absence of industrial unrest, labour problems or the existence of a harmonious cordial relationship or co-operation between workers and their employers. However, the problem of industrial peace is common to almost all the industrially developed and developing countries of the world and ever since industrialisation began, every country is making various efforts to find out solutions for establishing industrial peace.

The methods and ways used in solving the problem of industrial peace or industrial unrest differ from country to country depending upon its economic, social and political environment in existence. Still the problem has not been solved completely. On the contrary, with the advent of the industrial development, labour problems are becoming more and more complicated.

In India, the magnitude of labour problems has increased with the tempo of industrial activities and industrial development. Problems of wages, strikes and lock-outs, industrial housing, unemployment, trade unions etc. confront the Government as well as social reformers. These labour problems apart from their economic impact also have social and other repercussions.

The welfare of the working class in the industrial sector is important both to the industries as well as to the community at large. The Government concern for the welfare of the industrial workers in our country is evident from the fact that a large number of legislative enactments in this field have been passed or improved upon after 1947.

Several labour enactments have been promulgated by the central as well as state governments to safeguard the interests of the industrial workers. Payment of Wages Act, Minimum Wages Act, Industrial Disputes Act, Factories Act, Trade Unions Act, Workmen's Compensation Act, and Payment of Bonus Act are some of such Acts.

The Bombay Industrial Disputes Act, 1938 was passed in Maharashtra State previously. The provisions of this Act were availed of extensively by the employers as well as the employees in the textile industry. However, with the passage of time and on the strength of the experience gained after passing the Bombay Industrial Disputes Act of 1938, the Government felt it necessary to build further on the same foundations and hence 'The Bombay Industrial Relations Act of 1946' was passed. That Act also was found to be ineffective to deal fully with the growing problems of the industrial workers and hence 'The Maharashtra Recognition of Trade Unions and Prevention of Unfair Labour Practices Act of 1971' was passed to deal with the problems of trade unions and also to provide for the recognition of trade unions for facilitating collective bargaining for certain undertakings, to make clear their rights and obligations, to confer certain powers on unrecognised unions, to provide for declaring certain strikes and lock-outs as illegal strikes and lock-outs, to define properly certain unfair labour practices and to provide for their prevention, to constitute certain courts as independent machinery for carrying out the purposes of the Act etc.

The importance of this M.R.T.U. and P.U.L.P. Act is eminent from its title. Efforts have been made to cover many labour litigations under this Act. Now let us study important provisions of the M.R.T.U. and P.U.L.P. Act of 1971. However, before we study the Act's provisions let us first consider the important objects of passing the Act, its extent, commencement and the definitions as given in Sections 1, 2 and 3 of the Act.

2.2 Objects of the M.R.T.U. and P.U.L.P. Act of 1971

In the preamble of the Act, various objects of the Act are clearly mentioned. In the preamble, it is stated that –

"Act to provide for the recognition of trade unions for facilitating collective bargaining for certain undertakings, to state their rights and obligations; to confer certain powers on unrecognised unions; to provide for declaring certain strikes and lock-outs as illegal strikes and lock-outs; to define and provide for the prevention of certain unfair labour practices; to constitute courts (as independent machinery) for carrying out the purposes of according recognition to trade unions for enforcing the provisions relating to unfair practices; and to provide for matters connected with the purposes aforesaid."

WHEREAS, by Government Resolution, Industries and Labour Department, No. IDA. 1367 - LAB - II, dated the 14th February 1968, the Government of Maharashtra appointed a Committee called "The Committee on Unfair Labour Practices" for defining certain activities of employers and workers and their organisations which should be treated as unfair labour practices and for suggesting action which should be taken against employers or workers, or their organisations, for engaging in such unfair labour practices;

And WHEREAS, after taking into consideration the report of the Committee, Government is of opinion that it is expedient to provide for the recognition of trade unions for facilitating collective bargaining for certain undertakings; to state their rights and obligations; to confer certain powers on unrecognised unions; to provide for declaring certain strikes and lock-outs as illegal strikes and lock-outs; to define and provide for the prevention of certain unfair labour practices; to constitute courts (as independent machinery) for carrying out the purposes of according recognition to trade unions and for enforcing provisions relating to unfair practices; and to provide for matters connected with the purposes aforesaid; it is hereby enacted in the Twenty Second Year of the Republic of India.

Thus, from the preamble, we come to know about the following objectives behind passing the Act.

1. To provide for the recognition of trade unions for facilitating collective bargaining for certain undertakings covered by the Act;

2. To state the rights and obligations of trade unions;
3. To provide for declaring certain strikes and lock-outs as illegal strikes and lock-outs;
4. To define certain unfair labour practices and to provide for their prevention;
5. To constitute courts as independent machinery for carrying out the purposes of according recognition to trade unions for enforcing the provisions relating to unfair practices.

The Government of Maharashtra appointed a committee called 'the Committee on Unfair Labour Practices" in February 1968 for defining certain activities of employers, workers and their organisations which should be treated as unfair labour practices and also for suggesting actions which should be taken against the employers or workers or their organisations for engaging themselves in such unfair labour practices. The committee submitted its report. After considering the report submitted by the said committee, the Government of Maharashtra felt it essential to pass the M.R.T.U. and P.U.L.P. Act and as a result, the Act was passed to achieve various objectives stated above.

2.3 Extent, Commencement and Application of the Act

This M.R.T.U. and P.U.L.P. Act extends to the whole of the State of Maharashtra [Section 2 (1)], and

it came into force on 1st February, 1972 by the notification in the Official Gazette. The Government of Maharashtra is fully authorised to make applicable different provisions of this Act for different areas on different dates by notification in the Official Gazette [Section 2 (2)].

So far the application of this Act is concerned, Section 2 (3) states that "*Except as otherwise hereinafter provided, this shall apply to the industries to which the Bombay Industrial Relations Act, 1946, Bombay XI of 1947, for the time being applies, and also to any industrial dispute concerning such industry is the appropriate government under the Act.*

Section 2 (3) further provides that", *The State Government may, by notification in the Official Gazette, direct that the provisions of this Act shall cease to apply to any such industry from such date as may be specified in the notification and from that date, the provisions of this Act shall cease to apply to that industry and thereupon, Section 7 of the Bombay General Clauses Act, 1904, Bombay I of 1944, shall apply to such cessor as if this Act has been repealed in relation to such industry by a Maharashtra Act*" [Proviso to Section 2 (3)].

2.4 Definitions

In this Act, unless the context requires otherwise, the definitions of eighteen words or terms are given in Section (3) which are as follows:

1. Bombay Act: "Bombay Act" means the Bombay Industrial Relations Act, 1946, Bombay XI of 1947 [Section 3 (1)].

2. Central Act: "Central Act" means the Industrial Disputes Act, 1947, XIV of 1947 [Section 3 (2)].

3. Concern: "Concern" means any premises including the precincts thereof where any industry to which the Central Act applies is carried on [Section 3 (3)].

In the definition of 'concern', the words 'any premises' are used. But, they imply any one premise(s) and not more than one. The word 'concern' as defined in this sub-section implies any premises including the precincts thereof where any industry to which the Central Act i.e. the Industrial Disputes Act of 1947 applies is carried on and the expression 'any' in this context should mean only one premise and not more than one premises.

4. Court: "Court" for the purposes of Chapter VI and VII means the Industrial Court, or as the case may be, the Labour Court [Section 3 (4)].

5. Employee: "Employee" in relation to an industry to which the Bombay Act for the time being applies, means an employee as defined in clause (13) of Section 3 of the Bombay Act; and in any other case, means a workman as defined in clause (s) of Section 2 of the Central Act [Section 3 (5)].

The Section 4 (5) is explanatory. It merely states that the term 'employee', in relation to an industry to which the Bombay Industrial Relations Act applies, means an employee as defined in Section 3 (13) of the Bombay Industrial Relations Act and in other cases, an employee means a workman as defined under Section 2 (s) of the Industrial Disputes Act of 1947. Therefore, let us consider the definitions of an employee and a workman as given in both Acts.

According to Section 3 (13) of the Bombay Industrial Relations Act of 1946, "employee means any person employed to do any skilled or unskilled work for hire or reward in any industry, and includes:

(a) A person employed by a contractor to do any work for him in the execution of a contract with an employer within the meaning of sub-clause (e) of clause (14);

(b) A person who has been dismissed, discharged or retrenched or whose services have been terminated from employment on account of any dispute relating to change in respect of which notice is given or an application made under Section 42 whether before or after his dismissal, discharge, retrenchment or, as the case may be, termination from employment.

but does not include –

(i) A person primarily employed in a managerial, administrative, supervisory, or technical capacity drawing basic pay (excluding allowances) exceeding one thousand rupees per month;

(ii) Any other person or class of persons employed in the same capacity as those specified in clause (i) above irrespective of the amount of pay drawn by such persons which the State Government may, by notification in the Official Gazette, specify in this behalf.

The above mentioned definition of 'employee' is divided into two parts. The first part includes certain persons while the other part excludes certain persons from the scope of the definition of an employee.

It implies that an employee is any person who is employed directly or through a contractor to do any skilled or unskilled work and for that work, the employer must have paid him some amount to such person. The persons who have been dismissed, discharged, retrenched or terminated from service are also covered by the definition of an employee. While four kinds of persons i.e. persons who have been employed primarily in (1) managerial, (2) administrative, (3) supervisory and (4) technical capacity and drawing more than one thousand rupees per month have been excluded.

In the definition of "Employee" under M.R.T.U. and P.U.L.P. Act, it is also stated that "*in other case, an employee means a workman as defined in clause (s) of Section 2 of the Central Act*".

Section 2 (s) of the Central Act i.e. the Industrial Disputes Act of 1947 defines the term 'employee' as follows:

"Workman" means any person (including an apprentice) employed in any industry to do any manual, unskilled, skilled, technical, operational, clerical or supervisory work for hire or reward, whether the terms of employment be express or implied, and for the purposes of any proceeding under this Act, in relation to an industrial dispute, includes any such person who has been dismissed, discharged or retrenched in connection with, or as a consequence of, that dispute, or whose dismissal, discharge or retrenchment has led to that dispute. But "Workman" does not include any such person –

(i) Who is subject to the Air Force Act, 1950, or the Army Act, 1950, or the Navy Act, 1957; or

(ii) Who is employed in the police service or as an office or other employee of a prison; or

(iii) Who is employed mainly in a managerial or administrative capacity; or

(iv) Who, being employed in a supervisory capacity, draws wages exceeding one thousand six hundred rupees per mensem or exercises, either by the nature of the duties attached to the office or by reasons of the powers vested in him, functions mainly of a managerial nature.

The following test can be applied for the person to be considered as workman under Section 2 (s) of the Industrial Disputes Act, 1947.

If the person is employed by an industry, no matter where he is employed, shall be a workman. Thus, the definition of a workman presupposes the relationship of master and servant or employer and employee. This relationship of master and servant or employer and employee exists between them as a result of an agreement between them. Such agreement can be express or implied. By entering into such agreement, a workman remains under the supervision, control and direction of his master.

An employee is said to be under the control, direction and supervision of the employer if such an employee has to follow the orders of the employer –

1. Regarding the work entrusted to him and the details of work, and
2. The manner in which the work shall be executed or done or completed. From this point of view, the following persons are deemed to be workmen.

a. Salesmen receiving wages but not commission.
b. Employees of municipalities.
c. Transport engineers, Blending supervisors etc.
d. A time-keeper, a guard, *Malis* employed for looking after gardens attached with officers' bungalows, factories etc.
e. An auditor doing clerical work.
f. An employee occasionally doing supervisory work.
g. Accountants who are merely clerks with supervisory duties.
h. Assistant medical officers doing technical work.
i. Development officers of Life Insurance Corporation.
j. Retrenched workmen.

Thus, when the employee is employed to do manual, or clerical work; skilled or unskilled work; technical or non-technical work, he is considered as a workman even if he is employed in a supervisory capacity, unless his wages exceeds ₹ 1600/- or his duties are mainly of managerial nature. In different cases, the following persons were held not to be workmen.

(a) Persons authorised to assign duties and distribute works in various banks.
(b) Employees working in the head office of a managing agency which manages several concerns.
(c) Head clerk in the State Transport Authority.
(d) Casual and temporary workers after finishing their jobs.
(e) The staff members of seasonal factories who are not permanent; not workmen during off-season.
(f) Sales representatives, medical representatives who get commission are not workmen.
(g) Persons holding supervisory and managerial posts.
(h) Maintenance Engineers, performing supervisory work and authorise to make temporary appointments, grant leave; etc.
(i) Apprentices governed by Apprentices Act 1961.
(j) Blending supervisors and Fuelling superintendents.

6. Employer: "Employer" in relation to an industry to which the Bombay Act applies, means an employer as defined in clause (14) of Section 3 of the Bombay Act; and in any other case, means an employer as defined in clause (g) of Section 2 of the Central Act [Section 3 (6)].

Section 3 (14) of the Bombay Industrial Relations Act of 1946 defines the term 'Employer' as follows:

"Employer" includes –

(a) An association or a group of employers;

(b) Any agent of employers;

(c) Where an industry in conducted or carried on by a department of the State Government, the authority prescribed in that behalf, and where no such authority is prescribed, the head of the department;

(d) Where an industry is conducted or carried on by or on behalf of a local authority, the Chief Executive Officer of the authority;

(e) Where the owner of any undertaking in the course of or for the purpose of conducting the undertaking contracts with any person for the execution by or under the contractor of the whole or any part of any work which is ordinarily part of the undertaking, the owner of the undertaking.

While the Industrial Disputes Act, 1947 defines the term 'employer' under clause (g) of Section 2 which is as under "employer" means –

(i) In relation to an industry carried on by or under the authority of any department of the Central Government or a State Government the authority prescribed in this behalf, or where no authority is prescribed, the head of the department;

(ii) In relation to an industry carried on by or on behalf of a local authority, the chief executive officer of that authority.

The definition of an employer under Section 2 (g) of the Industrial Disputes Act of 1947 mentioned above is not exhaustive. But, it must be noted that it does not limit its sphere to businesses run by the Government or local authority. The Act applies to all industries carried on either by an individual or an association.

7. Industry: "Industry" in relation to an industry to which the Bombay Act applies means an industry as defined in clause (19) of Section 3 of the Bombay Act, and in any other case, means an industry as defined in clause (j) of Section 2 of the Central Act [Section 3 (7)].

In the M.R.T.U. and P.U.L.P. Act of 1971, the term 'Industry' has not been defined. But, the Act merely states that in relation to an industry to which the Bombay Industrial Relation Act applies, means an industry as defined in Section 3 (19) of Bombay I.R. Act and in other cases, an industry means an industry as defined in Section 2 (J) of the Industrial Disputes Act of 1947. Thus, an industry covers all the industries included in these two Acts. Therefore, let us consider the definitions of an industry as given in both the Acts.

The definition of 'Industry' as given in Section 3 (19) of the Bombay Industrial Relations Act of 1946 is as follows:

"industry" means –

(a) Any business, trade, manufacture of undertaking or calling of employers;

(b) Any calling, service employment, handicraft, or industrial occupation or avocation of employees;

and includes –

(i) Agriculture and agricultural operations;

(ii) Any branch of an industry or group of industries which the [State] Government may by notification in the Official Gazette declare to be an industry for the purposes of this Act.

While, in the Industrial Disputes Act 1947, the definition of 'Industry' is given in Section 2 (J) which is as follows:

"Industry" means any systematic activity carried on by cooperation between an employer and his workmen (whether such workmen are employed by such employer directly or by or through any agency, including a contractor) for the production, supply or distribution of goods or services with a view of satisfy human wants or wishes (not being wants or wishes which are merely spiritual or religious in nature), whether or not;

(i) Any capital that has been invested for the purpose of carrying on such industry; or

(ii) Such activity is carried on with a motive to make any gain or profit and includes –

(a) Any activity of the Dock Labour Board established under Section 5 A of the Dock Workers (Regulation of Employment) Act, 1948;

(b) Any activity relating to the promotion of sales or business or both carried on by an establishment,

but does not include –

1. Any agricultural operation except where such agricultural operation is carried on in an integrated manner with any other activity (being any such activity as is referred to in the foregoing provisions of this clause) and such other activity is the predominant one,

Explanation: For the purpose of this sub-clause, 'agricultural operation' does not include any activity carried on in a plantation as defined in clause (f) of Section 2 of the Plantations Labour Act, 1951; or

2. Hospitals or dispensaries; or

3. Educational, scientific, research or training institutions; or

4. Institutions owned and managed by organisations wholly or substantially engaged in any charitable, social or philanthropic service; or

5. Khadi or village industries; or

6. Any activity of the Government relatable to the sovereign functions of the Government including all the activities carried on by the departments of the Central Government dealing with defence research, atomic energy and space; or
7. Any domestic service; or
8. Any activity being a profession practiced by an individual or body of individuals if the number of persons employed by the individual or body of individuals in relation to such profession is less than ten; or
9. Any activity, being an activity carried on by a cooperative society or a club or any other like body of individuals, if the number of persons employed by the cooperative society, club or other like body of individuals in relation to such activity is less than ten;

From this definition of an industry as given in Section 2 (J) of the Industrial Disputes Act of 1947, it becomes clear that an industry means –

(a) Any systematic activity which is carried on by cooperation between an employer and his workmen.
(b) Such activity is carried on for the production, supply or distribution of goods and / or services with a view to satisfy human wants. Such wants must be material and not merely spiritual or religious in nature.
(c) Whether capital for carrying on such activity is invested or not is immaterial.
(d) Such industry may be carried on for profit or gain or there may be an absence of profit motive.
(e) Such industry may be the venture in the private, public, joint or in any other sector.

While deciding whether any industry comes within the purview of this Act or not, the true focus is functional and the decisive test is the nature of the activity carried on with special emphasis on the employee and employer relations.

8. Industrial Court: "Industrial Court" means on Industrial Court constituted under Section 4 of the M.R.T.U. and P.U.L.P. Act of 1971 [Section 3 (8)].

9. Investigating Officer: "Investigating Officer" means an officer appointed under Section 8 of the M.R.T.U. and P.U.L.P. Act of 1971 [Section 3 (9)].

10. Labour Court: 'Labour Court' means a Labour Court constituted under Section 6 of the M.R.T.U. and P.U.L.P. Act of 1971 [Section 3 (10)].

11. Member: 'Member' means a person who is an ordinary member of a union, and has paid a subscription to the union of not less than 50 *paise* per calendar month.

It is also provided that, no person shall at any time be deemed to be a member, if his subscription is in arrears for a period of more than three calendar months during the period of six months immediately preceding such time, and the expression "membership" shall be construed, accordingly [Proviso to the clause 11 of Section 3].

Explanation: A subscription for a particular calendar month shall, for the purpose of this clause, be deemed to be in arrears, if such subscription is not paid within three months after the end of the calendar month in respect of which it is due.

12. **Orders:** "Order" means an order of the Industrial or Labour Court [Section 3 (12)].

13. **Recognised Union:** "Recognised union" means a union which has been issued a certificate of recognition under Chapter III [Section 3 (13)].

14. **Schedule:** "Schedule" means a Schedule to this Act [Section 3 (14)].

15. **Undertaking:** "Undertaking" for the purposes of Chapter III, means any concern in industry to be one undertaking for the purpose of that Chapter [Section 3 (15)].

16. **Unfair Labour Practices:** "Unfair labour practices" means unfair labour practices as defined in Section 26 [Section 3 (16)].

17. **Union:** "Union" means a trade union of employee, which is registered under the Trade Unions Act, 1926 [Section 3 (17)].

It is made clear in clause 18 of Section 3 that "*words and expressions used in this Act and not defined therein, but defined in the Bombay Act, shall, in relation to an industry to which the provisions of the Bombay Act apply, have the meanings assigned to them by the Bombay Act; and in any other case, shall have the meanings assigned to them by the Central Act.*"

2.5 Authorities Under this Act

Industrial Court, Labour Court and Investigation Officers are the authorities under this M.R.T.U. and P.U.L.P. Act. Sections 4, 6 and 8 of the Act empower the State Government to constitute and appoint these authorities. Let us now consider the constitution, appointment, powers, duties etc. of these authorities.

2.6 Industrial Court – Its Constitution, Duties and Powers

2.6.1 Constitution of the Industrial Court and Qualifications of the Members of the Industrial Court

The State Government is empowered under this Act to constitute the Industrial Court. Provisions relating to the constitution and qualifications of the members of the Industrial Court have been made in Section 4 of the Act which are as follows :

1. The State Government shall by notification in the Official Gazette, constitute an Industrial Court.

2. The Industrial Court shall consist of not less than three members, one of whom shall be the President [Section 4 (2)].

3. Every member of the Industrial Court shall be a person who is not connected with the complaint referred to that Court, or with any industry directly affected by such complaint [Section 4 (3)].

It is also provided that, every member shall be deemed to be connected with a complaint or with an industry by reason of his having shares in a company which is connected with, or likely to be affected by, such complaint, unless he discloses to the State Government the nature and extent of the shares held by him in such company and in the opinion of the State Government recorded in writing such member is not connected with the complaint, or the industry [Proviso to Section 4 (3)].

    4.   Every member of the Industrial Court, shall be a person who is or has been a Judge of a High Court or is eligible for being appointed a Judge of such Court [Section 4 (4)].

It is further provided that one member may be a person who is not so eligible if he possesses in the opinion of the State Government expert knowledge of labour or industrial matters" [Proviso to Section 4 (4)].

Thus, by the notification in the Official Gazette, the State Government has constituted the Industrial Court. The Industrial Court consists of three members and one of them works as the President.

Sub-section (3) and (4) of Section 4 throw light on the qualifications of the members of the Industrial Court and also make clear certain restrictions on the State Government to appoint these members.

Section 2 (4) provides that every member of the Industrial Court must be a person who is or has been a Judge of the High Court or he must be such person who is eligible for being a Judge of the High Court. But it is also provided in clause 4 of Section 4 that there can be one member who is not so qualified. However, such member, in the opinion of the State Government, must have the expert knowledge of labour or industrial matters.

It is also provided in Section 2 (3) that any member of the Industrial Court must not be person who is connected with the complaint referred to that court or with any industry directly affected by such complaint.

Every member is considered to be connected with a complaint or with an industry by reason of his having shares in a company which is connected with or likely to be affected by, such complaint, unless such member discloses to the State Government the nature and the extent of his share holding in such company and in the opinion of the State Government recorded in writing such member is not connected with the complaint, or the industry [Proviso to Section 4 (3)].

2.6.2 Duties of the Industrial Court

There are certain duties entrusted to the Industrial Court under this Act. These duties are enumerated in Section 5 of this Act which are as follows:

Section 5 states that it shall be the duty of the Industrial Court:

(a) To decide an application by a union for grant of recognition to it;

(b) To decide an application by a union for grant of recognition to it in place of a union which has already been recognised under this Act;

(c) To decide an application from another union or an employer for withdrawal or cancellation of the recognition of a union;

(d) To decide complaints relating to excess unfair labour practice falling in item 1 of Schedule IV;

(e) To assign work and to give directions to the Investigating Officers in matters of verification of membership of unions and investigation of complaints relating to unfair labour practices;

(f) To decide references made to it on any point of law either by any civil or criminal court; and

(g) To decide appeals under Section 42.

From the above mentioned provisions of Section 5 of the M.R.T.U. and P.U.L.P. Act, we come to know that the Industrial Court constituted under this Act can decide certain matters. They are as follows:

1. Granting recognition to a union on the application made by such union to the Industrial Court.

2. Considering an application made to the Industrial Court by a union for recognition in place of a union already recognised, grant or otherwise the recognition to such union in place of a union already recognised.

3. Withdrawal or cancellation of the recognition of a union on the application from another union or an employer made to the Industrial Court.

4. Complaints relating to unfair labour practices except item No. I of Schedule IV. Section 26 of this Act, meaning of unfair labour practices is made clear and accordingly, unfair labour practices mean any of the practices listed in Schedules II, III and IV. These schedules are given elsewhere in this book. In schedule II, unfair labour practices on the part of the employers are given, in schedule III, unfair labour practices on the part of trade unions are given. While in schedule IV, general unfair labour practices on the part of employers are given.

5. It is also one of the duties of the Industrial Court constituted under this Act to decide references, if any, made to it by any Civil Court or Criminal Court on any point of law.

6. The duty of deciding appeals under Section 42 is also entrusted to the Industrial Court under Section 5 (g) of this Act.

Section 42 states that, "Notwithstanding anything contained in Section 40, the appeal shall lie to the Industrial Court :

(a) against a conviction by a Labour Court, by the person convicted,

(b) against the acquittal by a Labour Court in its special jurisdiction, by the complainant;

(c) for enhancement of a sentence awarded by a Labour Court in its special jurisdiction, by the State Government [Section 42 (1)].

Every appeal shall be made within thirty days from the date of conviction, acquittal or sentence, as the case may be. It is further provided that the Industrial Court may, for sufficient reason, allow an appeal after the expiry of the said period [Section 42 (2) and proviso of Section 42 (2)].

7. In Section 5 (e), it is mentioned that it is the duty of the Industrial Court to assign work and to give directions to the Investigating Officers in matters of verification of membership of unions and investigation of complaints relating to unfair labour practices. The provisions imply that the Industrial Court has the power to assign the work and to give directions to the investigation officers in the matters which are mentioned in Section 5 (e).

2.6.3 Powers of the Industrial Court

Section 30 (Chapter VII) of the Act deals with the powers of the Industrial Court and Labour Courts. It provides that if the Court draws the conclusion that any person named in the complaint has engaged in, or is engaging in, any unfair labour practice, the Court is empowered to pass necessary order against such person.

The Court is also empowered to pass such interim order as it thinks just and proper, pending final decision. Further powers of the Industrial Court relating to trying of offences under this Act are made clear in Sections 43, 44 and 45 (Chapter VIII) of this Act. These provisions relating to the powers of the Industrial Court are given below.

I. Powers of the Industrial Court according to the provisions of Section 30

1. Where a Court decides that any person named in the complaint has engaged in, or is engaging in, any unfair labour practice, it may in its order –

   (a) Declare that an unfair labour practice has been engaged in or is being engaged in by that person, and specify any other person who has engaged in, or is engaging in the unfair labour practice;

   (b) Direct all such persons to cease and desist from such unfair labour practice, and take such affirmative action (including payment of reasonable compensation to the employee or employees affected by the unfair labour practice, or reinstatement of the employee or employees with or without back wages, or the payment of reasonable compensation), as may in the opinion of the Court be necessary to effectuate the policy of the Act.

   (c) where a recognised union has engaged in or is engaging in, any unfair labour practice, direct that its recognition shall be cancelled or that all or any of its rights under sub-section (1) of Section 20 or its right under Section 23 shall be suspended [Section 30 (1)].

2. In any proceeding before it under this Act, the Court may pass such interim order (including any temporary relief or restraining order) as it deems just and proper (including directions to the person to withdraw temporarily the practice complained of, which is an issue in such proceeding), pending final decision [Section 30 (2)].

It is further provided that, the Court may, on an application in that behalf, review any interim order passed by it [Proviso to Section 30 (2)].

3. For the purpose of holding an enquiry or proceeding under this Act, the Court shall have the same powers as are vested in Court in respect of –

(a) Proof of facts by affidavit;
(b) Summoning and enforcing the attendance of any person, and examining him on oath;
(c) Compelling the production of documents; and
(d) Issuing commissions for the examination of witnesses [Section 30 (3)].

4. The Court shall also have powers to call upon any of the parties to proceedings before it to furnish in writing, and, in such forms as it may think proper, any information, which is considered relevant for the purpose of any proceedings before it, and the party so called upon shall thereupon furnish the information to the best of its knowledge and belief, and if so required by the Court to do so, verify the same in such manner as may be prescribed [Section 30 (4)].

II. Powers of the Industrial Court when the concerned parties to the suit do not appear before the Court [Section 31]:

The Industrial Court is empowered either to adjourn the matter or proceed ex-parte and to pass necessary orders as it thinks fit. Provisions of Section 31 are as follows:

Consequences of Non-appearance of Parties:

1. Where in any proceeding before the Court, if either party, inspite of notice of hearing having been duly served on it, does not appear, when the matter is called on for hearing the Court may either adjourn the hearing of the matter to a subsequent day, or proceed *ex parte*, and made such order as it think fit [Section 31 (1)].

2. Where any order is made *ex parte* under sub-section (1), the aggrieved party may, within thirty days of the receipt of the copy thereof, make an application to the Court to set aside such order.

If the Court is satisfied that there was sufficient cause for non-appearance of the aggrieved party, it may set aside the order so made, and shall appoint a date for proceeding with the matter [Section 31 (2)].

It is also provided that, no order shall be set aside on any such application as aforesaid, unless notice thereof has been served on the opposite party [Proviso to Section 31 (2)].

III. The Power of the Industrial Court to decide all Connected Matters [Section 32]

Section 32 confers the power to the Industrial Court which is in addition to the powers given under other provisions of this Act. The Industrial Court can decide all matters which are not covered under the other provisions of the Act and also can deal with various matters arising out of any application or complaint, if any, referred to it.

It must be noted here that the Industrial Court has the power to invoke the provisions only if there is no specific provision or if the Act is silent about the power of the Court and the matter is referred to the Court. This implies that Section 32 does not enlarge the jurisdiction of the Industrial Court beyond what is conferred upon it by the other provisions of this Act.

For example, the Industrial Court has no jurisdiction to deal with the unfair labour practices mentioned in item 1 of schedule IV appended to this Act. Section 32 does not confer any power to the Industrial Court to deal with the unfair labour practices mentioned in item 1 on the Schedule IV of this Act. Section 32 is reproduced below for your information.

Power of the Industrial Court to decide all connected matters: "*Notwithstanding anything contained in this Act, the Court shall have the power to decide all matters arising out of any application or a complaint referred to it for the decision under any of the provisions of this Act*".

IV. The power of the Industrial Court to make Regulation [Section 33]

The Industrial Court is empowered to make regulation consistent with the provisions of this Act and rules made thereunder regulating its procedure [Section 33 (1)].

Section 33 (2) further states that "*in particular, and without prejudice to the generality of the foregoing power, such regulations may provide for the formation of Benches consisting of one or more of its members (including provision of formation of a Full Bench consisting of three or more members) and the exercise by such Bench of the jurisdiction and powers vested in them*".

It is also provided that, "*no Bench shall consist only of a member, who has not been, and at the time of his appointment, was not eligible for appointment as a Judge of a High Court*" [Proviso to Section 33 (2)].

Section 33 (3), "*every regulation made under this section shall be published in the Official Gazette*".

It is made clear in Section 33 (4) that, "*every proceeding before the Court shall be deemed to be a judicial proceeding within the meaning of Sections 192, 193 and 228 of the Indian Penal Code, XLV of 1860*".

The Industrial Court shall have power to direct by whom the whole or any part of the costs of any proceeding before it shall be paid [Section 33 (5)].

It is further provided that, "*no such cost shall be directed to be paid for the services of any legal adviser engaged by any party*" [Proviso to Section 33 (5)].

It should be noted that the regulations framed under Section 33 by the Industrial Court are for its own procedure. These rules cannot be regarded as equivalent to statutory provisions governing the rights and obligations of the parties before the Court [B. M. Dhup. General Secretary, Maharashtra Majdoor Congress, Bombay V. Vegetable Vitamins Food Company Pvt. Limited and others – 1979 I –] [LLJ – 24].

V. The Power of the Industrial Court under Section 43

Section 43 (1) empowers the Industrial Court in an appeal under Section 42 made to it to confirm, modify, add to or rescind any order of the Labour Court appealed against and may pass such order thereon as the Industrial Court may deem fit. We have already considered the provisions of Section 42 while studying the duties of the Industrial Court.

Section 43 (2) States that, "*in respect of offences punishable under this Act, the Industrial Court shall have all the powers of the High Court of Judicature at Bombay under the Code of Criminal Procedure, 1898, V of 1898.*"

"*A copy of the order passed by the Industrial Court shall be sent to the Labour Court*" [Section 43 (3)]. This implies that the Industrial Court has to send a copy of the order passed by it according to the provisions of Section 43 to the Labour Court.

VI. Power of the Industrial Court to Exercise Superintendence over Labour Courts [Section 44]

Section 44 states that, "the Industrial Court shall have superintendence over all Labour Courts and it may –

(a) Call for returns;

(b) Make and issue general rules and prescribe forms for regulating the practice and procedure of such Courts in matters not expressly provided for by this Act, and in particular, for securing the expeditious disposal of the cases;

(c) Prescribe form in which books, entries and accounts shall be kept by officers of any Courts; and

(d) Settle a table of fees payable for process issued by a Labour Court or the Industrial Court.

Thus, Section 44 confers wide powers of superintendence over the Labour courts. These powers help the Industrial Court to have administrative and judicial control over all Labour Courts and also include the powers to direct the Labour Courts to carry out the orders given.

VII. Power of the Industrial Court to Transfer Proceedings [Section 45]

Section 45 empowers the Industrial Court to transfer proceedings from one Labour Court to another. It states that, – "*The Industrial Court may by order in writing, and for reasons to be stated therein, withdraw any proceeding under this Act pending before a Labour Court, and transfer the same to another Labour Court for disposal and the Labour Court to which the proceedings is so transferred may dispose of the proceeding, but subject to any special direction in the order of transfer, proceed either de novo or from the stage at which it was so transferred*".

It is made clear in Section 46 that "*no order of the Industrial Court in appeal in respect of offences tried by it under this Act shall be called in question in any Criminal Court*".

2.7 Labour Court – Its Constitution, Duties and Powers

2.7.1 Constitution of Labour Court

The State Government is empowered under this Act to constitute one or more Labour Courts and to appoint persons to preside over such Courts. The provisions relating to the constitution of Labour Courts and to the appointment of persons to preside over such Courts, their qualifications have been made in Section 6 which are as follows:

"The State Government shall by notification in the Official Gazette, constitute one or more Labour Courts, having jurisdiction in such local areas, as may be specified in such notification, and shall appoint persons having the prescribed qualifications to preside over such Courts".

So far as qualifications of persons to be appointed to preside over Labour Courts under this Act, it is provided that, *"no person shall be so appointed, unless he possesses qualifications (other than the qualification of age), prescribed under Article 234 of the Constitution for being eligible to enter the judicial service of the State of Maharashtra; and is not more than sixty years of age"* [Proviso to Section 6].

2.7.2 Duties of Labour Court

Certain duties have been entrusted to the Labour Court or Labour Courts constituted under this Act. These are as given below:

(a) To decide complaints relating to unfair labour practices which are mentioned or described in item 1 of the Schedule IV; and

(b) To try offences punishable under the Act.

Section 7 lays down that, *"It shall be the duty of the Labour Court to decide complaints relating to unfair labour practices described in item 1 of Schedule IV and to try offences punishable under this Act".*

Thus, the jurisdiction of the Labour Courts appointed under this Act is limited to give decisions in respect of the complaints relating to unfair labour practices described in item 1 of the Schedule IV appended to this Act and also to try offences punishable under this Act.

In Schedule IV appended to this Act, various general unfair labour practices on the part of employers are given. But the duty of the Labour Courts constituted under this Act is to decide complaints only relating to unfair labour practices described in item 1 of this schedule IV. This item 1 of the said schedule provides that the discharge or dismissal of employees by the employer shall amount to an unfair labour practice if such discharge or dismissal is :

1. By way of victimisation;
2. not in good faith, but in the colourable exercise of the employer's rights;
3. By falsely implicating an employee in a criminal case on the false evidence or on concocted evidence;
4. For patently false reasons;
5. On untrue or trumped up allegations of absence without leave;

6. In utter disregard of the principles of natural justice in the conduct of domestic enquiry or with undue haste;
7. For misconduct of a minor or technical character, without having any regard to the nature of the particular misconduct, so as to amount to a shockingly disproportionate punishment.

2.7.3 Powers of the Labour Court

Section 30 (Chapter III) of the Act deals with the powers of the Labour Courts as well as the Industrial Court. It provides that if the court draws the conclusion that any person named in the complaint has engaged in, or is engaging in, any unfair labour practice, the court is empowered to pass necessary order against such person. The Court is also empowered to pass such interim order as it thinks fit, just and proper; pending final decision.

Further, the power of the Labour Courts relating to trying of offences under this Act are made clear in Sections 38, 39, 40, 41 [Chapter VIII] of this Act. The provisions relating to the powers of the Labour Courts are given below:

I. Powers of the Labour Court according to the provisions of Section 30:

1. Where a Court decides that any person named in the complaint has engaged in, or is engaging in, any unfair labour practice, it may in its order –

   (a) Declare that an unfair labour practice has been engaged in or is being engaged in by that person, and specify any other person who has engaged in, or is engaging in the unfair labour practice;

   (b) Direct all such persons to cease and desist from such unfair labour practice, and take such affirmative action (including payment of reasonable compensation to the employee or employees affected by the unfair labour practice, or reinstatement of the employee or employees with or without back wages, or the payment of reasonable compensation), as may in the opinion of the Court necessary to effectuate the policy of the Act.

   (c) Where a recognised union has engaged in or is engaging in, any unfair labour practice, direct that its recognition shall be cancelled or that all or any of its rights under sub-section (1) of Section 20 or its rights under Section 23 shall be suspended [Section 30 (1)].

2. In any proceeding before it under this Act, the Court may pass such interim order including any temporary relief or restraining order) as it deems just and proper (including directions to the person to withdraw temporarily the practice complained of, which is an issue in such proceeding), pending final decision [Section 30 (2)].

It is further provided that, the Labour Court may, on an application in that behalf, review any interim order passed by it [Proviso to Section 30 (2)].

3. For the purpose of holding an enquiry or proceeding under this Act, the Court shall have the same powers as are vested in Court in respect of –

   (a) proof of facts by affidavit;
   (b) summoning and enforcing the attendance of any person, and examining him on oath;
   (c) compelling the production of documents; and
   (d) issuing commissions for the examination of witnesses [Section 30 (3)].

4. The Court shall also have powers to call upon any of the parties to proceedings before it to furnish in writing, and, in such forms as it may think proper, any information, which is considered relevant for the purpose of any proceedings before it, and the party so called upon shall thereupon furnish the information to the best of its knowledge and belief, and if so required by the Court to do so, verify the same in such manner as may be prescribed [Section 30 (4)].

II. Powers of Labour Courts in relation to offences [Section 38]:

Section 38 empowers the Labour Courts constituted under this Act to try offences which are punishable under this Act. The provisions of Section 38 are as follows:

A Labour Court shall have power to try offences punishable under this Act [Section 38 (1)].

Every offence punishable under this Act shall be tried by a Labour Court within the limits of whose jurisdiction it is committed [Section 38 (2)].

Thus, section 38 provides the forum to try various offences punishable under this M.R.T.U. and P.U.L.P. Act of 1971. It is only the Labour Court which has jurisdiction to try all such offences, which have been committed within the limits of its jurisdiction.

III. Powers of the Labour Courts to take cognizance of offences [Section 39]

Section 39 states that, "*No Labour Court shall take cognizance of any offence except on a complaint of facts constituting such offence made by the person affected thereby or a recognised union or on report in writing by the Investigating Officer*".

Thus, this Section 39 empowers the Labour Court to take cognizance of offences punishable under this Act. However, Section 39 lays down two important conditions. The Labour Court can take cognizance of offences only on fulfillment to these two conditions. These two conditions are –

1. There must be a complaint of facts constituting an offence under this Act; and
2. Such complaint must have been made by
   (a) the person affected thereby, or
   (b) a recognised union, or
   (c) by the investigating officer on submitting his report in writing.

IV. Powers and Procedure of the Labour Courts in Trials [Section 40]

In Section 40, provisions relating to the power and procedure of the Labour Courts in trial have been made clear. It states that, "In respect of offences punishable under this Act, a Labour Court shall have all the powers under the Code of Criminal Procedure, 1898, V of 1898, of a Presidency Magistrate in Greater Bombay and a Magistrate of the First Class elsewhere, and in the trial of every such offence, shall follow the procedure laid down for in Chapter XXII of the said Code of summary trial in which an appeal lies; and the rest of the provisions of the Code shall so far as may be, apply to such trial".

Thus, Section 40 confers upon the Labour Courts all powers of a Presidency Magistrate in Greater Bombay and Magistrate of the First Class elsewhere in respect of offences punishable under this Act. These powers are as provided under the Code of Criminal Procedure of 1898.

However, the provisions have been made in Section 42 to make an appeal to the Industrial Court notwithstanding anything contained in Section 40. Section 42 is reproduced below:

1. Notwithstanding anything contained in Section 40, an appeal shall lie to the Industrial Court –

    (a) Against a conviction by a Labour Court, by the person convicted;

    (b) Against an acquittal by a Labour Court in its special jurisdiction, by the complainant;

    (c) For enhancement of a sentence awarded by a Labour Court in its special jurisdiction, by the State Government [Section 42 (1)].

2. Every appeal shall be made within thirty days from the date of conviction, acquittal or sentence, as the case may be [Section 42 (2)].

It is provided that, the Industrial Court may, for sufficient reason, allow an appeal after expiry of the said period [Proviso to Section 42 (2)].

V. Powers of Labour Courts to impose higher punishment [Section 41]

Any Labour Court is empowered to pass sentence authorised under this Act even in excess of its powers under Section 32 of the Code of Criminal Procedure of 1898. Section 41 says that, "Notwithstanding anything contained in Section 32 of the Code of Criminal Procedure, 1898, V of 1898, it shall be lawful for any Labour Court to pass sentence authorised under this Act in excess of its powers under Section 32 of the said Code".

2.8 Investigating Officers – Their Appointment, Duties and Powers

2.8.1 Appointment of the Investigation Officers

The Investigating Officers are appointed by the State Government to assist the Industrial Court and Labour Courts in discharge their duties. Such Investigating Officers are appointed for different areas as the State Government considers necessary. The provisions relating to the appointment to Investigating Officers are made in Section 8 which is as follows.

"The State Government may, by notification in Official Gazette, appoint such number of Investigating Officers for any area as it may consider necessary, to assist the Industrial Courts and Labour Courts in the discharge of their duties".

2.8.2 Duties of Investigating Officers

1. The Investigating Officer shall be under the control of the Industrial Court, and shall exercise powers and perform duties imposed on him by the Industrial Court [Section 9 (1)].

2. It shall be the duty of an Investigating Officer to assist the Industrial Court in matters of verification of membership of unions, and assist the Industrial and Labour Courts for investigating into complaints relating to unfair labour practices [Section 9 (2)].

3. It shall also be the duty of an Investigating Officer to report to the Industrial Court, or as the case may be, the Labour Court the existence of any unfair labour practices in any industry or undertaking, and the names and addresses of the persons said to be engaged in unfair labour practices and any other information which the Investigating Officer may deem fit to report to the Industrial Court, or as the case may be, the Labour Court [Section 9 (3)].

The Investigation Officers work under the control of the Industrial Court and they exercise various powers and perform certain duties as imposed on them by the Industrial Court. Their important duties are as follows:

1. The Investigation Officers have to assist the Industrial Court in the matters which are mentioned below:
   (a) Verification of membership of unions.
   (b) Investigation into complaints relating to unfair labour practices in order to assist the Industrial as well as Labour Courts [Section 9 (2)].

2. The duty of the Investigating Officers is to report to the Industrial Court or the Labour Court, as the case may be, relating to the following matters:
   (a) The existence of any unfair labour practices in any industry or undertaking;
   (b) Information relating to the names and addresses of persons said to be engaged in unfair labour practices; and
   (c) Any other information which the Investigation Officers deem fit to report to the Industrial Court or the Labour Court, as the case may be [Section 9 (3)].

2.8.3 Powers of the Investigating Officers

We have seen above that Section 9 of the M.R.T.U. and P.U.L.P. Act of 1971 lays down certain duties of the Investigating Officers appointed under this Act. At the same time Section 37 provides for certain powers conferred on the Investigating Officers in order to enable them to discharge their official duties as may be assigned to them by the Industrial Court. The powers of the Investigating Officers according to Section 37 are as follows:

Powers of Investigating Officer: 1. An Investigating Officer shall exercise the powers conferred on him by or under this Act, and shall perform such duties as may be assigned to him, from time to time, by the Court [Section 37 (1)].

2. For the purpose of exercising such powers and performing such duties, an Investigating Officer may, subject to such conditions as may be prescribed, at any time during working hours, and outside working hours after reasonable notice, enter and inspect –
   (a) Any place used for the purpose of any undertaking;
   (b) Any place used as the office of any union;
   (c) Any premises provided by an employer for the residence of his employees; and shall be entitled to call for and inspect all relevant documents which he may deem necessary for the due discharge of his duties and powers under this Act [Section 37 (2)].

3. All particulars contained in, or information obtained from, any document inspected or called for under sub-section (2) shall, if the person, in whose possession the document was, so requires, be treated as confidential [Section 37 (3)].

4. An Investigating Officer may, after giving reasonable notice, convene a meeting of employees for any of the purposes of this Act, on the premises where they are employed, and may require the employer to affix a written notice of the meeting at such conspicuous place in such premises as he may order, and may also himself affix or cause to be affixed such notice.

The notice shall specify the date, time and place of the meeting, the employees or class of employees affected, and the purpose for which the meeting is convened [Section 37 (4)].

It is further provided that, during the continuance of a lock-out which is not illegal, no meeting of employees affected thereby shall be convened on such premises without the employer's consent [Proviso to Section 37 (4)].

5. An Investigating Officer shall be entitled to appear in any proceeding under this Act [Section 37 (5)].

6. An Investigating Officer may call for and inspect any document which he has reasonable ground for considering to be relevant to the complaint or to be necessary for the purpose of verifying the implementation of any order of the Court or carrying out any other duty imposed on him under this Act and for the aforesaid purposes the Investigating Officer shall have the same powers as are vested in a civil court under the Code of Civil Procedure, 1908, V of 1908 in respect of compelling the production of documents [Section 37 (6)].

Apart from the powers, duties etc. discussed so far, chapter III of the Industrial Court Regulations of 1975 [Regulations from 46 to 72] elaborately lays down the powers, functions and duties of the Investigating Officers. For your information, these regulations are reproduced below.

Chapter III of the Industrial Court Regulations of 1975
POWERS, FUNCTIONS AND DUTIES OF THE INVESTIGATING OFFICERS

46. Every Investigating Officer may be allocated one or more areas in which he may exercise the powers and perform the duties.

47 (i) The Investigating Officer shall maintain a register entering therein all the 'Undertakings' with their names and addresses within the local area in the jurisdiction.

(ii) The Register shall be in Form 14 which is as follows:

FORM 14
(Regulation No. 47)
Register of Undertaking to be maintained by Investigating Officer
1. Serial No.
2. Name of the Undertaking
3. Address of the Undertaking
4. No. of employees found on premises on date of visit
5. Date of visit
6. Name of Recognised Trade Union, if any
7. Trade Union of employees, if any
8. Industry of business of the undertaking

---

48. Entries in the register shall be periodically checked, verified and corrected by the Investigating Officers, at least once in six months every year.

49. The Investigating Officers shall keep in touch with the employer, the employees and the recognised union or other union of the undertaking within his area to find out if any unfair labour practices mentioned in Schedules II, III and IV are engaged in by any person.

50. As soon as an Investigating Officer receives information about any unfair labour practice being engaged in by any person, the Investigating Officers shall visit the undertaking concerned and verify the correctness of the information by personal inquiry. If there is reason to believe that any person is engaged or has engaged in an unfair labour practice, the Investigating Officer may obtain a complaint in writing from any one affected by such unfair labour practice.

51. On receipt of a complaint in writing or otherwise the Investigating Officers may proceed to make enquiries and for that purpose record statements of persons willing to give information.

52. The Investigating Officer shall record in a register, the steps taken and progress of his inquiry on a complaint from day to day. Investigating Officers may at any time be required to produce this register before the Court. Entries in this register shall be signed by Investigating Officers every day.

53. As far as possible Investigating Officer shall hold enquiry at the premises of the undertaking or the office of the union, depending upon the subject matter to be investigated.

54. The employees or employer or other persons acquainted with the acts relating to the unfair labour practice of which complaint has been made may be called upon by the Investigating Officers to attend his office for recording statements wherever necessary.

55. If an Investigating Officer finds that person whose statement it necessary to be recorded is not attending the office, a notice shall be issued to such person by the

Investigating Officers and on receipt of such notice such person shall be bound to appear before the Investigating Officers and make a statement.

Notice to appear shall be in Form 15 which is given below.

FORM 15
(Regulation No. 55)
Notice to appear before Investigating Officer

Before the Investigating Officer, appointed by Industrial Court, at ....

Application (MRTU) No. .... of 20...

Complaint (ULP) NO. .... of 20...

Name of the Applicant Union/Complainant with full address	Applicant
	....
	Complainant

Versus

Name of the Opponent/Respondent with full address	Opponent
	....
	Respondent

In the matter of: An application/A complaint for ......

NOTICE

Please take notice that whereas Shri .... Investigating Officers at .... has informed that you are likely to be in possession of information in connection with enquiries being conducted by such Investigating Officer you are required to appear before Investigating Officer on .... 20 .... at 10.30 a.m. or at such time immediately thereafter according to the convenience of the Investigating Officer, in the .... at ....

(Seal)　　　　　　　　　　　Signature of Officer authorised to sign notice

---

56. Any person whose statement has been recorded by the Investigating Officers shall be called upon to sign the statement, but before obtaining the signature the statements shall be read over or interpreted to the person making the statement and endorsement to the effect shall be made by Investigating Officers below the statement. As far as possible signature of person making the statement should be attested by some persons other than Investigating Officers. If the person making the statement refuses to sign the statement Investigating Officers shall make an endorsement to that effect immediately.

57. Any document produced by any person making a complaint regarding unfair labour practice or any document required to be produced by the Investigating Officers shall be received and marked by the Investigating Officers and the fact of production and the date thereof shall be noted in the date of production shall be endorsed and initialled by Investigating Officers on the document itself. As far as possible copies of original documents

duly certified by the person producing the same as true copies may be kept on record unless retention of original documents or record is considered necessary by the Investigating Officers.

58. The Investigating Officer is expected to complete the enquiry into an unfair labour practices as expeditiously as possible, in any case within one month of the receipt of the information relating to subject matter of the investigation or within such further time as may be allowed by the Industrial Court or the Labour Court.

59. The Investigating Officers shall make an attempt to find out basic causes leading to the alleged unfair labour practice and may ascertain from each party, separately if necessary, the basis on which a settlement may be reached. The Investigating Officers may thereafter arrange a joint meeting of both the parties to explore the prospects of a settlement.

60. If a settlement is reached it shall be recorded in writing and duly authenticated by each party and also by the Investigating Officers. A copy of such settlement shall be furnished to Industrial Court or Labour Court as the case may be.

61. (i) If a settlement is not possible, the Investigating Officer shall make a report giving facts found by him and reasons for the failure of the settlement. The report shall also state whether the investigating Officer proposes to file a complaint.

(ii) Every Investigating Officer shall keep a separate record of any unfair labour practice brought to his notice but not covered by Schedules II, III or IV of the Act, the circumstances in which an unfair labour practice *was notice and relief which according to Investigating Officer should be available to a person adversely affected by such unfair labour practice.*

(iii) Such record shall be made in a separate register to be maintained by the Investigating Officers.

62. The Investigating Officers may enter and inspect any place used for the purpose of an undertaking of any place used as the Office of any union or any premises provided by the employer for the residence of his employees at any time during working hours. If it is necessary to enter and inspect any such places or premises, outside the working hours the Investigating Officers shall give a notice to that effect to the person incharge of the place or premises and thereafter enter and inspect the premises.

63. (i) The Investigating Officer may call for and inspect any relevant document in the custody of any person, production of which is considered necessary for due discharge of his duties by the Investigating Officers.

(ii) A notice to produce document may be given by the Investigating Officers in Form 16 which is given as follows.

FORM 16

(Regulation No. 63)

Notice to produce documents before Investigating Officer

Before the Investigating Officer, appointed by Industrial

Court, at ....

Application (MRTU) No .... of 20...

Complaint (ULP) NO .... of 20...

Name of the Applicant Union / Complainant with full address   Applicant

                                                                                                          ....

                                                                                                          Complainant

versus

Name of the Opponent/Respondent with full address   Opponent

                                                                                                 ....

                                                                                                 Respondent

In the matter of: An application / A complaint for ....

NOTICE

Please take notice that Investigating Officer at .... hereby requires you to produce before him the following documents alleged to be in your custody or power:

1. Description of documents.
2. Description of documents.
3. Description of documents.

The above documents shall be produced by you or by any person authorised by you on .... at 10.30 a.m. or at such time immediately thereafter according to the convenience of the Investigating Officer.

(Seal)   Signature of Officer authorised to sign notice

---

64. The Investigating Officers shall not disclose the particulars contained in any document or information obtained from any person if the person in whose possession the document was found or gave information so required.

65. (i) If the Investigating Officer considers it expedient or necessary to convene a meeting of the employees in an undertaking the Investigating Officers shall give a notice to that effect to the employer requiring the employer to affix a written notice for such a meeting at a conspicuous place in the premises. The notice shall be in Form 17 which is as follows.

FORM 17

(Regulation No. 65)

Notice from Investigating Officer to Employer

to affix notice of meeting of employees

Before the Investigating Officer, appointed by Industrial

Court, at ....

Application (MRTU) No .... of 20...

Complaint (ULP) NO .... of 20...

Name of the Applicant Union / Complainant with full address   Applicant

....

Complainant

versus

Name of the Opponent/Respondent, with full address   Opponent

....

Respondent

In the matter of: An application / A complaint for ....

NOTICE

Please take notice that you are hereby required to display at a prominent place/Notice Board for accompanying the notice of meeting of employees called by the Investigating Officer immediately and report compliance within three days.

(Seal)   Signature of Officer authorised to sign notice

(ii) The employer to whom such notice is sent shall be bound to display such a notice on the conspicuous place of the premises or on the usual notice board for the information of the employees in the undertaking.

(iii) Such a notice shall specify the date, the time and the place of the meeting and the employees or category of employees covered by such notice and the purpose for which the meeting has been convened.

66. The Investigating Officer may call for and inspect any document in possession of the employer of an undertaking or employees of the undertaking or any union whose members are employees in that undertaking if he has reasonable ground for considering such document to be relevant for any inquiry under the Act.

67. The Investigating Officers may call upon any trade union which claims membership of the employees of the undertaking to produce register of members and such other

documents as may be necessary for verification of membership of the employees of the Union.

68. The Investigating Officers may issue a notice in Form 16 to any person having documents alleged to be containing information in respect to membership of the employees of a union to produce such documents before the Investigating Officers within a time to be fixed in the notice. Any person to whom such notice is issued shall be bound to produce the document within the time fixed in the notice or within such other time as may be extended by the Investigating Officers.

69. If a meeting of the employees is convened by the Investigating Officers in the premises of the undertaking or at some other place, the Investigating Officers shall keep a brief record of the proceeding of such meeting, the number of employees present at such a meeting and the decisions, if any, arrived at such a meeting.

70. If the Investigating Officers so requires a person to whom notice is issued for production of any document shall be bound to tender the document in original or a true copy of such document for being used by the Investigating Officers against a receipt for such document. The receipt shall be in Form 18.

FORM 18
(Regulation No. 70)
Receipt for Documents produced before Investigating Officer

The Documents as per list of documents have been produced by Shri. .... before Investigating Officers .... on.....................

Date:

Place:

Signature of Officer, receiving the documents

71. The Investigating Officers shall be bound to carry out the orders of Industrial Court or Labour Court and perform such other duties as may be assigned by such Court / Courts.

72. If the Investigating Officer in his discretion decides to appear in any proceeding under the Act before the Industrial Court or the Labour Court, the Investigating Officer shall make a brief record of the reasons why the Investigating Officers decide to appear in any proceedings under the Act and shall produce the same before the Court.

The Investigating Officer may be directed by the Industrial Court or Labour Court to appear in any proceeding in which it is necessary to make enquiry into complaint of an alleged unfair labour practice or otherwise to assist the Court.

2.9 Recognition of Unions

Provisions relating to the recognition of unions have been made in Chapter III of M.R.T.U. and P.U.L.P. Act. Section 10 throws light on the conditions under which the provisions of Sections 11 and 18 included in Chapter III are made applicable to the undertakings covered by this Act.

Section 10 (1) states that, "*Subject to the provisions of sub-sections (2) and (3), the provisions of this Chapter shall apply to every undertaking, wherein fifty or more employees are employed, or were employed on any day of the proceeding twelve months*".

It is further provided that, "*the State Government may, after giving not less than sixty days' notice of its intention so to do, by notification in the Official Gazette, apply the provisions of this Chapter to any undertaking, employing such number of employees less than fifty as may be specified in the notification*" [Proviso to Section 10 (1)].

Thus, subject to the provisions of sub-sections (2) and (3) of Section 10, the provisions of Sections 11 to 18 of Chapter III are applicable to every undertaking wherein fifty or more employees are employed or were employed on any day of the preceding twelve months. It is also provided that the State Government, after giving sixty days notice and by giving notification in the Official Gazette, may apply to provisions of Chapter III to any undertaking even though the number of employees employed is less than fifty.

It is further made clear that, "*The provisions of this Chapter shall not apply to undertakings in industries to which the provisions of the Bombay Act for the time being apply*" [Section 10 (2)].

Thus, the provisions of this Chapter III are not applicable to undertakings in industries to which the provisions of the Bombay Industrial Relations Act is applicable.

"*If the number of employees employed in any undertaking to which the provisions of this Chapter apply at any time falls below fifty continuously for a period of one year, those provisions shall cease to apply to such undertaking*" [Section 10 (3)].

The provisions of Section 10 (3) clearly indicate that any undertaking to which the provisions of Chapter III apply; if in such undertaking, the number of employees employed falls below fifty continuously for a period of one year, then the provisions of this Chapter III shall not apply to such undertaking. Thus, the provisions of Section 10 make clear the scope of Chapter III.

2.9.1 Application for Recognition of an Union [Section 11]

In Section 11, essential conditions for making an application to the Industrial Court for getting recognition to a union as a registered recognised union are stated.

Section 11 (1) states that, "*Any union (hereinafter referred to as the "applicant-union") which has for the whole of the period of six calendar months immediately preceding the calendar month in which it so applies under this section a membership of not less than thirty per cent of the total number of employees employed in any undertaking may apply in the prescribed form to the Industrial Court for being registered as a recognised union for such undertaking".*

These provisions of Section 11 (1) imply that the following two important conditions must be fulfilled by the applicant union before making the application for recognition as the registered recognised union and on the fulfillment of these conditions, such union can make an application in the prescribed form to the Industrial Court.

1. Union having for the whole period of six calendar months a membership of not less than thirty percent of the total number of employees employed in any undertaking, and

2. Such membership of thirty percent must be for six months immediately preceding the calendar month in which it makes application to the Industrial Court.

Besides these two conditions, the applicant union has to fulfill certain other conditions which have been provided in Sections 12 (5); 12 (6) and 19. The relevant provisions of these sections are as follows:

"The Industrial Court shall not recognise any union, if it is satisfied that the application for its recognition is not made bonafide in the interest of the employees, but is made in the interest of the employer, to the prejudice of the interest of the employees" [Section 12 (5)].

"The Industrial Court shall not recognise any union, if, at any time, within six months immediately preceding the date of the application for recognition, the union has instigated, aided or assisted the commencement or continuation of the strike which is deemed to be illegal under this Act" [Section 12 (6)].

Thus, efforts have been made to protect the interest of employees by making provisions in Section 12 (5). It has been made obligatory for the union to make the application for recognition bona fide in the interest of the employees.

Section 19 of the Act also imposes certain obligations upon the recognised union to provide for four matters in the rules and the observance of these rules by the union seeking recognition.

Section 19 states that, *"The rules of a union seeking recognition under this Act shall provide for the following matters, and the provisions thereof shall be duly observed by the union, namely:*

1. That the membership subscription shall not be less than fifty paise per month;
2. The Executive committee shall meet at intervals of not more than three months;
3. All resolutions passed, whether by Executive Committee or the General Body of the union, shall be recorded in a minute book kept for the purpose;
4. An auditor appointed by the State Government may audit its account at least once in each financial year".

After fulfilling the conditions mentioned above, any union can make an application in the prescribed form i.e. "form A" to the Industrial Court. Format of Form A is given below for your information.

FORM A

(Section 11, Rule 4)

(Application by a union For registration as a recognised union)

Industrial Case No.

In the Industrial Court at ..   ..   ..

Name and address of the applicant union) ...   . Applicants;

versus

1. (Name and address of the employer undertaking   ... Non-applicant
2. (Name and address of other trade union)   ... Non-applicant

Application for registration as a Recognised Union

The applicant union begs to submit as follows:

1. The applicant union is registered under the Indian Trade Unions Act on .... under certificate No. issued by the Registrar of Trade Unions.

2. The applicant union has the following office-bearers elected on ....

President	–
Vice-President (if any)	–
General Secretary (if any)	–
Treasurer (if any)	–
Members of the Executive Committee	–

3. The applicant union has the following membership in the undertaking called .... for the whole of the period of six calendar months immediately preceding month in which this application is made:

Month	Number of members	Percentage of the total number of employees in undertaking
1.		
2.		
3.		
4.		
5.		
6.		

A list of all such employees who are members of the applicant union for each month, alphabetically arranged, is filed with this application.

4. At a general meeting of the members of the applicant union/meeting of the Executive Committee of the applicant union which was held at .... on .... day of .... 20..., it was decided that the union should apply for registration as a recognised union for ....

(Here insert the name of the Undertaking)

5. The undertaking for which this trade union seeks recognition as a Recognised union is engaged in ………………… industry/trade. The undertaking is known as ………. and is located at the following address –

Address ………………………………………………………………………

………………………………………………………………………

6. The undertaking is a proprietary concern/partnership concern / company and is owned by the following persons:

………………………………………………………………………

………………………………………………………………………

7. The constitution of the application union provides for the matters mentioned in Section 19 of the Act. A copy of the Constitution is attached.

8. The applicant union hereby tenders the prescribed fee of ₹ ……for this application / the applicant union has paid the prescribed fee of ₹ ……. for this application by Money Order, receipt for which is enclosed.

9. The applicant union has not instigated, aided or assisted the commencement or continuation of a strike among the employees in the undertaking for which the applicant union seeks recognition which is deemed to be illegal under the Act within six months immediately preceding the date of this application.

10. The applicant union had/had not made an application for registration as a recognised union before any Industrial Court under the Act.

11. (i) A member of the applicant union has to pay a monthly subscription of ₹ ……. …………………….. every month.

(ii) The Executive Committee of the applicant union met on the following dates during the twelve months preceding the date of the application.

(iii) The applicant union maintains minute book in which all resolutions passed by the Executive Committee or the General Body of the union are recorded.

(iv) The applicant union maintains accounts and such accounts were last audited by ………. on ………. and the certificate of the auditor is enclosed.

(v) The year of account of the applicant union is from ………. to ………….

12. The applicant union is a recognised union for the following undertakings/is not a recognised union for any other undertaking ……………. ……… …………….. …………….. …………….. …………….

……………. ……………. ……………. ……………. ……………. ……. Names of the undertaking ……………….. ………….

……………. ………….. ……………. ……………. ……………. ……………. ………….

13. The applicant union has/has not on its roll of members employees employed in undertaking other than the undertaking for which the application is filed.

14. The applicant union herewith files the following documents with a list:

(i) Registered address of the applicant union.

(ii) A list of members of the applicant union who are employed in the undertaking for which recognition is sought arranged alphabetically with a date of such employees joining as a member.

(iii) A true copy of certificate of registration as a trade union.

(iv) Authority of the person for filling this application.

(v) A true copy of the Constitution of the applicant union.

VERIFICATION

I . ... who is holding office as .... in the applicant union hereby verify that the contents in the above application in paras .... are written from my knowledge and are true and those in paras .... are written from information obtained from .... and believed to be true. I have signed this at .... on .... date of the application.

Signature of the person

authorisd to make application

*Presented by .. .. ..

on .. .. ..

*Signature of the office authorised to receive application

(*To be filled when the application is presented in person).

Section 11 (2) provides that as far as possible, the Industrial Court shall dispose of the application for recognition of union within the period of three months where the undertaking for which recognition applied for is situated in the same local area and in any other case, within the period of four months from the receipt of the application.

Section 11 (2) is reproduced below:

"*Every such application shall be disposed of by the Industrial Court as far as possible within three months from the date of receipt of the application, where a group of concerns in any industry which is notified to be one undertaking for which recognition is applied for is situated in the same local area; and in any other case, within four months*".

'Local area' for the purposes of this sub-section means the area which the State Government may, by notification in the Official Gazette, specify in the notification. [Explanation to Section 11 (2)]

2.9.2 Recognition of Union [Section 12]

Section 12 prescribes the procedure to be followed by the Industrial Court while deciding an application for recognition of union. The Industrial Court is also empowered to refuse to grant recognition on specific conditions which are mentioned in Section 12 (5) and (6).

The provisions of Section 12 are as follows:

1. On receipt of an application from a union for recognition under Section 11 and on payment of the prescribed fees, not exceeding rupees five the Industrial Court shall, if it finds the application on a preliminary scrutiny to be in order, cause notice to be displayed on the notice board of the undertaking, declaring its intention to consider the said application on the date specified in the notice, and calling upon the other union or unions, if any, having membership of employees in that undertaking and the employers and employees affected by the proposal to show cause, within a prescribed time, as to why recognition should not be granted to the applicant-union [Section 12 (1)].

2. If, after considering the objections, if any, that may be received under sub-section (1) from any other union (hereinafter referred to as "other union") or employers or employees, if any, and if after holding such enquiry in the matters as it deems fit, the Industrial Court comes to the conclusion that the conditions requisite for registration specified in Section 11 are satisfied, and the applicant-union also complies with the conditions specified in Section 19 of this Act, the Industrial Court shall, subject to the provisions of this section, grant recognition to the applicant-union under this Act, and issue a certificate of such recognition in such form as may be prescribed [Section 12 (2)].

3. If the Industrial Court comes to the conclusion; that any of the other unions has the largest membership of employees employed in the undertaking, and the said other union has notified to the Industrial Court its claim to be registered as a recognised union for such undertaking, and if it satisfies the conditions requisite for recognition specified in Section 11, and also complies with the conditions specified in Section 19 of this Act, the Industrial Court shall, subject to the provisions of this section, grant such recognition to the other union, and issue a certificate of such recognition in such form as may be prescribed [Section 12 (3)].

For the purpose of this sub-section, the other union shall be deemed to have applied for recognition in the same calendar month as the applicant-union [Explanation to Section 12 (3)].

4. There shall not, at any time, be more than one recognised union in respect of the same undertaking [Section 12 (4)].

5. The Industrial Court shall not recognise any union, if it satisfied that the application for its recognition is not made bona fide in the interest of the employees, but is made in the interest of the employer, to the prejudice of the interest of the employees [Section 12 (5)].

6. The Industrial Court shall not recognise any union, if, at any time, within six months immediately preceding the date of the application for recognition, the union has instigated, aided or assisted the commencement or continuation of the strike which is deemed to be illegal under this Act [Section 12 (6)].

Labour Laws - III   M.R.T.U. & P.U.L.P. Act 1971

The certificate of recognition to be issued to a union under Section 12 (5) is in 'Form B' which is given below:

FORM – B
(Section 12 (5), Rule 7)
(Certificate of Recognition)

Name and full address of the Union ....

Registration No. ....

It is hereby certified that ....

(Here insert the name and full address of the Union)

has been registered as a recognised union under Section 12 of the Maharashtra Recognition of Trade Unions and Prevention of Unfair Labour Practices Act, 1971, for the Undertaking ......

(Here insert the name and address of the undertaking)

as per order of the Industrial Court at .... passed on .... This certificate is given this .... day of .... of the Year ....

Place

Date

[Seal]

Signature of the Registrar of the Industrial Court

2.9.3 Cancellation of Recognition and Suspension of Rights [Section 13]

Provisions have been made in Section 13 of this Act relating to cancellation of recognition and suspension by empowering an Industrial Court either to cancel the recognition of a union or to suspend any or all of its rights under certain circumstances. The grounds for cancellation of recognition and suspension of rights of a union are given in Section 13 (1). This Section 13 also lays down the procedure and the manner in which the Industrial Court and exercises its power in that respect.

The provisions of Section 13 are given below:

Section 13: Cancellation of Recognition and Suspension of Rights

(1) The Industrial Court shall cancel the recognition of a union if after giving notice to such union to show cause why its recognition should not be cancelled and after holding an inquiry, it is satisfied.

1. That it was recognised under mistake, misrepresentation or fraud; or
2. That the membership of the union has, for a continuous period of six calendar months, fallen below the minimum required under Section 11 for its recognition:

Provided that, where a strike (not being an illegal strike under the Central Act) has extended to a period exceeding fourteen days in any calendar month, such month shall be excluded in computing the said period of six months:

Provided further that, the recognition of a union shall not be cancelled under the provisions of this sub-clause, unless its membership for the calendar month in which show cause notice under this section was issued was less than such minimum; or
3. That the recognised union has, after its recognition, failed to observe any of the conditions specified in Section 19; or
4. That the recognised union is not being conducted bona fide in the interest of employees, but in the interest of employer to the prejudice of the interest of employees; or
5. That it has instigated, aided, or assisted the commencement or continuation of a strike which is deemed to be illegal under this Act,; or
6. That its registration under the Trade Union Act, XVI of 1926, is cancelled; or
7. That another union has been recognised in place of a union recognised under this Chapter.

Thus, from the provisions of Section 13 (1), we come to know the following seven grounds on which the Industrial Court is empowered to cancel the recognition of a union even after giving the notice to such union to show cause as to why its recognition should not be cancelled.

After holding an inquiry, if the Industrial Court is satisfied that the Union –
1. Was recognised under mistake, misrepresentation or fraud, or
2. Its membership has fallen below the minimum required under Section 11, or
3. It failed to observe any of the conditions specified in Section 19, or,
4. It acted against the interest of the employees and in the interest of the employer, or
5. It has instigated, aided or assisted the commencement or continuation of a strike deemed to be illegal, or
6. Its registration is cancelled under the Trade Unions Act, 1926; or
7. Another union has been recognised in its place under this chapter. However, the proviso to sub-section (1) lays down that :
   (a) where a strike extends for more than fourteen days in any calendar month such month shall be excluded in computing the period of six months, or
   (b) its recognition shall be cancelled and its membership falls down for the calendar month in which show cause notice under this section was issued, the Industrial Court is empowered to cancel the recognition of such union.

Section 13 (2) states that, "*The Industrial Court may cancel the recognition of a union if, after giving notice to such union to show cause why its recognition should not be cancelled, and after holding an inquiry, it is satisfied, that it has committed any practice which is, or has been declared as, an unfair labour practice under this Act*".

It is further provided that, in having regard to the circumstances in which such practice has been committed, the Industrial Court is of opinion that instead of cancellation of the recognition of the union, it may suspend all or any of its rights under sub-section (1) of Section 20 or under Section 23, the Industrial Court may pass an order accordingly, and specify the period for which such suspension may remain in force [Proviso to Section 13 (2)].

Thus, Section 13 (2) provides that the recognition can also be cancelled if the union has committed any practice which is, or has been declared as an unfair labour practice under this Act.

However, considering the circumstances, if the Industrial Court is of the opinion that there is no need of cancellation of the recognition of the union, it may suspend all or any of its rights under Section 20 (1) or 23 by passing the necessary orders and specifying the period for which such suspension shall remain in force.

2.9.4 Recognition of Other Union [Section 14]

Section 14 provides for granting the status of a recognised union to other union in place of a recognised union which is already registered as such subject to certain essential conditions. These conditions are laid down in Section 14 in clauses (1) to (4).

In brief, these conditions are as follows:
1. Applicant union must have largest membership of employees;
2. A period of two years must have elapsed since the date of registration of the recognised union, or/and;
3. A period of one year has elapsed since the date of disposal of the provisions application of that union;
4. The applicant union complies with the conditions necessary for recognition, as specified in Sections 11 and 19 of this Act;
5. Its membership during the whole period of six months, immediately preceding the calendar month in which it made application was larger than the membership of the recognised union.

Section 14 also lays down the procedure to be followed by the Industrial Court while taking action in respect of recognition of other union. Section 14 is reproduced below in order to understand fully the essential conditions and the procedure to be followed while giving recognition to other union.

Section 14: Recognition of Other Union

1. If any union makes an application to the Industrial Court for being registered as a recognised union in place of a recognised union already registered as such (hereinafter in this section referred to as the (recognised union) for an undertaking, on the ground that it has the largest membership of employees employed in such undertaking, the Industrial Court shall, if a period of two years has elapsed since the date of registration of the recognised union, call upon the recognised union by a notice in writing to show cause, within thirty days of the receipt of such notice, as to why the union now applying should not be recognised in its place. An application made under this sub-section shall be accompanied by such fee not exceeding rupees five as may be prescribed.

Provided that, the Industrial Court may not entertain any application for registration of a union, unless a period of one year has elapsed since the date of disposal of the previous application of that union.

2. If, on the expiry of the period of notice under sub-section (1), the Industrial Court finds, on preliminary scrutiny, that the application made is in order, it shall cause notice to be displayed on the notice board of the undertaking, declaring its intention to consider the said application on the date specified in the notice, and calling upon other union or unions, if any, having membership of employees in that undertaking, employer and employees affected by the proposal to show cause within a prescribed time as to why recognition should not be granted.

3. If, after considering the objections, if any, that may be received under sub-section (2) and if, after holding such enquiry as it deems fit (which may include recording to evidence of witness and hearing of parties), the Industrial Court comes to the conclusion that the union applying complies with the conditions necessary for recognition specified in Section 11 and that its membership was, during the whole of the period of six calendar months immediately preceding the calendar month, in which it made the application under this section, larger than the membership of the recognition union, then the Industrial Court shall, subject to the provisions of Section 12 and this section recognise the union applying in place of the recognised union and issue a certificate of recognition in such form as may be prescribed.

FORM – D
(Section 43 (3), rule 11)

(Certificate of Recognition)

Name and full address of the Union ....

Registration No. ....

It is hereby certified that ....

(Here insert the name and full address the Union)

has been registered as a recognised union under Section 14 of the Maharashtra Recognition of Trade Unions and Prevention of Unfair Labour Practices Act, 1971, in place of ....

(Here insert the name and full address of the Union registered earlier)

as per order of the Industrial Court at .... passed on .... This certificate is given this .... day of .... of the Year ....

Place ....

Date ....

| Seal |

Signature of the Registrar of the Industrial Court

---

4. If the Industrial Court comes to the conclusion that any of the other unions have the largest membership of employees employed in the undertaking, and such other union has notified to the Industrial Court its claim to be registered as a recognised union for such

undertaking, and if, such other union satisfies the conditions requisite for recognition under Section 11 and complies with the conditions specified in Section 19 of this Act, the Industrial Court shall grant such recognition to such other union and issue a certificate of such recognition in such form as may be prescribed.

Explanation: For the purpose of this sub-section, the other union shall be deemed to have applied for recognition in the same calendar month as the applicant union.

5. Every application under this section shall be disposed of by the Industrial Court as far as possible, within three months from the date of receipt of the application, where a group of concerns in any industry which is notified to be undertaking for which recognition is applied for is situated in same local area; and in any other case, within four months.

Explanation: "Local area" for the purposes of this sub-section means the area which the State Government may, by notification in the Official Gazette, specify in such notification.

The application by another union for recognition under Section 14 is required to be submitted in 'Form-C' which is given below and the fee payable by a union for registration under Section 14 is ₹ Five only.

FORM C
(Section 14, Rule 8)
(Application by another union for recognition)
Industrial Case No.

In the Industrial Court at ..   ..   ..

(Name and address of the applicant union) ...   . Applicants;

versus

1. (Name and address of the employer undertaking)   ... Non-applicant
2. (Name and address of other trade union)   ... Non-applicant

Application for registration as a Recognised Union

The applicant union begs to submit as follows:

1. The applicant union is registered under the Indian Trade Unions Act on .... under certificate No. .... issued by the Registrar of Trade Unions.

2. The applicant union has the following office-bearers elected on ....

   President   –
   Vice-President (if any)   –
   General Secretary (if any)   –
   Treasurer (if any)   –
   Members of the Executive Committee   –

3. The applicant union has the following membership in the undertaking called .... for the whole of the period of six calendar months immediately preceding month in which this application is made:

Month	Number of members	Percentage of the total number of employees in undertaking
1.		
2.		
3.		
4.		
5.		
6.		

A list of all such employees who are members of the applicant/union for each month, alphabetically arranged, is filed with this application.

4. At a general meeting of the members of the applicant union/meeting of the Executive Committee of the applicant union which was held at .... on .... day of .... 20..., it was decided that the union should apply for registration as a recognised union for ....

(Here insert the name of the undertaking)

5. The undertaking for which this trade union seeks recognition as a Recognised Union is engaged in .... industry/trade. The undertaking is known as .... and is located at the following address:

Address ....
....

6. The undertaking is a proprietory concern/partnership concern / company and is owned by the following persons:

....
....

7. The constitution of the application union provides for the matters mentioned in Section 19 of the Act. A copy of the Constitution of the union is attached.

8. The applicant union hereby tenders the prescribed fee of ₹ ......for this application / the applicant union has paid the prescribed fee of ₹ .... for this application by Money Order, receipt for which is enclosed.

9. The applicant union has not instigated, aided or assisted the commencement or continuation of a strike among the employees in the undertaking for which the applicant union seeks recognition which is deemed to be illegal under the Act within six months immediately preceding the date of this application.

10. The applicant union had/had not made an application for registration as a recognised union before any Industrial Court under the Act.

11. (i) A member of the applicant union has to pay a monthly subscription of ₹ .... every month.

(ii) The Executive Committee of the applicant union met on the following dates during the twelve months preceding the date of the application.

(iii) The applicant union maintains minute book in which all resolutions passed by the Executive Committee or the General Body of the union are recorded.

(iv) The applicant union maintains accounts and such accounts were last audited by .... on .... and the certificate of the auditor is enclosed.

(v) The year of account of the applicant union is from .... to ....

12. The applicant union is a recognised union for the following undertakings/is not a recognised union for any other undertaking ....

Names of the undertakings ....

13. The applicant union has/has not on its roll of members employees employed in undertaking other than the undertaking for which the application is filed.

14. The applicant union herewith files the following documents with a list:

(i) Registered address of the applicant union.

(ii) A list of members of the applicant union who are employed in the undertaking for which recognition is sought and arranged alphabetically with a date of such employees joining as a member.

(iii) A true copy of certificate of registration as a trade union.

(iv) Authority of the person for filing this application.

(v) A true copy of the Constitution of the applicant union.

15. Trade Union called .... has been registered as a recognised union for the above undertaking ....

16. This union claims that it has the largest majority of employees employed in the same undertaking in which .... is registered as a recognised union.

17. This union had/had not made an application for registration as a recognised union in place of an already recognised union registered as such. Such application was disposed of on

...   .

VERIFICATION

I . ... who is holding office as .... in the applicant union hereby verify that the contents in the above application in paras .... are written from my knowledge and are true and those in paras .... are written from information obtained from .... and believed to be true. I have signed this at .... on .... date of the application.

Signature of the person authorised to make application

*Presented by ..   ..   ..

on ..   ..   ..

*Signature of the office authorised to receive application

(*To be filled when the application is presented in person).

2.9.5 Application for Re-recognition [Section 15]

Section 15 is a remedial section and it makes available a remedy to the union of which the recognition has been cancelled on the grounds mentioned in Section 13, clauses (I) and (II).

Section 13 (2) provides that a union, the recognition of which has been cancelled on any other ground shall not be entitled to apply for re-recognition within the period of one year from the date of the cancellation of its recognition. But such union can apply for re-recognition within the period of one year if the Industrial Court grants it the permission to do so. Section 15 is as follows:

Application for re-recognition: 1. Any union the recognition of which has been cancelled on the aground that it was recognised under a mistake or on the ground specified in clause (ii) of Section 13, may, at any time after three months from the date of such cancellation, and on payment of such fees as may be prescribed apply again to the Industrial Court from recognition; and thereupon the provisions of Sections 11 and 12 shall apply in respect of such application as they apply in relation to an application under Section 11 [Section 15 (1)].

2. A Union, the recognition of which has been cancelled on any other ground shall not, save with the permission of the Industrial Court, be entitled to apply for re-recognition within a period of one year from the date of such cancellation [Section 15 (2)].

Application for re-recognition of a union under Section 15 (1) is required to be submitted in Form-E which is given below and the fee payable by a union for that purpose is ₹ Five only.

FORM – E
(See rule 12)
(Application for re-recognition by a union)
Industrial Case No.

In the Industrial Court at ....
(Name and address of the applicant union) .... Applicant;

versus

1. (Name and address of the employer undertaking)   ... Non-applicant
2. (Name and address of other trade union)   ... Non-applicant

The applicant union begs to submit as follows:

1. The applicant union is registered under the Indian Trade Unions Act, on .... under certificate No. .... issued by the Registrar of Trade Unions.

2. The applicant union has the following office-bearers elected on ....
    President   ....
    Vice-President (if any)   ....
    General Secretary (if any)   ....
    Treasurer (if any)   ....
    Members of the Executive Committee   ....

3. The applicant union has the following membership in the undertaking called .... for the whole of the period of six calendar months immediately preceding month in which this application is made:

Month	Number of members	Percentage of the total number of employees in undertaking
1.		
2.		
3.		
4.		
5.		
6.		

A list of all such employees who are members of the applicant union for each month, alphabetically arranged, is filed with this application.

4. At a general meeting of the members of the applicant union/meeting of the Executive Committee of the applicant union which was held at .... on .... day of .... 20..., it was decided that the union should apply for registration as a recognised union for ....

(Here insert the name of the Undertaking)

5. The undertaking for which this trade union seeks recognition as a Recognised Union is engaged in .... industry/trade. The undertaking is known as .... and is located at the following address –

Address ....

....

6. The undertaking is a proprietary concern/partnership concern / company and is owned by the following persons:

....

....

7. The Constitution of the application union provides for the matters mentioned in Section 19 of the Act. A copy of the Constitution of the Union is attached.

8. The applicant union hereby tenders the prescribed fee of ₹ ......for this application / the applicant union has paid the prescribed fee of ₹ .... for this application by Money Order, receipt for which is enclosed.

9. The applicant union has not instigated, aided or assisted the commencement or continuation of a strike among the employees in the undertaking for which the applicant union seeks recognition which is deemed to be illegal under the Act within six months immediately preceding the date of this application.

10. The applicant union had/had not made an application for registration as a recognised union before any Industrial Court under the Act after its recognition was cancelled.

11. (i) A member of the applicant union has to pay a monthly subscription of ₹ .... every month.

(ii) The Executive Committee of the applicant union met on the following dates during the twelve months preceding the date of the application.

(iii) The applicant union maintains minute book in which all resolutions passed by the Executive Committee or the General Body of the union are recorded.

(iv) The applicant union maintains accounts and such accounts were last audited by .... on .... and the certificate of the auditor is enclosed.

(v) The year of account of the applicant union is from .... to ....

12. The applicant union is a recognised union for the following undertakings/is not a recognised union for any other undertaking ....

Names of the undertakings ....

13. The applicant union has/has not on its roll of members employees employed in undertaking other than the undertaking for which the application is filed.

14. The applicant union herewith files the following documents with a list:

(i) Registered address of the applicant union.

(ii) A list of members of the applicant union who are employed in the undertaking for which recognition is sought and arranged alphabetically with a date of such employees joining as a member.

(iii) A true copy of certificate of registration as a trade union.

(iv) Authority of the person for filling this application.

(v) A true copy of the Constitution of the applicant union.

15. The recognition of the applicant union was cancelled by an order of the Industrial Court at ..... on .... A copy of the order is enclosed herewith.

16. It is prayed that inquiry may be made and the applicant union may be registered again as a recognised union for the undertaking.

VERIFICATION

I . ... who is holding office as .... in the applicant union hereby verify that the contents in the above application in *paras .... are written from my knowledge and are true and those in paras .... are written from information obtained from .... and believed to be true. I have signed this at .... on ....

Date of the application.

Signature of the person
authorisd to make application

*Presented by ....

        on ....

*Signature of the officer authorised to receive application

(*To be filled when the application is presented in person).

2.9.6 Liability of Union or Members not Relieved by Cancellation [Section 16]

Section 16 states that, "*Notwithstanding anything contained in any law for the time being in force the cancellation of the recognition of a union shall not relieve the union or any member thereof from any penalty or liability incurred under this Act prior to such cancellation*".

2.9.7 Publication or Order [Section 17]

Every order passed under Sections 12, 13, 14 or 15 shall be final, and shall be caused to be published by the Industrial Court in the prescribed manner.

2.9.8 Recognition of Union for more than One Undertaking

"*Subject to the foregoing provisions of this Chapter, a union may be recognised for more than one undertaking*" [Section 18].

2.10 Obligations and Rights of Recognised and Other Unions

Provisions relating to obligations and rights of recognised unions, other unions and certain employees are embodied in Sections 19 to 23 of Chapter IV of the Act.

Section 19 deals with the obligations of the recognised unions while Sections 20 and 21 make clear the rights of the recognised unions.

Section 22 provides for the rights of unrecognised unions. Let us consider the provisions of these sections in brief.

2.10.1 Obligations of Recognised Unions [Section 19]

According to the provisions of Section 19 which relates to the obligations of a recognised union, "*The rules of a union seeking recognition under this Act shall provide for the following matters, and the provisions thereof shall be duly observed by the union, namely:*

1. The membership subscription shall be not less than fifty paise per month;
2. The Executive committee shall meet at intervals of not more than three months;
3. All resolutions passed, whether by Executive Committee or the General Body of the union, shall be recorded in a minute book kept for the purpose;
4. An auditor appointed by the State Government may audit its account at least once in each financial year".

The above mentioned four conditions have been imposed upon a union seeking recognition under this Act. But so far as the last condition i.e. an auditor appointed by the State Government may audit its account at least once in each financial year is concerned this condition is not within the control of the union as it is the State Government who appoints the auditor for the purpose of auditing its accounts.

If the State Government appoints any auditor, it is obligatory on the part of a union seeking recognition under this Act to get its account duly audited.

Section 13 (1) (iii) empowers the Industrial Court to cancel the recognition or to suspend the rights of a recognised union if it fails to observe the conditions mentioned in Section 19.

Thus, a recognised union or any union seeking recognition must comply with the conditions as are laid down in Section 19.

Besides these conditions, a union seeking recognition has to fulfill the conditions mentioned in Section 12 of this Act. Provisions of Section 12 have been already discussed.

2.10.2 Rights of Recognised Union [Section 20]

Recognised unions enjoy certain rights. The provisions relating to such rights have been made in Section 20 of the Act. Section 20 lays down that,

(1) Such officers, members of the office staff and members of a recognised union as may be authorised by or under rules made in this behalf by the State Government shall, in such manner and subject to such conditions as may be prescribed, have a right:

- (a) To collect sums payable by members to the union on the premises, where wages are paid to them;
- (b) To put up or cause to be put up a notice board on the premises of the undertaking in which its members are employed and affix or cause to be affixed notice thereon;
- (c) For the purpose of the prevention or settlement of an industrial dispute:
- (i) To hold discussion on the premises of the undertaking with the employees concerned, who are the members of the union but so as not to interfere with the due working of the undertaking;
- (ii) To meet and discuss, with an employer or any person appointed by him in that behalf, the grievances of employees employed in this undertaking;
- (iii) To inspect, if necessary, in an undertaking any place where any employee of the undertaking is employed;
- (d) To appear on behalf of any employee or employees in any domestic or departmental inquiry held by the employer [Section 20 (1)].

2. Where there is a recognised union for any undertaking:

- (a) That union alone shall have the right to appoint its nominees to represent workmen on the Works Committee constituted under Section 3 of the Central Act;
- (b) No employee shall be allowed to appear or act or be allowed to be represented in any proceedings under the Central Act (not being a proceedings in which the legality or propriety of an order to dismissal, discharge, removal retrenchment, termination of service, or suspension of an employee is under consideration), except through the recognised union and the decision arrived at, or order made, in such proceeding shall be binding on all the employees in such undertaking; and accordingly, the provisions of the Central Act, that is to say, the Industrial Disputes Act, 1947, XIV of 1947, shall stand amended in the manner and to the extent specified in Schedule I [Section 20 (2)].

Section 21 provides for the right to appear or act in the proceeding relating to certain unfair labour practices. It states that,

1. No employee in an undertaking to which the provisions of the Central Act for the time being apply, shall be allowed to appear or act or allowed to be represented in any proceeding relating to unfair labour practices specified in items 2 and 6 of Schedule IV of this Act except through the recognised union [Section 21 (1)].

It is further provided that where there is no recognised union to appear, the employee may himself appear or act in any proceeding relating to any such unfair labour practices [Proviso to Section 21 (1)].

2. Notwithstanding anything contained in the Bombay Act, no employee in any industry to which the provisions of the Bombay Act, for the time being apply, shall be allowed to appear or act or allowed to be represented in any proceeding relating to unfair labour practices specified in items 2 and 6 of Schedule IV of this Act except through the representative of employees entitled to appear under Section 30 of the Bombay Act [Section 21 (2)].

2.10.3 Rights of Unrecognised Unions [Section 22]

Unrecognised unions also enjoy certain rights under this Act. Such rights are given in Section 22 which are as follows:

"Such officers, members of the office staff and members of any union (other than a recognised union) as may be authorised by or under the rules made in this behalf by the State Government shall, in such manner and subject to such conditions as may be prescribed, have a right –

(i) To meet and discuss with an employer or any person appointed by him in that behalf, the grievances of any individual member relating to his discharge, removal, retrenchment, termination of service and suspension;

(ii) To appear on behalf of any of its members employed in the undertaking in any domestic or departmental inquiry held by the employer" [Section 22].

Thus, the officers, members of the office staff and members of a recognised union have a right to :

(1) discuss with an employer in the matters related to discharge, removal, retrenchment, termination of service and suspension of any individual member, and

(2) to appear on behalf of its members in any domestic or departmental inquiry held by the employer under Section 22.

2.10.4 Employees Authorised by Recognised Union to Appear or Act in Certain Proceedings to be Considered as on Duty [Section 23]

Section 23 lays down that, *"Not more than two members of a recognised union duly authorised by it in writing who appear or act on its behalf in any proceeding under the Central Act or the Bombay Act or under this Act shall be deemed to be on duty on the days on which such proceedings actually take place, and accordingly, such member or members shall, on production of a certificate from the authority of the court before which he or they appeared or acted to the effect that he or they so appeared or acted on the days specified in the certificate, be entitled to be paid by his or their employer his or their salary and allowances which would have been payable for those days as if he or they had attended duty on those days.*

Explanation: For the purpose of this section "recognised union" includes a representative union under the Bombay Act".

2.11 Illegal Strikes and Lock-outs

Strike is an effective weapon in the hands of workmen. The workmen can bring pressure on their employer to fulfill their demands. While lock-out is a weapon which is used by an employer against his workmen to make an appropriate settlement in his favour. This implies that the workmen as well as employers use these weapons i.e. strikes and lock-outs, to protect their own interest and also to bring about the settlements in their favour.

Provisions of Section 24 lays down the conditions under which a strike or a lock-out becomes illegal. Let us first consider the conditions under which a strike becomes illegal according to the provisions of Section 24 (1).

2.11.1 Illegal Strikes

Section 24 (1) states that, "*In this Act, unless the context requires otherwise "illegal strike" means a strike which is commenced or continued –*

(a) Without giving to the employer notice of strike in the prescribed form, or within fourteen days of the giving of such notice;

(b) Where there is a recognised union, without obtaining the vote of the majority of the members of the union, in favour of the strikes before the notice of the strike is given;

(c) During the pendency of conciliation proceeding under the Bombay Act or the Central Act and seven days after the conclusion of such proceeding in respect of matters covered by the notice of strike;

(d) Where submission in respect of any of the matters covered by the notice of strike is registered under Section 66 of the Bombay Act, before such submission, is lawfully revoked;

(e) Where an industrial dispute in respect of any of the matters covered by the notice of strike has been referred to the arbitration of a Labour Court or the Industrial Court voluntarily under sub-section (6) of Section 58 or Section 71 of the Bombay Act, during the arbitration proceeding or before or the date on which the arbitration proceedings are completed or the date on which the award of the arbitrator comes into operation, whichever is later;

(f) During the pendency of arbitration proceedings before an arbitrator under the Central Act and before the date on which the arbitration proceedings are concluded, if such proceedings are in respect of any of the matters covered by the notice of strike;

(g) In cases where an industrial dispute has been referred to the arbitration of a Labour Court or the Industrial Court under Sections 72, 73 or 73-A of the Bombay Act, during such arbitration proceedings or before the date on which the proceeding is completed or the date on which the award of the Court comes into operation, whichever is later, if such proceedings are in respect of any of the matters covered by the notice of strike;

(h) In case where an industrial dispute has been referred to the adjudication of the Industrial Tribunal or Labour Court under the Central Act, during the pendency of such proceeding before such authority and before the conclusion of such proceeding, if such proceeding is in respect of any of the matters covered by notice of strike.

It is further provided that, nothing in clauses (g) and (h) shall apply to any strike where the union has offered in writing to submit the industrial dispute to arbitration under sub-section (6) of Section 58 of the Bombay Act or Section 10-A of the Central Act, and –

(i) The employer does not accept the offer, or

(ii) The employer accepts the offer but disagreeing on the choice of the arbitrator, does not agree to submit the dispute to arbitration without naming an arbitrator as provided in the Bombay Act,

and thereafter, the dispute has been referred for arbitration of the Industrial Court under Section 73-A of the Bombay Act, or where the Central Act applies, while disagreeing on the choice of the arbitrator, the employer does not agree to submit the dispute to arbitration of the arbitrator recommended by the State Government in this behalf, and thereafter, the dispute has been referred to adjudication of the Industrial Tribunal or the Labour Court, as the case may be, under the Central Act; or

(iii) During any period in which any settlement or award is in operation, in respect of any of the matters covered by the settlement or award; [Proviso to Section 24 (1)].

Provisions of clauses (a) and (b) of Section 24 (1) imply that if the following conditions for commencement or continuation of a strike are not fulfilled, such strike becomes illegal.

(a) Before giving the notice of a strike, where there is a recognised union, it must obtain the vote of majority of its members in favour of the strike;

(b) The notice of the strike must be given to the employer in the prescribed form. Rule 22 of the M.R.T.U. and P.U.L.P. Rules of 1975 prescribes that the notice of the strike must be in Form I and the same must be sent to the employer by the registered post. The format of Form I is as follows:

FORM – I
(See Rule 22)

Name of the Trade Union:
Names of 5 elected representatives of the workmen, where no Trade Union exists:
Address: ....
Dated the .... day of .... 20 ......
To,
    (Here mention name of the employer and full address of the undertaking)
Dear Sir (s)/Madam,

    In accordance with the provisions contained in sub-section (1) of Section 24 of the Maharashtra Recognition of Trade Unions and Prevention of Unfair Labour Practices Act, 1971, I/we.
(Here insert name of the persons (s))
hereby give you Notice that I/we propose to call a strike of the workmen employed in you undertaking propose to go on strike along with the other workmen employed in your undertaking from the .... day of .... 20 .... , for the reason (s) explained in the Annexure attached hereto.

    2. This Union being a recognised Union in your undertaking has obtained the vote of majority of the members in your undertaking in favour of the strike, before serving this notice on you, under clause (b) of sub-section (2) of Section 24 of the Act.

Yours faithfully,

Place ....

Signature
General Secretary/Secretary
....
(Here insert name of the Union)

*Strike off whichever is not applicable.

Annexure
Statement of Reasons

Copy to:
1. The Investigating Officer
   (Here enter office address of the Investigating Officer, for the area concerned)
2. The Registrar, Industrial Court, Maharashtra, Bombay.
3. The Judge, Labour Court ....
   (Here enter address of the Labour Court, of the area concerned).
4. The Commissioner of Labour, Bombay.

(c) The strike should not be commenced or continued within 14 days of giving such notice clauses (c) to (h) of Section 24 (1) imposes various restrictions on the commencement or continuation of strike during the pendency of the proceedings and within certain period from the conclusion of such proceedings.

2.11.2 Illegal Lock-outs

Provisions of Section 24 (2) lay down the conditions under which a lock-out becomes illegal. Section 24 (2) states that, *"illegal lock-out" means a lock-out which is commenced or continued* –

(a) Without giving to the employees, a notice of lock-out in the prescribed form or within fourteen days of the giving of such notice;

(b) During the pendency of conciliation proceeding under the Bombay Act or the Central Act and seven days after the conclusion of such proceeding in respect of any of the matters covered by the notice of lock-out;

(c) During the period when a submission in respect of any of the matters covered by the notice of lock-out is registered under Section 66 of the Bombay Act, before such submission is lawfully revoked;

(d) Where an industrial dispute in respect of matter covered by the notice of lock-out has been referred to the arbitration of a Labour Court or the Industrial Court voluntarily under sub-section (6) of Section 58 or Section 71 of the Bombay Act, during the arbitration proceeding or before the date on which the arbitration proceeding is completed or the date on which the award of the arbitrator comes into operation, whichever is later;

(e) During the pendency of arbitration proceedings before an arbitrator under the Central Act and before the date on which the arbitration proceedings are concluded, if such proceedings are in respect of any of the matters covered by the notice of lock-out;

(f) In cases where an industrial dispute has been referred to the arbitration of a Labour Court of the Industrial Court compulsory under Sections 72, 73 or 73-A of the Bombay Act, during such arbitration proceeding or before the date on which the proceeding is completed, or the date on which the award of the Court comes into operation whichever is later, if proceedings are in respect of any of the matters covered by the notice of lock-out; or

(g) In cases where an industrial dispute has been referred to the adjudication of the Industrial Tribunal or Labour Court under the Central Act, during the pendency of such proceeding before such authority and before the conclusion of such proceeding, if such proceeding is in respect of any of the matters covered by the notice of lock-out;

Provided that, nothing in clauses (f) and (g) shall apply to any lock-out where the employer has offered in writing to submit the industrial dispute to arbitration under sub-section (6) of Section 58 of the Bombay Act, or Section 10-A of the Central Act; and

(i) The union does not accept the offer;

(ii) The union accepts the offer, but disagreeing on the choice of the arbitrator does not agree to submit the dispute to arbitration without naming an arbitrator as provided in the Bombay Act,

and thereafter, the dispute has been referred for arbitration of the Industrial Court under Section 73-A of the Bombay Act, or where the Central Act applies, while disagreeing on the choice of the arbitrator, the union does not agree to submit the dispute to arbitration of the arbitrator recommended by the State Government in his behalf, and thereafter, the dispute has been referred to adjudication of the Industrial Tribunal or the Labour Court, as the case may be, under the Central Act;

    (h) During any period in which any settlement or award is in operation, in respect of any of the matters covered by the settlement or award".

Clause (a) of Section 24 (2) makes it clear that if the lock-out is commenced or continues without giving the notice to the employees in the prescribed form or within fourteen days of giving such notice, such lock-out is considered illegal. Such notice of lock-out must be given in Form – J which is prescribed under Rule 23 of the M.R.T.U. and P.U.L.P. Rules of 1975. Moreover, the reasons of lock-out are required to be given in the annexure annexed to the notice, and further the date on which the lock-out is to be intended is required to be mentioned in the notice. The format of the Form-J is as follows:

FORM – J
(See Rule 23)
Notice of lock-out

Name of the employer: ....
Full address of the undertaking: ....
Dated the .... day of .... 20 ....

In accordance with the provisions of sub-section (2) of Section 24 of the Maharashtra Recognition of Trade Unions and Prevention of Unfair Labour Practices Act, 1971, I/We .... hereby give notice to all concerned that it is my/our intention to effect a lock-out in .... departments (s)/sections (s) of my/our undertakings, with effect from .... day of ..... 20 ... for the reasons explained in the Annexure attached thereto.

                                                 Signature ....

Place: ....

                                                 Designation ....
                                   (Here insert name of the undertakings)

Annexure
Statement of Reasons

Copy to –
    1. The Investigating Officer: ....
       (Here enter office address of the Investigating Officer for the area concerned)
    2. The Registrar, Industrial Court, Maharashtra, Bombay ....
    3. The judge, Labour Court ....
    4. The Commissioner of Labour, Bombay ....
Copy forwarded to:
    1. Investigating Officer of the area at ....
    2. Commissioner of Labour ....
    3. Labour Court at ....

Thus, clauses (a) to (h) of Section 24 (2) make clear the circumstances under which the lock-out declared by the employer becomes illegal.

2.11.3 Reference to the Labour Court for Declaration Whether the Strike or Lock-out is Illegal [Section 25]

The provisions of Section 25 are passed for the purpose of getting a declaration whether the strike and lock-out which are in contravention of the provisions of this Act are illegal. After such declaration is made, an opportunity is given to the concerned erring employer or employees to rectify the error with the promise that thereupon the illegality in the action already taken would be withdrawn [Section 25 (5)]. Now let us consider the provisions of Section 25.

Section 25 (1) lays down that "*Where the employees in any undertaking have proposed to go on strike or have commenced a strike, the State Government or the employer of the undertaking may make a reference of the Labour Court for a declaration that such strike is illegal*".

Where the employer of any undertaking has proposed a lock-out or has commenced a lock-out, the State Government or the recognised union or, where there is no recognised union, any other union of the employees in the undertaking may a reference to the Labour Court for a declaration whether such lock-out will be illegal [Section 25 (2)].

For the purposes of this section recognised union includes a representative union under the Bombay Act [Explanation to Section 25 (2)].

No declaration shall be made under this section, save in the open [Section 25 (3)].

The declaration made under this section, shall be recognised as binding, and shall be followed in all proceeding under this Act [Section 25 (4)].

Where any strike or lock-out declared to be illegal under this section is withdrawn within forty-eight hours of such declaration, such strike or lock-out shall not, for the purposes of this Act, be deemed to be illegal under this Act [Section 25 (5)].

2.12 Unfair Labour Practices

2.12.1 Meaning of Unfair Labour Practices and Various Unfair Labour Practices [Section 26]

In this Act, unless the context requires otherwise, unfair labour practices mean any of the practices listed in Schedules II, III and IV [Section 26]. It is laid down in Section 27 that "*no employer or union and no employee shall engage in any unfair labour practice*".

Various unfair labour practices on the part of the employers are given in Schedule II.

SCHEDULE II

Unfair Labour Practices on the Part of the Employers

1. To interfere with, restrain or coerce employees in the exercise of their right to organise, form, join or assist a trade union and to engage in concerted activities for the purposes of collective bargaining or other mutual aid or protection, that is to say –

   (a) Threatening employees with discharge or dismissal, if they join a union;

   (b) Threatening a lock-out or closure, if a union should be organised;

(c) Granting wage increase to employees at crucial periods of union organisation, with a view to undermining the efforts of the union at organisation.

2. To dominate, interfere with, or contribute, support - financial or otherwise - to any union, that is to say –

(a) An employer taking an active interest in organising a union of his employees; and
(b) An employer showing partiality or granting favour to one of several unions attempting to organise his employees or to its members, where such a union is not a recognised union.

3. To establish employer sponsored unions.

4. To encourage or discourage membership in any union by discriminating against any employee, that is to say -

(a) Discharging or punishing an employee because he urged other employees to join or organise a union;
(b) Discharging or dismissing an employee for taking part in any strike (not being a strike which is deemed to be an illegal strike under this Act);
(c) Changing seniority rating of employee because of union activities;
(d) Refusing to promote employees to higher posts on account of their union activities;
(e) Giving unmerited promotions to certain employees, with a view to show discord amongst the other employees, or to undermine the strength of their union;
(f) Discharging office-bearers or active union members, on account of their union activities.

5. To refuse to bargain collectively, in good faith, with the recognised union.
6. Proposing or continuing a lock-out deemed to be illegal under this Act.

Various unfair labour practices on the part of trade unions are given in Schedule III.

SCHEDULE III

Unfair Labour Practices on the part of Trade Unions

1. To advise or actively support or instigate any strike deemed to be illegal under this Act.

2. To coerce employees in the exercise of their right to self-organisation or to join unions or refrain from joining any union, that is to say –

(a) for a union or its members to picketing in such a manner that non-striking employees are physically debarred from entering the workplace;
(b) to indulge in acts of force or violence or to hold out threats of intimidation in connection with a strike against non-striking employees or against managerial staff.

3. For a recognised union to refuse to bargain collectively in good faith with the employer.

4. To indulge in coercive activities against certification of a bargaining representative.

5. To stage, encourage or instigate such forms of coercive actions as willful "go-slow" squatting on the work premises after working hours or of "gherao" of any of the members of the managerial staff.

6. To stage demonstrations at the residence of the employers or the managerial or other staff members.

In Schedule IV, the general unfair labour practises on the part of employers are given.

SCHEDULE IV

General Unfair Labour Practices on the Part of employers

1. To discharge or dismiss employees –
(a) By way of victimisation;
(b) Not in good faith, but in the colourable exercise of the employer's rights;
(c) By falsely implicating an employee in a criminal case on false evidence or on concocted evidence;
(d) For patently false reasons;
(e) On untrue or trumped up allegations of absence without leave;
(f) In utter disregard of the principles of natural justice in the conduct of domestic enquiry or with undue haste;
(g) For misconduct of a minor or technical character, without having any regard to the nature of the particular misconduct or the past record of service of the employee, so as to amount to a shockingly disproportionate punishment.

2. To abolish the work of a regular nature being done by employees, and to give such work to contractors as a measure of breaking a strike.

3. To transfer an employee *malafide* from one place to another place, under the guise following management policy.

4. To insist upon individual employees, who were on legal strike, to sign a good conduct-bond, as a pre-condition to allowing them to resume work.

5. To show favouritism or partiality to one set of workers, regardless of merits.

6. To employ employees as "*badlis*", casuals or temporaries and to continue them as such for years, with the object of depriving them of the status and privileges of permanent employees.

7. To discharge or discriminate against any employee for filing charges or testifying against an employer in any enquiry or proceeding relating to any industrial dispute.

8. To recruit employees during a strike which is not an illegal strike.

9. Failure to implement award, settlement or agreement.

10. To indulge in act of force or violence.

2.12.2 Provisions Relating to Modification of Schedules

Provisions relating to modifications of various schedules appended to this Act have been done in Section 53 of the Act. These provisions are as under:

1. The State Government may, after obtaining the opinion of the Industrial Court, by notification in the Official Gazette, at any time make any addition to, or alteration, in any Schedule II, III or IV and may, in the like manner, delete any item therefrom [Section 53 (1)].

It is also provided that, before making any such addition, alteration or deletion, a draft of such addition, alternation or deletion shall be published for the information of all persons likely to be affected thereby, and the State Government shall consider any objections or suggestions that may be received by it from any person with respect thereto [Proviso to Section 53 (1)].

2. Every such notification shall, as soon as possible after its issue, be laid by the State Government before the Legislature of the State [Section 53 (2)].

2.12.3 The Procedure to be followed for Dealing with Complaints Relating to Unfair Labour Practices [Section 28]

While dealing with the complaints relating to unfair labour practices, the following procedure is to be followed according to the provisions of Section 28 of the Act.

1. Where any person has engaged in or is engaging in any unfair labour practice, then any union or any employee or any employer or any Investigating Office may, within ninety days of the occurrence of such unfair labour practice, file a complaint before the Court competent to deal with such complaint either under Section 5, or as the case may be, under Section 7, of this Act;

Provided that, the Court may entertain a complaint after the period of ninety days from the date of the alleged occurrence, if good and sufficient reasons are shown by the complainant for the late filing of the complaint.

2. The Court shall take a decision on every such complaint as far as possible within a period of six months from the date of receipt of the complaint.

3. On receipt of a complaint under sub-section (1), the Court may, if it so considers necessary, first cause an investigation into the said complaint to be made by the Investigating Officer, and direct that a report in the matter may be submitted by him to the Court, within the period specified in this direction.

4. While investigating into any such complaint, the Investigating Officer may visit the undertaking, where the practice alleged is said to have occurred, and make such enquiries as he considers necessary. He may also make efforts to promote settlement of the complaint.

5. The Investigating Officer shall, after investigating into the complaint under sub-section (4) submit his report to the Court, within the time specified by it, setting out the

full facts and circumstances of the case, and the efforts made by him in settling the complaint. The Court shall, on demand and on payment of such fee as may be prescribed by rules, supply a copy of the report to the complainant and the person complained against.

6. If, on receipt of the report of the Investigating Officer, the Court finds that the complaint has not been settled satisfactorily, and that facts and circumstances of the case require, that the matter should be further considered by it, the Court shall proceed to consider it, and give its decision.

7. The decision of the Court, which shall be in writing, shall be in the form of an order. The order of the Court shall be final and shall not be called in question in any civil or criminal court.

8. The Court shall cause its order to be published in such manner as may be prescribed. The order of the Court shall become enforceable from the date specified in the order.

9. The Court shall forward a copy of its order to the State Government and such officers of the Stage Government as may be prescribed.

2.12.4 Parties on Whom an Order of the Court is Binding

Section 29 of the Act specifically mentions the parties on whom the orders of the Court are binding. These provisions of Section 29 are made in order to avoid any ambiguity for identifying the persons or parties to be made liable to obey or to comply with the orders at the Court.

Section 29 is reproduced below from which we come to know the parties or persons on whom the orders of the Court are binding.

Section 29: Parties on whom Order or Court shall be binding:

An order of the Court shall be binding on –

(a) All parties to the complaint;

(b) All parties who were summoned to appear as parties to the complaint whether they appear or not, unless the Court is of opinion that they were improperly made parties;

(c) In the case of an employer who is a party to the complaint before such Court in respect of the undertaking to which the complaint relates, his heirs, successors or assigns in respect of the undertaking to which the complaint relates; and

(d) Where the party referred to in clause (a) or clause (b) is composed of employees, all persons, who, on the date of the complaint are employed in the undertaking to which complaint relates and all persons who may be subsequently employed in the undertaking.

From the provisions of Section 29, we come to know that on the following parties or persons, an order of the Court is binding.

1. All parties to the complaint.
2. All parties who have been summoned to appear as parties to the complaint. But if the parties who have been summoned are, in the opinion of the court, found improperly made parties, then such parties are not bound by the order of the court.
3. An employer who is a party to the complaint. Here, an employer includes his heirs, successors.
4. All persons who are employed on the date of the complaint and all other persons subsequently employed in the undertaking where the party referred to in clause (a) or clause (b) of Section 29 is composed of employees.

2.13 Penalties

Provisions relating to penalties for,

(1) disclosure of confidential information,

(2) contempts of the Industrial or Labour Courts and

(3) obstructing officers from carrying out their duties and for failure to produce documents or the compliance with requision or order have been made in Sections 47, 48 and 49 respectively. These sections are given below:

2.13.1 Penalty for Disclosure of Confidential Information

If an Investigating Officer or any person present at, or concerned, in any proceeding under this Act wilfully discloses any information or the contents of any document in contravention of provisions of this Act, he shall, on conviction, on a complaint made by the party who gave the information or produced the document in such proceeding, be punished with fine which may extend to one thousand rupees [Section 47].

2.13.2 Penalty for Contempts of the Industrial or Labour Courts [Section 48]

The main object of Section 48 is to impose certain legal obligations upon the concerned persons or parties to comply with the orders of the Industrial or Labour Courts, as the case may be. If the persons or parties do not comply with the orders of the Industrial or Labour Courts, that leads to the contempt of the Court punishable under this Act. The punishments for contempt of the Industrial or Labour Courts according to the provisions of Section 48 are as under.

1. Any person who fails to comply with any other of the Court under clause (b) of sub-section (1) or sub-section (2) of Section 30 of this Act shall, on conviction, be punished with imprisonment which may extend to three months or with fine which may extend to five thousand rupees.

2. If any person,

(a) When ordered by the Industrial Court or a Labour Court to produce or deliver up any document or to furnish information being legally bound so to do, intentionally omits to do so; or

(b) When required by the Industrial Court or a Labour Court to bind himself by an oath or affirmation to state the truth refuse to do so;

(c) Being legally bound to state the truth on any subject to the Industrial Court or a Labour Court refuses to answer any question demanded of him touching such subject by such Court; or

(d) Intentionally offers any insult or causes any interruption to the Industrial Court or a Labour Court at any stage of its judicial proceeding, he shall, on conviction, be punished with imprisonment for a term which may extend to six months or with fine which may extend to one thousand rupees or with both.

3. If any person refuses to sign any statement made by him, when required to do so by the Industrial Court or a Labour Court, he shall, on conviction, be punished with imprisonment for term which may extend to three months or with fine which may extend to five hundred rupees or with both.

4. If any offence under sub-section (2) or (3) is committed in the view or presence of the Industrial Court or as the case may be, a Labour Court, such Court may, after recording the facts constituting the offence and the statement of the accused as provided in the Code of Criminal Procedure, 1898, V of 1898 forward the case to a Magistrate having jurisdiction to try the same, and may require security to be given for the appearance of the accused person before such Magistrate or, if sufficient security is not given, shall forward such person in custody to such Magistrate. The magistrate to whom any case is so forwarded shall proceed to hear the complaint against the accused person in the manner provided in the said Code or Criminal Procedure.

5. If any person commits any act or publishes any writing which is calculated to improperly influence the Industrial Court, or a Labour Court or to bring such Court or a member of a Judge thereof into disrepute or contempt or to its or his authority, or to interfere with the lawful process of any such Court, such person shall be deemed to be guilty of contempt of such Court.

6. In the case of contempt of itself, the Industrial Court shall record the facts constituting such contempt, and make a report in that behalf to the High Court.

7. In the case of contempt of a Labour Court, such Court shall record the facts constituting such contempt, and make a report in that behalf to the Industrial Court; and thereupon, the Industrial Court may, if it considers it expedient to do so, forward the report to the High Court.

8. When any intimation or report in respect of any contempt is received by the High Court under sub-sections (6) or (7), the High Court shall deal with such contempt as if it were contempt of itself, and shall have and exercise in respect of it the same jurisdiction, powers and authority in accordance with the same procedure and practice as it has and exercises in respect of contempt of itself.

2.13.3 Penalty for Obstructing Officers from Carrying out their Duties and for Failure to Produce Documents or to Comply with Requisition or Order [Section 49]

Any person who wilfully:

1. Prevents or obstructs officers, members of the office staff, or members of any union from exercising any of their rights conferred by this Act;
2. Refuses entry to an Investigating Officer to any place which he is entitled to enter;
3. Fails to produce any document which he is required to produce; or
4. Fails to comply with any requisition or order issued by him or under the provisions of this Act or the rules made thereunder; shall, on conviction, be punished with fine which may extend to five hundred rupees.

2.14 Recovery of Money Due from Employer and Recovery of Fines

2.14.1 Recovery of Money Due from Employer

Where any money is due to an employee from an employer under an order passed by the Court under Chapter VI, the employee himself or any other person authorised by him in writing in this behalf, or in the case of death of the employee, his assignee or heirs may, without prejudice to any other mode of recovery, make an application to the Court for the recovery of money due to him, and if the Court is satisfied that any money is so due, it shall issue a certificate for that amount to the Collector, who shall, proceed to recover the same in the same manner as an arrear of land revenue [Section 50].

It is provided that, every such application shall be made within one year from the date on which the money became due to the employee from the employer [Proviso 1 to Section 50].

It is further provided further that, any such application may be entertained after the expiry of the said period of one year, if the Court is satisfied that the applicant had sufficient cause for not making the application within the said period [Proviso 2 to Section 50].

2.14.2 Recovery of Fines

The amount of any fine imposed under this Chapter shall be recoverable as arrears of land revenue [Section 51].

Points to Remember

- This Act came into force on 1-2-1972 and it extends to the whole State of Maharashtra.
- The Industrial Court, the Labour Court, and the Investigating Officers are the Authorities appointed under this Act. The provisions relating to the appointment, duties and powers are also made in the Act.
- There are the provisions relating to unions, their resignations, recognition etc. in the Act.
- Provisions relating to illegal strike and lock-outs have been made in Sections 24 and 25.
- Various unfair trade practices on the part of employers, trade unions, employees are given in the schedules.
- Penalties for various offences are given in Sections 47, 48 and 49.
- How to recover any amount due to from an employer is made clear in Section 50 of the Act.

Questions for Discussion

1. Explain the objects of the M.R.T.U. and P.U.L.P. Act.
2. Explain the extent and application of the M.R.T.U. and P.U.L.P. Act.
3. Define and explain the following terms as used in the M.R.T.U. and P.U.L.P. Act.
   (a) Employee;
   (b) Employer;
   (c) Industry;
4. What are the authorities under the M.R.T.U. and P.U.L.P. Act?
5. Explain the constitution, duties and powers of the Industrial Court under this Act.
6. Explain in brief the constitution, duties and powers of the Labour Court under this Act.
7. Explain the provisions relating to appointment, duties and powers of the Investigating Officers of the M.R.T.U. and P.U.L.P. Act of 1971.
8. Explain the provisions of the M.R.T.U. and P.U.L.P. Act relating to recognition of unions.
9. What are the essential conditions for making an application to the Industrial Court for getting recognition to a union as a registered union?
10. What is the procedure to be followed by the Industrial Court while deciding an application for the recognition of a union?
11. Describe the obligations and rights of recognised and other unions under this Act.
12. Explain the provisions of the M.R.T.U. and P.U.L.P. Act relating to (a) illegal strikes and (b) illegal lock-outs.
13. Explain the meaning of unfair labour practices and state various unfair labour practices under the M.R.T.U. and P.U.L.P. Act.

14. Explain the procedure to be followed for dealing with complaints relating to unfair labour practices under M.R.T.U. and P.U.L.P. Act.
15. What are the provisions of this Act relating to penalties for disclosure of confidential information and for contempts of the Industrial and Labour Courts?
16. Write a note on the following:
    (a) Cancellation of recognition and suspension of rights of a union.
    (b) Recognition of other unions under the M.R.T.U. and P.U.L.P. Act.
    (c) Application for re-recognition of a union.
    (d) Rights of unrecognised unions.
    (e) Provisions of the M.R.T.U. and P.U.L.P. Act relating to reference to the Labour Court for declaration whether the strike or lock-out is illegal.
    (f) Unfair labour practices on the part of the employers.
    (g) Unfair labour practices on the part of the trade unions.
    (h) General unfair labour practices on the part of employers.
    (i) Provisions relating to modifications of schedules appended to the M.R.T.U. and P.U.L.P. Act.
    (j) Punishment for the contempts of the Industrial or Labour Court.

Practical Problems

1. Mr. X is the employee of a Cooperative Bank. He files a compliant of unfair labour practices about five years thereafter. He does not mention any adequate reason for delay in his complaint. Can his complaint be heard?

   [**Hint:** No. This case is similar to that of Pune District Central Co-operative Bank V. H. R. Gaikwad [(1999) 81 FLR 611 (Bom. H.C.)] case. In that case, the Labour Court erred in condoning the delay. Consequently the complaint was dismissed].

2. Mr. X fails and refuses to produce the necessary documents which he is required to produce. What is the penalty for this offence?

   [**Hint:** He, on conviction, can be punished with a fine which may extend to ₹ five hundred].

3. Mr. Y intentionally causes unnecessary interruption to the Industrial Court in its judicial proceeding. What is the punishment for this offence?

   [**Hint:** He can be punished under Section 48(2) (d) with imprisonment for a term which may extend to six months or with fine which may extend to five hundred rupees or with both].

Chapter **3**...

The Payment of Gratuity Act, 1972 (Social Security Legislation)

Contents ...

- 3.1 Introduction
- 3.2 Nature of Gratuity Payment
- 3.3 The Basic Objects of the Payment of Gratuity Act, 1972
- 3.4 The Salient Features and Important Provisions of the Act
- 3.5 Scope and Extent of the Act
- 3.6 Definitions
- 3.7 Payment of Gratuity
    - 3.7.1 When is Gratuity Payable?
    - 3.7.2 Rate of Gratuity
    - 3.7.3 Maximum Amount of Gratuity
- 3.8 Calculation of Gratuity
- 3.9 Provisions Relating to Better Terms of Gratuity
- 3.10 Forfeiture of Gratuity
- 3.11 Power of an Appropriate Government to Exempt
- 3.12 Compulsory Insurance [Section 4-A]
- 3.13 Nomination
- 3.14 Determination of the Amount of Gratuity
    - 3.14.1 Direction of Payment of Gratuity
    - 3.14.2 Maintenance of Records of Cases by the Controlling Authority
- 3.15 Recovery of Gratuity
    - 3.15.1 Application for Recovery of Gratuity
- 3.16 Protection of Gratuity
- 3.17 Appointment and Powers of Inspectors
    - 3.17.1 Appointment of Inspectors
    - 3.17.2 Powers of Inspectors
- 3.18 Penalties
- 3.19 Exemption of the Employer from Liability in Certain Cases
- 3.20 Cognizance of Offences [Section 11]
- 3.21 Protection of Action Taken in Good Faith

3.22 Act to Override Other Enactments

3.23 Power to Make Rules

3.24 Display of Abstract of the Act and Rules
- Points to Remember
- Questions for Discussion
- Practical Problems

Learning Objectives...

After going through this chapter, you will be able to know:
- The Nature of Gratuity Payment
- Important Objects of the Act
- Calculation of the Gratuity payable under this Act
- Provisions of the Act relating to Forfeiture of Gratuity
- Powers of the Inspectors appointed under this Act
- Offences and Penalties for the Offences under the Act
- Various Rules which are given in Form 'U'

3.1 Introduction

Labour welfare and Social security are the major aspects of national programmes towards bettering the lot of workers and creating a life and work environment of decent comfort for this class of population. Social security of workers refers to protection provided to the workers against providential mishaps over which they have no control.

The idea of social security implies that the State shall make itself responsible for ensuring some minimum standard of material welfare to its citizens to cover various main contingencies of life. Childhood and old age are the two stages of dependency in the life of a man. The social security system aims to help individuals in such time of dependency. Besides this, there are many risks of insecurity to which human life is liable.

The main risks of insecurity are incidents of life occurring right from childhood up to old age and death and they mainly include sickness, invalidity, accidents, industrial disease, unemployment, old age, death of the bread-winner and other such emergencies. Considering these aspects, various social security measures are required to be introduced and implemented. In India, there is a network of legislation which provides for social security for the workers.

The Worksmen's Compensation Act of 1923; The Employee's State Insurance Act of 1948; The Maternity Benefit Act of 1961; The Employee's Provident Funds and Miscellaneous Provisions Act of 1952; The Payment of Gratuity Act of 1972 and; other such Acts have been passed to provide social security to workers in India. In this chapter, various important provisions of the Payment of Gratuity Act of 1972 are considered.

Prior to enactment of the Payment of Gratuity Act of 1972, there was no Central Act in existence to regulate the payment of gratuity to industrial workers except the Working Journalists (Conditions of Service) and Miscellaneous Provisions Act of 1955. However, the Government of Kerala enacted legislation in 1970-71 for the payment of gratuity to workers employed in factories, plantations, shops and establishments.

The Governor of West Bengal promulgated an ordinance on 3rd June, 1971 prescribing a scheme of gratuity. The ordinance was subsequently replaced by the West Bengal Payment of Compulsory Gratuity Act of 1971. After the enactment of the above mentioned two Acts, some other State Governments also voiced their intention of enacting similar measures in their respective states. Therefore, a central law on the subject became necessary to ensure a uniform pattern of payment of gratuity to the employees throughout the country. As a result, the Payment of Gratuity Act of 1972 was passed by the Parliament in August, 1972. It came into force on 16th September, 1972. It was amended in 1984, 1987, 1994, 1998 and the latest amendment in the Act has been made in 2010.

3.2 Nature of Gratuity Payment

Provident Fund, pension are retirement benefits. Gratuity is also one of the kinds of retirement benefits. It is, in fact, a payment to be made to the employees to help them after their retirement whether such retirement is the result of the rules of superannuation or of some physical disability.

Any employee should be entitled to claim a certain amount of payment as a retirement benefit for his faithful service over a certain period of his employment is the general principle underlying any gratuity scheme. This implies that a gratuity is received by an employee as a reward for meritorious and long service.

3.3 The Basic Objects of the Payment of Gratuity Act of 1972

The basic objects of the Payment of Gratuity Act of 1972 are –

(1) To ensure a uniform pattern of payment of gratuity to the employees throughout the country.

(2) To avoid different treatment to the employees of establishment which have branches in more than one State when the employees are liable to transfer from one State to another State under the conditions of their service.

(3) To provide, according to the provisions of the Act, to pay the amount of gratuity to an employee on his superannuation, or on his retirement, or on his resignation, or on his death, or total disablement due to accident or disease as the case may be.

3.4 The Salient Features and Important Provisions of the Act

There is a network of laws which provide for social and economic security for the works in India. The Workmen's Compensation Act, the Employees' State Insurance Act, the Maternity Benefit Act are some such laws.

The Payment of Gratuity Act of 1972 is also one of such Acts which provides social and economic security to employees and also helps to increase employee welfare. Besides this, the important features of the Act are as follows:

(i) By making the nature of gratuity payment, there is an attempt to ensure a uniform pattern of payment of gratuity to the employees to whom the Act is applicable.

(ii) It is provided in the Act to pay the amount of gratuity to employees on their superannuation, or on their retirement, or on their resignations, or on their death, or total disablement due to accidents or diseases as the case may be.

(iii) The Payment of Gratuity Act of 1972 is a Central Law.

(iv) In the Act, provisions have been made relating to the payment of gratuity, nomination, determination of the amount of the payment of gratuity, protection of gratuity, etc.

(v) There are also provisions in the Act to enforce the Act by appointing inspectors under the Act and by giving them necessary powers.

(vi) Provisions have been made in the Act for imposing penalties for various offences related to the different matters related to the gratuity.

(vii) The following points throw light on the important provisions of the Act.

(a) Meaning and Nature of Gratuity:

Gratuity is a lump-sum payment to an employee when he retires or leaves his service. It is basically a retirement benefit to an employee so that he can live life comfortably after his retirement. However, gratuity is payable even to an employee who resigns after completing at least **Five** years of service under the Payment of Gratuity Act of 1972.

Provident Fun and pension are retirement benefits. Gratuity is also a kind of retirement benefit. It is, in fact, a payment to be made to employees to help them after their retirement whether such retirement is the result of the rules of superannuation or of some physical disability.

Any employee should be entitled to claim a certain amount of payment as a retirement benefit for his faithful service over a certain period of his employment is the general principle underlying any gratuity scheme. This implies that a gratuity is received by an employee as a reward for meritorious and long service.

(b) Application of the Act:

The Act applies to every factory, mine, plantation, shop and establishment when ten or more persons are employed. It is also applicable to motor transport undertakings, club, chambers of commerce and associates, local bodies, solicitors' offices employing 10 or more persons.

(c) Basic Objects of the Payment of Gratuity Act of 1972:

The basic objects of the Payment of Gratuity Act of 1972 are –

(1) To ensure a uniform pattern of payment of gratuity to the employees throughout the country.

(2) To avoid different treatment to the employees of establishments which have branches in more than one State when the employees are liable to transfer from one State to another State under the conditions of their service.

(3) To provide, according to the provisions of the Act, to pay the amount of gratuity to an employee on his superannuation, or on his retirement, or on his resignation, or on his death, or total disablement due to accident or disease as the case may be.

(d) Employees Eligible for Gratuity:

The Act applies to all employees and workers employed in all those organisations to which this Act is applicable.

Gratuity is payable to an employee on:

(i) resignation,

(ii) termination of service on account of death or disablement due to accident or disease,

(iii) retirement.

Gratuity is normally payable only after an employee completes five years of continuous service. However, in case of death or disablement of an employee, the condition of minimum service of Five years is not applicable. The Act is applicable to all employees irrespective of the amount of his salary. Earlier ceiling on the amount of salary was there. But that ceiling on salary of ₹ 2,500 was removed w.e.f. 24th May, 1994 by amending the Act.

(e) Requirement of the Act in respect of 'Continuous Service':

One of the essential conditions for the purpose of the payment is that an employee must be in continuous service. But when an employee remains absent on account of leave, accident, sickness, lay-off, lock-out or strike, the employee is treated on 'continuous service'.

(f) Amount of Gratuity Payable:

Gratuity is payable @ **Fifteen** days' wages for every year of completed service. If the employee has completed more than **six** months in the last year of his service, it will be treated as full year for the purpose of gratuity.

In the case of seasonal employment, gratuity is payable @ **Seven** days wages for each season. Wages for the purpose of gratuity consist of basic salary plus D.A. as per last drawn salary. Allowances like bonus, H.R.A., overtime, commission, etc. are not considered for the purpose of calculating gratuity. It should be noted that employees who are paid on monthly wages basis, wages per day should be calculated by dividing monthly salary by **Twenty six** days in order to arrive at daily wages.

At present, the maximum gratuity payable under the Act is ₹ **Ten** lakhs. However, employers can offer better terms to their employees than those specified under the Act.

(g) Compulsory Insurance of Gratuity Liability:

Provisions have been made in the Act for compulsory insurance of employer's liability to pay gratuity to his employees or in the alternate for setting up of a gratuity funds in relation to establishments employing 500 or more employees in Section 4-A. This Section 4-A has been inserted by the Payment of Gratuity Amendment Act of 1987 made effective from 1st October 1987.

(h) Nomination:

We find the provisions relating to nomination in Section 6 of the Payment of Gratuity Act of 1972. Rules relating to nominations have also been made in Payment of Gratuity (Central) Rules, 1972.

(i) Payment of the Amount of Gratuity:

Section 4 (1) provides for the time of payment of gratuity. It states that, *"Gratuity shall be payable to an employee on the termination of his employment after he has rendered continuous service for not less than five years –*

(a) on his superannuation, or

(b) on his retirement or resignation, or

(c) on his death or disablement due to accident or disease

It is provided that the completion of continuous service of five years shall not be necessary where the termination of the employment of any employee is due to death or disablement [Proviso 1 to Section 4 (1)].

It is further provided further that in the case of death of the employee, gratuity payable to him shall be paid to his nominee or, if no nomination has been made, to his heirs, and where any such nominees or heirs is a minor, the share of such minor, shall be deposited with the controlling authority who shall invest the same for the benefit of such minor in such bank or other financial institution, as may be prescribed, until such minor attains majority [Proviso 2 to Section 4 (1)].

For the purposes of this section, disablement means such disablement as incapacitates an employee for the work which he was capable of performing before the accident or disease resulting in such disablement [Explanation to Section 4 (1)]. The employer is under obligation to pay the gratuity within **Thirty** days from the date it becomes payable.

(j) Gratuity cannot be Attached:

Gratuity payable to an employee cannot be attached in execution of any decree or order of any civil, revenue or criminal court according to the provisions of Section 13 of the Payment of Gratuity Act of 1972.

(k) Forfeiture and Deduction of Gratuity:

Provisions relating to forfeiture and deduction of gratuity have been made in Section 4 (6). This section states the case in which gratuity payable to an employee can be forfeited; notwithstanding anything contained in Section 4 (1).

According to Section 4 (6) (a), *"the gratuity of an employee, whose services have been terminated for any act, willful omission or negligence causing any damage or loss to, or destruction of, property belonging to the employer, shall be forfeited to the extent of the damage or loss so caused"*.

While Section 4 (6) (b) states that, *"the gratuity payable to an employee may be wholly or partially forfeited"* –

- (i) if the services of such an employee have been terminated for his riotous or disorderly conduct or any other act of violence on his part, or
- (ii) if the services of such employee have been terminated for any act which constitutes an offence involving moral turpitude, provided that such an offence is committed by him in the course of his employment.

Gratuity is paid to the employees besides other objectives for their good behaviour or conduct in their period of employment which must be more than five years. But, when an employee is dismissed for misconduct, he cannot be deprived altogether of the benefit of gratuity to be received for his services. He must be paid his dues of gratuity after deducting the loss, if any, caused because of his misconduct to his employer. However, in the case of theft, which is an offence involving moral turpitude, the gratuity payable to an employee under the provisions of this Act stands forfeited in view of Section 4 (6) (b) (ii).

(l) Recovery of Gratuity:

As gratuity is a compulsory payment according to the provisions of this Act, it must be paid to an employee on fulfilling the conditions laid down in the Act by his employer. If the amount of gratuity payable under this Act is not paid by the employer within the time limit prescribed for the payment, he must make an application to the controlling authority.

On receiving the application by the aggrieved person, the controlling authority issues the certificate for that amount to the collector who recovers the same together with compound interest.

The provisions relating to the recovery of the amount of gratuity are made in Section 8 which are as follows:

"If the amount of gratuity payable under this Act is not paid by the employer, within the prescribed time, to the person entitled thereto, the controlling authority shall, on an application made to it in this behalf by the aggrieved person, issue a certificate for that amount to the Collector, who shall recover the same, together with compound interest thereon at such rate as the Central Government may, by notification, specify from the date of expiry of the prescribed time, as arrears of land revenue and pay the same to the person entitled thereto" [Section 8].

It is also provided that the controlling authority shall, before issuing a certificate under this section, give the employer a reasonable opportunity of showing cause against the issue of such certificate [Proviso 1 to Section 8].

It is also provided that the amount payable under this Section 8 shall, in no case, exceed the amount of gratuity payable under this Act.

(m) Appoint of Inspectors:

Provisions have been made in the Act to appoint Inspectors. Necessary powers are given to the Inspectors to perform the duties entrusted to them under the Act.

(n) Provisions for Imposing Penalties:

Provisions have been made in Section 9 of this Act for imposing penalties for false statement, for false representation and also for contravention of the provisions of the Act.

3.5 Scope and Extent of the Act

The Act expressly provides for a scheme of compulsory payment of gratuity by the managements of factories, mines, oilfields, plantations, ports, railway companies, shops and other establishments to which the Act applies in the event of superannuation, retirement, resignation and death or disablement due to accident or disease.

As regards the quantum of gratuity, the Act provides that for every completed year of service or part thereof in excess of six months, the employer is liable to pay his employee at the rate of fifteen days wages for every completed year of service or part thereof in excess of six months subject to a maximum of ₹ Ten Lakhs.

Though a workman has the right to claim gratuity, this right to claim gratuity of a workman can be forfeited by his employer under certain circumstances [Section 4 (6)]. The gratuity of an employee can be forfeited to the extent of the damages or loss caused to the property of the employer by the willful negligence or omission by his employee whose services have been terminated for any such act.

The gratuity of an employee can be wholly forfeited provided that the services of such employee have been terminated for his disorderly conduct or riotous conduct or for any other violent act on his part or for any offence involving moral turpitude committed by him during the course of his employment. However, provisions have been made in the Act relating to grant of exemption by notification of Appropriate Government and also for the settlement of any dispute relating to the amount of gratuity payable to an employee under the Act. Provisions also have been made in the Act relating to the admissibility of any claim for payment of gratuity, recovery of gratuity from defaulting employer's penalties for offences, protection of action in good faith etc.

Section 1 (2), makes it clear that the Act extends to the whole of India. However, it is expressly provided that in so far as it relates to plantations or ports, it shall not extend to the State of Jammu and Kashmir.

Scope of coverage of this Act is made clear in Sections 1 (3) and 3 (A).

Section 1 (3) states that the Act shall apply to –
- (a) every factory, mine, oilfield, plantation, port and railway company;
- (b) every shop or establishment within the meaning of any law for the time being in force in relation to shops and establishments in a State, in which ten or more persons are employed, or were employed, on any day of the preceding twelve months;
- (c) such other establishments or class of establishments, in which ten or more employees are employed, or were employed, on any day of the preceding twelve months, as the Central Government may, by notification, specify in this behalf.

While Section 3 (A) states that, "*A shop or establishment to which this Act has become applicable shall continue to be governed by this Act notwithstanding that the number of persons employed therein at any time after it has become so applicable falls below ten*".

The main intention to make this provision is obviously to check the tendency among the employers to reduce artificially the number of employees so as to get out of coverage under this Payment of Gratuity Act. It should also be noted that the municipalities are also covered by Section 1 (3) in view of giving more extensive application as this Act is a social legislation.

The Act has been applied to the following establishments in which ten or more persons are employed or were employed on any day of the preceding twelve months w.e.f. the dates and the notifications against each.

(1)	Motor Transport	w.e.f. 8-4-1974	G.S.R. 415, dt. 8-4-1974
(2)	Clubs	w.e.f. 8-10-1979	G.S.R. 1255, dt. 17-9-1979
(3)	Chambers of Commerce and Industry and Associated / Federation of Chambers of Commerce and Industry	w.e.f. 15-11-1980	S.O. 3203, dt. 30-10-1980
(4)	Inland Water Transport Establishments	w.e.f. 10-1-1981	S.O. 133, dt. 24-12-1980
(5)	Local Bodies	w.e.f. 23-1-1982	S.O. 239, dt. 8-1-1982
(6)	Solicitor's offices	w.e.f. 9-1-1982	S.O. 111, dt. 28-12-1982

However, the Act does not apply to apprentices and persons holding civil posts under the Central Government or a State Government and are governed by any other Act or by the rules provided for the payment of gratuity.

Section 5 (1) empowers the Government to exempt, subject to the conditions as may be specified in the notification, any establishment, factory, mine etc. to which this Act is applicable from the operation of the provisions of this Act, if in the opinion of the Appropriate Government, the employees in such establishment, factory, mine etc. are in receipt of gratuity or pensionary benefits not less favourable than the benefits conferred under this Act.

3.6 Definitions

The definitions of various terms, words, concepts pertaining to the provisions of this Act are given in Section two. These definitions are as follows:

- **Appropriate Government [Section 2 (a)]:**

    "Appropriate Government", means –
    (i) in relation to an establishment -
    - (a) belonging to, or under the control of the Central Government,
    - (b) having branches in more than one State,
    - (c) of a factory belonging to, or under the control of the Central Government,
    - (d) of a major port, mine, oilfield or railway company, the Central Government,

    (ii) in any other case, the State Government.

    Thus, in relation to establishments mentioned above in (a) to (d) clauses, the Central Government is an Appropriate Government. While in any other case, the State Government is an Appropriate Government.

- **Continuous Service [Section 2 (c) and Section 2-A]:**

    The payment of gratuity is a retirement benefit. For the purpose of getting this benefit, the service of an employee should be a continuous one. However, interrupted service because of the reason of leave, sickness, lay-off, strike etc. not due to any fault of an employee concerned should not be treated as a break in his continuous service.

    Considering this point, the concept of continuous service is defined. According to Section 2 (c), continuous service means continuous service as defined in Section 2-A. Section 2-A is as follows:

    "For the purposes of this Act –

    (1) an employee shall be said to be in continuous service for a period if he has, for that period, been in uninterrupted service, including service which may be interrupted on account of sickness, accident, leave, absence from duty without leave (not being absent in respect of which an order treating the absence as break in service has been passed in accordance with the standing orders, rules or regulations governing the employees of the establishment), lay-off, strike or a lock-out or cessation of work not due to any fault of the employee, whether such uninterrupted or interrupted service was rendered before or after the commencement of this Act [Section 2-A (1)];

    (2) where an employee (not being an employee employed in a seasonal establishment) is not in continuous service within the meaning of clause (1), for any period of one year or six months, he shall be deemed to be in continuous service under the employer –
    - (a) for the said period of one year, if the employee during the period of twelve calendar months preceding the date with reference to which calculation is to be made, has actually worked under the employer for not less than –

      (i) one hundred and ninety days, in the case of an employee employed below the ground in a mine or in an establishment which works for less than six days in a week; and

      (ii) two hundred and forty days, in any other case;

  (b) for the said period of six months, if the employee during the period of six calendar months preceding the date with reference to which the calculation is to be made, has actually worked under the employer for not less than –

      (i) ninety five days, in the case of an employee employed below the ground in a mine or in an establishment which works for less than six days in a week; and

      (ii) one hundred and twenty days, in any other case [Section 2-A (2)];

For the purposes of clause (2), the number of days on which an employee has actually worked under an employer shall include the days on which –

  (i) he has been laid-off under an agreement or as permitted by standing orders made under the Industrial Employment (Standing Orders) Act, 1946 (20 of 1946), or under the Industrial Disputes Act, 1947 (14 of 1947), or under any other law applicable to the establishment;

  (ii) he has been on leave with full wages, earned in the previous year;

  (iii) he has been absent due to temporary disablement caused by accident arising out of and in the course of his employment; and

  (iv) in the case of a female, she has been on maternity leave; so, however, that the total period of such maternity leave does not exceed twelve weeks [Explanation to Section 2-A (2)].

(3) where an employee, employed in a seasonal establishment, is not in continuous service within the meaning of clause (1), for any period of one year or six months, he shall be deemed to be in continuous service under the employer for such period if he has actually worked for not less than seventy five per cent of the number of days on which the establishment was in operation during such period [Section 2-A (3)].

- **Completed Year of Service [Section 2 (b)]:**

According to Section 2 (b), completed year of service means a continuous service for one year.

- **Controlling Authority [Section 2 (d)]:**

Controlling authority means an authority appointed by the Appropriate Government under Section 3. Section 3 is reproduced as follows.

"The appropriate Government, may, by notification, appoint any officer to be a controlling authority, who shall be responsible for the administration of this Act and different controlling authorities may be appointed for different areas".

The provision of Section 3 implies that the controlling officer is responsible for the administration of this Act.

- **Employee [Section 2 (e)]:**

"Employee" means any person (other than an apprentice) employed on wages in any establishment, factory, mine, oilfield, plantation, port, railway company or shop, to do any skilled, semi-skilled, or unskilled, manual, supervisory, technical or clerical work, whether the terms of such employment are expressed or implied, and whether or not such person is employed in a managerial or administrative capacity, but does not include any such person who holds a post under the Central Government or a State Government and is governed by any other Act or by any rules providing for payment of gratuity [Section 2 (e)].

The definition of an employee is quite comprehensive. An employee does not include an apprentice neither any such person holding a post under the Central or State Government and is governed by any other Act or by any other rules providing payment of gratuity. Explanation to this Section 2 (e) making clear the wage limit of an employee has been omitted by the Payment of Gratuity Amendment Act of 1994 with effect from 24th May, 1994.

- **Employer [Section 2 (f)]:**

According to Section 2 (f)

"Employer" means, in relation to any establishment, factory, mine, oilfield, plantation, port, railway company or shop –

(i) belonging to, or under the control of the Central Government or a State Government, a person or authority appointed by the Appropriate Government for the supervision and control of employees, or where no person or authority has been so appointed, the head of the Ministry or the Department concerned,

(ii) belonging to, or under the control of, any local authority, the person appointed by such authority for the supervision and control of employees or where no person has been so appointed, the chief executive officer of the local authority,

(iii) in any other case, the person, who, or the authority which, has the ultimate control over the affairs of the establishment, factory, mine, oilfield, plantation, port, railway company or shop, and where the said affairs are entrusted to any other person, whether called a manager, managing director or by any other name.

- **Factory [Section 2 (g)]:**

For the purposes of this Act, 'Factory' has the same meaning as assigned to it in clause (m) of Section 2 of the Factories Act of 1948.

According to Section 2 (g), 'Factory' means any premises including the precincts thereof –

(i) wherein 10 or more workers are working or were working on any day of the preceding 12 months, and in any part of which a manufacturing process is being carried on with the aid of power, or is ordinarily so carried on, or

(ii) wherein 20 or more workers are working or were working on any day of the preceding 12 months, and in any part of which a manufacturing process is being carried on without the aid of power, or is ordinarily so carried on.

The term 'factory' does not include a mine subject to the operation of the Indian Mines Act, 1952 or a mobile unit belonging to the armed forces of the Union, a railway running shed or a hotel, restaurant or eating place.

- **Family [Section 2 (h)]:**

According to Section 2 (h), "family", in relation to an employee, shall be deemed to consist of –

(i) in the case of a male employee, himself, his wife, his children, whether married or unmarried, his dependant parents [and the dependant parents of his wife and the widow] and children of his pre-deceased son, if any,

(ii) in the case of a female employee, herself, her husband, her children, whether married or unmarried, her dependant parents and the dependant parents of her husband and the widow and children of her pre-deceased son, if any.

However, where the personal law of an employee permits the adoption by him of a child, any child lawfully adopted by him shall be deemed to be included in his family, and where a child of an employee has been adopted by another person and such adoption is, under the personal law of the person making such adoption, lawful, such child shall be deemed to be excluded from the family of the employee [Explanation to Section 2 (f)].

- **Major Port [Section 2 (i)]:**

"Major port" has the meaning assigned to it in clause (8) of Section 3 of the Indian Ports Act, 1908 (15 of 1908);

- **Mine [Section 2 (j)]:**

"Mine" has the meaning assigned to it in clause (j) of sub-section (1) of Section 2 of the Mines Act, 1952 (35 of 1952);

- **Notification [Section 2 (k)]:**

"Notification" means a notification published in the Official Gazette;

- **Oilfield [Section 2 (l)]:**

"Oilfield" has the meaning assigned to it in clause (e) of Section 3 of the Oilfields (Regulation and Development) Act, 1948 (53 of 1948);

- **Plantation [Section 2 (m)]:**

"Plantation" has the meaning assigned to it in clause (f) of Section 2 of the Plantations Labour Act, 1951 (69 of 1951);

- **Port [Section 2 (n)]:**

"Port" has the meaning assigned to it in clause (4) of Section 3 of the Indian Ports Act, 1908 (15 of 1908);

- **Prescribed [Section 2 (o)]:**

    "Prescribed" means prescribed by rules made under this Act;

- **Railway Company [Section 2 (p)]:**

    "Railway company" has the meaning assigned to it in clause (5) of Section 3 of the Indian Railways Act, 1890 (9 of 1890);

- **Retirement [Section 2 (q)]:**

    "Retirement" means termination of the service of an employee otherwise than on superannuation;

- **Superannuation [Section 2 (r)]:**

    "Superannuation", in relation to an employee, means

    (i) the attainment by the employee of such age as is fixed in the contract or conditions of service as the age on the attainment of which the employee shall vacate the employment.

    (ii) in any other case, the attainment by the employee of the age of fifty-eight years;

- **Wages [Section 2 (s)]:**

    "Wages" means all emoluments which are earned by an employee while on duty or on leave in accordance with the terms and conditions of his employment and which are paid or are payable to him in cash and includes dearness allowance but does not include any bonus, commission, house rent allowance, overtime wages and any other allowance.

3.7 Payment of Gratuity

Section 4 of the Act throws light on the circumstances in which gratuity becomes payable to an employee. The payment of gratuity by an employer to his employees as defined under this Act is mandatory. However, provisions have been made in this Act to forfeit the gratuity. Section 4 also deals with cases where gratuity can be forfeited.

3.7.1 When is Gratuity Payable?

Section 4 (1) provides for the time of payment of gratuity. It states that, "*Gratuity shall be payable to an employee on the termination of his employment after he has rendered continuous service for not less than five years –*

(a) on his superannuation, or

(b) on his retirement or resignation, or

(c) on his death or disablement due to accident or disease

It is provided that the completion of continuous service of five years shall not be necessary where the termination of the employment of any employee is due to death or disablement [Proviso 1 to Section 4 (1)].

It is further provided that in the case of death of the employee, gratuity payable to him shall be paid to his nominee or, if no nomination has been made, to his heirs, and where any such nominees or heirs is a minor, the share of such minor, shall be deposited with the controlling authority who shall invest the same for the benefit of such minor in bank or other financial institution, as may be prescribed, until such minor attains majority [Proviso 2 to Section 4 (1)].

For the purposes of this section, disablement means such disablement as incapacitates an employee for the work which he was capable of performing before the accident or disease resulting in such disablement [Explanation to Section 4 (1)].

Important points relating to the payment of gratuity are as follows:

(1) Gratuity is payable to an employee:

- (a) on the termination of his employment after he has rendered continuous service for not less than five years. The meaning of continuous service is given in Section 2-A; or
- (b) on his superannuation, where an employee continues in the service even after the date of superannuation, he is entitled to receive gratuity for the full period of his service and not merely upto the age of superannuation; or
- (c) on his resignation; or
- (d) on his retirement; or
- (e) on his death; or
- (f) on becoming disable due to accident or disease. Here, disablement implies such disablement which incapacitates an employee to do the work which he was capable of doing before the accident or disease resulting such disablement.

(2) The completion of continuous service of five years is not necessary when the termination of the employment of any employee is due to either death or disablement.

(3) In the case of the death of an employee, gratuity payable to him must be paid to his nominee. However, if no such nomination is made, it is to be paid to his heirs. If any of such nominees or heirs is a minor, the share of such minor is to be deposited with the controlling authority. The Appropriate Government appoints, by notification, an officer as a controlling authority who is responsible for the administration of this Act. Different controlling authorities are appointed for the different areas. It is the responsibility of the concerned controlling authority to invest the amount of gratuity for the benefit of a minor in such bank or in any other financial institutions, as may be prescribed, until such minor attains majority.

(4) Section 4 (4) provides for the computation of the gratuity payable to an employee employed on reduced wages after his disablement. It states that, "*for the purpose of computing the gratuity payable to an employee who is employed, after his disablement, on reduced wages, his wages for the period preceding his disablement shall be taken to be the wages received by him during that period, and his wages for the period subsequent to his disablement shall be taken to be the wages as so reduced*".

3.7.2 Rate of Gratuity

Section 4 (2) deals with the rate of gratuity. While making the provisions relating to fixing the rate of gratuity to be paid to employees, attention has also been paid to the piece-rated employees and employees working in seasonal establishments.

Section 4 (2) lays down that, *"for every completed year of service or part thereof in excess of six months, the employer shall pay gratuity to an employee at the rate of fifteen days' wages based on the rate of wages last drawn by the employee concerned"*.

It is provided that in the case of a piece-rated employee, daily wages shall be computed on the average of the total wages received by him for a period of three months immediately preceding the termination of his employment, and, for this purpose, the wages paid for any overtime work shall not be taken into account [Proviso 1 to Section 4 (2)].

It is further provided that in the case of an employee who is employed in a seasonal establishment and who is not so employed throughout the year, the employer shall pay the gratuity at the rate of seven days' wages for each season [Proviso 2 to Section 4 (2)].

In the case of a monthly rated employee, the fifteen day's wages shall be calculated by dividing the monthly rate of wages last drawn by him by twenty six and multiplying the quotient by fifteen [Explanation to Section 4 (2)].

A month is a period of 30 days including days of rest and holidays. If wages are to be calculated on monthly rate, 15 days' wages would be what an employee would earn within the period of 15 days and not in 15 working days [Swamy V. Controlling Authority, Hyderabad, 1978. Lab. I.C. 1285].

3.7.3 Maximum Amount of Gratuity

The amount of gratuity payable to an employee shall not exceed ₹ Three Lakhs and Fifty Thousand [Section 4 (3)]. The Amendment Act of 1987 replaced the then existing ceiling of 20 months' wages for payment of gratuity by a monetary ceiling of Rupees Fifty Thousand. Then the Amendment Act of 1994 (w.e.f. 24th May, 1994) increased the amount of maximum gratuity to rupees one lakh and thereafter, the Payment of Gratuity (Amendment) Act of 1998 further increased this limit to rupees three lakhs and fifty thousand. Further amending the Act, in 2010, the limit has been increased to ₹ Ten Lakhs. Thus, the maximum amount of gratuity is ₹ Ten Lakhs.

3.8 Calculation of Gratuity

We have considered various aspects such as when the gratuity is payable, rate of gratuity, maximum amount of gratuity etc. Now, let us study how the amount of gratuity payable to an employee is calculated by taking a few illustrations.

Illustration 1:

Mr. A is the employee whose last drawn salary which included basic salary and DA is ₹ 5,200/- per month. He has completed **Thirty Five** years of service. Calculate the amount of gratuity payable to him.

Solution:

The last drawn salary which includes basic salary and D.A. is ₹ 5,200 per month. Hence, his salary per day is ₹ 200 [₹ 5,200 divided by 26].

Therefore, he is entitled to get the gratuity of ₹ 3,000 [15 days multiplied by ₹ 200] for every year of completed service. He has served for 35 years continuously. So, he is entitled to get a gratuity of ₹ 1,05,000 [₹ 3,000 multiplied by 35 years].

Thus, the gratuity payable to Mr. A is ₹ 1,05,000.

Illustration 2:

Mr. Malik has served 30 years continuously and retired. His basic salary is ₹ 2,000, D.A. ₹ 1,120. Commission ₹ 1,000, House Rent ₹ 700 per month on his retirement. Calculate the amount of gratuity payable to Mr. Malik.

Solution :

For the purpose of calculating gratuity payable to Mr. Malik, we have to consider only his basic salary and D.A. Other allowances like H.R.A.; Commission etc. are not being considered for calculating the amount of gratuity.

Hence, his last drawn salary comes to ₹ 3,120 [Basic Salary ₹ 2,000 plus D.A. ₹ 1,120]. It means his salary per day is ₹ 120 [₹ 3,120 divided by 26] and he is entitled to get the gratuity of ₹ 1,800 [15 days multiplied by ₹ 120] for every year of completed service.

As his total eligible service for the purpose of getting gratuity is 30 years, he is entitled to receive the gratuity of ₹ 54,000 [₹ 1,800 multiplied by 30 years].

Thus, the gratuity payable to Mr. Malik is ₹ 54,000/-.

Illustration 3:

Mr. Parag Ghamandi's whose monthly wages at the time of retirement were ₹ 4,004. He retired after 20 years and 4 months continuous service. Calculate the amount of gratuity payable to him.

Solution:

Facts:

1. Mr. Parag Ghamandi's last drawn monthly salary - ₹ 4,004.
2. His continuous service on retirement - 20 years and 4 months. But for calculating gratuity his continuous service - 20 years. It is so because if an employee completes more than **six** months in the last year of his service, then it is treated as a full year for the purpose of gratuity.
3. His salary per day - ₹ 154 [₹ 4,004 ÷ 26 days]
4. He is entitled to get gratuity for every year of completed service –
   ₹ 2,310 [₹ 154 daily salary × 15 days].
5. Total gratuity payable to him - ₹ 46,200 [₹ 2,310 multiplied by 20 years of continuous service].

Thus, the gratuity payable to Mr. Parag Ghamandi is ₹ 46,200/-.

3.9 Provisions Relating to Better Terms of Gratuity

Sometimes, an employee may get more amount and better terms of gratuity under an award or contract or agreement with his employer. Hence, it is stated in Section 4 (5) that, "*Nothing in this section shall affect the right of an employee to receive better terms of gratuity under any award or agreement or contract with the employer*".

This simply implies that the provisions of Section 4 do not affect any right of an employee if he is to get more beneficial terms of gratuity from his employer under contract or agreement made with him. Thus, the scheme envisaged by the enactment not only secures the minimum of gratuity for the employees but the Act also provides for the better terms of gratuity wherever possible.

3.10 Forfeiture of Gratuity

Provisions relating to forfeiture of gratuity have been made in Section 4 (6). This section states the case in which gratuity payable to an employee can be forfeited; notwithstanding anything contained in Section 4 (1).

According to Section 4 (6) (a), "*the gratuity of an employee, whose services have been terminated for any act, willful omission or negligence causing any damage or loss to, or destruction of, property belonging to the employer, shall be forfeited to the extent of the damage or loss so caused*".

While Section 4 (6) (b) states that, "*the gratuity payable to an employee may be wholly or partially forfeited*" –

(i) if the services of such an employee have been terminated for his riotous or disorderly conduct or any other act of violence on his part, or

(ii) if the services of such employee have been terminated for any act which constitutes an offence involving moral turpitude, provided that such an offence is committed by him in the course of his employment.

Gratuity is paid to the employees besides other objectives for their good behaviour or conduct in their period of employment which must be more than five years. But, when an employee is dismissed for misconduct, he cannot be deprived altogether of the benefit of gratuity to be received for his services. He must be paid his dues of gratuity after deducting the loss, if any, caused because of his misconduct to his employer. However, in the case of theft, which is an offence involving moral turpitude, the gratuity payable to an employee under the provisions of this Act stands forfeited in view of Section 4 (6) (b) (ii).

3.11 Power of an Appropriate Government to Exempt

There are three sub-sections of Section 5 which throw light on the power of an Appropriate Government to exempt.

Section 5 (1) empowers the Appropriate Government to exempt by notification in the Official Gazette, any establishment, factory, mine etc. to which this Act applies from the operation of the provisions of this Act under certain circumstances.

Section 5 (2) has been incorporated in the Act by the Payment of Gratuity (Second) Amendment Act of 1984 which authorises the Appropriate Government to exempt any employee or class of employees in similar circumstances.

While Section 5 (3) authorises the Appropriate Government to issue notification retrospectively. However, it is also made clear that such notification shall not be issued so as to prejudicially affect the interests of any person. Section 5 is reproduced as follows.

"The Appropriate Government may, by notification, and subject to such conditions as may be specified in the notification, exempt any establishment, factory, mine, oilfield, plantation, port, railway company or shop to which this Act applies from the operation of the provisions of this Act if, in the opinion of the Appropriate Government, the employees in such an establishment, factory, mine, oilfield, plantation, port, railway company or shop are in receipt of gratuity or pensionary benefits not less favourable than the benefits conferred under this Act" [Section 5 (1)].

"The appropriate Government may, by notification and subject to such conditions as may be specified in the notification, exempt any employee or class of employees employed in any establishment, factory, mine, oilfield, plantation, port, railway company or shop to which this Act applies from the operation of the provisions of this Act, if, in the opinion of the Appropriate Government, such employee or class of employees are in receipt of gratuity or pensionary benefits not less favourable than the benefits conferred under this Act" [Section 5 (2)].

"A notification issued under sub-section (1) or sub-section (2) may be issued retrospectively, a date not earlier than the date of commencement of this Act, but no such notification shall be issued so as to prejudicially affect the interests of any person" [Section 5 (3)].

3.12 Compulsory Insurance [Section 4-A]

Provisions have been made in the Act for compulsory insurance of employer's liability to pay gratuity to his employees or in the alternate for setting up of a gratuity funds in relation to establishments employing 500 or more employees in Section 4-A.

This Section 4-A has been inserted by the Payment of Gratuity Amendment Act of 1987 made effective from 1st October 1987. Section 4-A is as follows:

(1) With effect from such date as may be notified by the Appropriate Government in this behalf, every employer, other than an employer or an establishment belonging to, or under the control of, the Central Government or a State Government, shall, subject to the provisions of sub-section (2), obtain an insurance in the manner prescribed, for his liability for payment towards the gratuity under this Act, from the Life Insurance Corporation of India established under the Life Insurance Corporation of India Act, 1956 (31 of 1956) or any other prescribed insurer [Section 4-A (1)].

It is provided that different dates may be appointed for different establishments or class of establishments or for different areas [Proviso to Section 4-A (1)].

(2) The appropriate Government may, subject to such conditions as may be prescribed, exempt every employer who had already established an approved gratuity fund in respect of his employees and who desires to continue such arrangement, and every

employer employing five hundred or more persons who establishes an approved gratuity fund in the manner prescribed from the provisions of sub-section (1) [Section 4-A (2)].

(3) For the purpose of effectively implementing the provisions of this section, every employer shall within such time as may be prescribed get his establishment registered with the controlling authority in the prescribed manner and no employer shall be registered under the provisions of this section unless he has taken an insurance referred to in sub-section (1) or has established an approved gratuity fund referred to in sub-section (2) [Section 4-A (3)].

(4) The Appropriate Government may, by notification, make rules to give effect to the provisions of this section and such rules may provide for the composition of the Board of Trustees of the approved gratuity fund and for the recovery by the controlling authority of the amount of the gratuity payable to an employee from the Life Insurance Corporation of India or any other insurer with whom an insurance has been taken under sub-section (1), or as the case may be, the Board of Trustees of the approved gratuity fund [Section 4-A (4)].

(5) Where an employer fails to make any payment by way of premium to the insurance referred to in sub-section (1) or by way of contribution to an approved gratuity fund referred to in sub-section (2), he shall be liable to pay the amount of gratuity due under this Act (including interest, if any, for delayed payments) forthwith to the controlling authority [Section 4-A (5)].

(6) Whoever contravenes the provisions of sub-section (5) shall be punishable with a fine which may extend to rupees ten thousand and in the case of a continuing offence with a further fine which may extend to rupees one thousand for each day during which the offence continues [Section 4-A (6)].

Explanation: In this section, "approved gratuity fund" shall have the same meaning as in clause (5) of Section 2 of the Income-tax Act, 1961 (43 of 1961) [Explanation to Section 4-A].

Thus, according to Section 4-A (1), it is the responsibility of every employer to obtain an insurance for his liability in respect of payment of gratuity under this Act from the Life Insurance Corporation or any other prescribed insurer as notified by the Appropriate Government in this behalf. It may further be noted that provisions of Section 4-A (1) do not apply to an employer or an establishment belonging to, or under the control of the Central or State Government.

However, according to the provisions of Section 4-A (2), the Appropriate Government may exempt (1) every employer who has already established an approved gratuity fund in respect of his employees and desiring to continue such agreement and (2) every employer employing 500 or more persons who establishes an approved gratuity fund in the manner prescribed from the provisions of Section 4-A (1).

Provisions of Section 4-A (3) make it clear that every employer has to get his establishment registered within such time as may be prescribed with the controlling authority in the prescribed manner. An employer shall not be registered under the provisions of Section 4-A unless he has taken insurance referred to in Section 4-A (1) or established an approved gratuity fund referred to in Section 4-A (2).

The Appropriate Government is empowered to make rules by notification in the Official Gazette to give effect to the provisions of this Section [Section 4-A (4)]. Section 4-A (4) further provides that the rules thus, made may provide for the composition of the Board of Trustees of the approved controlling authority of the amount of the gratuity payable to an employee from the Life Insurance Corporation or any other insurer with whom an insurance has been taken under Section 4-A (1) or as the case may be, the Board of Trustees of the approved gratuity fund.

The provisions also have been made in Section 4-A (5) for the failure to pay insurance premium or contribution, if any. It states that where an employee fails to make any payment by way of premium to the insurance referred to in Section 4-A (1) or by way of contribution to an approved gratuity fund as referred to in Section 4-A (2), such an employer is liable to pay the amount of gratuity due under this Act, including interest for delayed payments, forthwith to the controlling authority. Whoever contravenes these provisions of Section 4-A (5), is punishable with a fine which may extend to rupees ten thousand and in the case of continuing offence with a further fine which may extend to rupees one thousand for each day during which the offence continues [Section 4-A (6)].

3.13 Nomination

The provisions relating to nomination in Section 6 of the Payment of Gratuity Act of 1972 are given in this section. Rules relating to nominations have also been made in Payment of Gratuity (Central) Rules, 1972. The provisions of Section 6 and rules pertaining to nominations are given below.

Section 6: Nomination:

(1) Each employee, who has completed one year of service, shall make, within such time, in such form and in such manner, as may be prescribed, nomination for the purpose of the second proviso to sub-section (1) of Section 4 [Section 6 (1)].

(2) An employee may, in his nomination, distribute the amount of gratuity payable to him under this Act amongst more than one nominee [Section 6 (2)].

(3) If an employee has a family at the time of making a nomination, the nomination shall be made in favour of one or more members of his family, and any nomination made by such employee in favour of a person who is not a member of his family, shall be void [Section 6 (3)].

(4) If at the time of making a nomination the employee has no family, the nomination may be made in favour of any person or persons but if the employee subsequently acquires a family, such a nomination shall forthwith become invalid and the employee shall make, within such time as may be prescribed, a fresh nomination in favour of one or more members of his family [Section 6 (4)].

(5) A nomination may, subject to the provisions of sub-sections (3) and (4) be modified by an employee at any time, after giving to his employer a written notice in such form and in such manner as may be prescribed, of his intention to do so [Section 6 (5)].

(6) If a nominee predeceases the employee, the interest of the nominee shall revert to the employee who shall make a fresh nomination, in the prescribed form, in respect of such interest [Section 6 (6)].

(7) Every nomination, fresh nomination or alteration of nomination, as the case may be, shall be sent by the employee to his employer, who shall keep the same in his safe custody [Section 6 (7)].

Rule 6 which pertains to nominations is given below:

Rule 6: Nominations:

(1) A nomination shall be in Form 'F' and submitted in duplicate by personal service by the employee, after taking proper receipt or by sending through registered post acknowledgement due to the employer –

- (i) in the case of an employee who is already in employment for a year or more on the date of commencement of these rules, ordinarily within ninety days from such date, and
- (ii) in the case of an employee who completes one year of service after the date of commencement of these rules, ordinarily, within thirty days of the completion of one year of service.

Provided that nomination in Form 'F' shall be accepted by the employer after the specified period, if filed with reasonable grounds for delay, and no nomination so accepted shall be invalid merely because it was filed after the specified period.

(2) Within thirty days of the receipt of a nomination in Form 'F' under sub-rule (1), the employer shall get the service particulars of the employee, as mentioned in the form of nomination, verified with reference to the records of the establishment and return to the employee, after obtaining a receipt thereof, the duplicate copy of the nomination in Form 'F' duly attested either by the employer or an officer authorised in this behalf by him, as a token of recording of the nomination by the employer and the other copy of the nomination shall be recorded.

(3) An employee who has no family at the time of making a nomination shall, within ninety days of acquiring a family, submit in the manner specified in sub-rule (1), a fresh nomination, as required under sub-section (4) of Section 6, in duplicate in Form 'G' to the employer, and thereafter the provisions of sub-rule (2) shall apply *mutatis mutandis* as if it was made under sub-rule (1).

(4) A notice of modification of a nomination, including cases where a nominee predeceases an employee, shall be submitted in duplicate in Form 'H' to the employer in the manner specified in sub-rule (1), and thereafter the provisions of sub-rule (2) shall apply *mutatis mutandis* as if it was made under sub-rule (1).

(5) A nomination or a fresh nomination or a notice of modification of nomination shall be signed by the employee or, if illiterate, shall bear his thumb-impression, in the presence of two witnesses, who shall also sign a declaration to that effect in the nomination, fresh nomination or notice of modification of nomination, as the case may be.

(6) A nomination, fresh nomination or notice of modification of nomination shall take effect from the date of receipt thereof by the employer.

Various forms in which information pertaining to nominations are given below:

FORM 'F'
[*See sub-rule* (1) of Rule 6]

Nomination

To,

(Give here name or description of the establishment with full address)

1. Shri/Shrimati/Kumari ....

(name in full here)

whose particulars are given in the statement below, hereby nominate the person(s) mentioned below to receive the gratuity payable after my death as also the gratuity standing to my credit in the event of my death before the amount payable, or having become payable has not been paid and direct that the said amount of gratuity shall be paid in the proportion indicated against the name(s) of the nominee(s).

2. I hereby certify that the person(s) mentioned is/are a member(s) of any family within the meaning of clause (*h*) of Section 2 of the Payment of Gratuity Act, 1972.

3. I hereby declare that I have no family within the meaning of clause (*h*) of Section 2 of the said Act.

4. (a) My father/mother/parents is/are not dependant on me.

   (b) My husband's father/mother/parents is/are not dependant on my husband.

5. I have excluded my husband from my family by a notice dated .... to the controlling authority in terms of the proviso to clause (*h*) of Section 2 of the said Act.

6. Nomination made herein invalidates my previous nomination.

Nominee(s)

Name in full with full address of nominee(s)	Relationship with the employee	Age of nominee	Proportion by which the gratuity will be shared
(1)	(2)	(3)	(4)
1.			
2.			
3.			
:			
:			

Statement

1. Name of the employee in full
2. Gender
3. Religion
4. Whether unmarried/married/widow/widower
5. Department/Branch/Section where employed
6. Post held with Ticket or Serial Number if any
7. Date of appointment
8. Permanent address:

      Village ....   Thana ....   Sub-division ......

      Post office ....   District .....   State ......

Place ....   Signature/Thumb-impression of the

Date ....   Employee

Declaration by Witnesses

Nomination signed/thumb-impressed before me

Name in full and full address of witnesses   Signature of witnesses

1.   1.

2.   2.

Place ....

Date ....

Certificate by the Employer

Certified that the particulars of the above nomination have been verified and recorded in this establishment.

Employer's Reference Number if any   Signature of the Employer/Officer authorised Designation

Date ....   Name and address of the establishment or rubber stamp thereof

Acknowledgement by the Employee

Received the duplicate copy of nomination in Form 'F' filed by me and duly certified by the employer.

Date ....   Signature of the Employee

Note: Strike out the words/paragraphs not applicable.

FORM 'G'

[*See* sub-rule (3) of Rule 6]

Fresh Nomination

To,

(Give here name or description of the establishment with full address)

1. Shri/Shrimati/Kumari ....

(Name in full here)

whose particulars are given in the statement below, have acquired a family within the meaning of clause (*h*) of Section 2 of the Payment of Gratuity Act, 1972 with effect from .... (date here) .... in the manner indicated below and therefore nominate between the person(s) mentioned below to receive the gratuity payable after my death as also the gratuity standing to my credit in the event of my death before the amount has become payable, or having become payable has not been paid and direct that the said amount of gratuity shall be paid in the proportion indicated against the name(s) of the nominee(s).

2. I hereby certify that the person(s) mentioned is/are a member(s) of any family within the meaning of clause (*h*) of Section 2 of the said Act.

3. (a) My father/mother/parents is/are not dependant on me.

    (b) My husband's father/mother/parents is/are not dependant on my husband.

4. I have excluded my husband from my family by a notice dated the .... to the Controlling Authority in terms of the proviso to clause (*h*) of Section 2 of the said Act.

Nominee(s)

Name in full with full address of nominee(s)	Relationship with the employee	Age of nominee	Proportion by which the gratuity will be shared
(1)	(2)	(3)	(4)
1.			
2.			
3.			
:			
:			

Manner of acquiring a "Family"

(Here give details as to how a family was acquired, i.e. whether by marriage or parents being rendered dependant or through any other process like adoption).

Statement

1. Name of the employee in full
2. Sex
3. Religion
4. Whether unmarried/married/widow/widower
5. Department/Branch/Section where employed
6. Post held with Ticket or Serial Number, if any
7. Date of appointment
8. Permanent address:

Village	Thana	Sub-division ......
Post office	District	State ......

Place ....

Date ....

Signature/Thumb-impression of the Employee

Declaration by Witnesses

Fresh nomination signed/thumb-impressed before me.

Name in full and full address of witnesses	Signature of witnesses
1.	1. ....
2.	2. ....

Place ....

Date ....

Certificate by the Employer

Certified that the particulars of the above nomination have been verified and recorded in this establishment.

Employer's Reference Number, if any   Signature of the Employer/Officer authorised
                                          Designation ....

Date ....   Name and address of the establishment or
                                          rubber stamp thereof

Acknowledgement by the Employee

Received the duplicate copy of nomination in Form ...... filed by me on ......, duly certified by the employer.

Date ....   Signature of the Employee

Note: Strike out the words/paragraphs not applicable.

FORM 'H'

[See sub-rule (4) of Rule 6]

Modification of Nomination

To,

(Give here name or description of the establishment with full address)

I, Shri/Shrimati/Kumari ....

(Name in full here)

whose particulars are given in the statement below, hereby give notice that the nomination filed by me on .... and recorded under your reference Number .... dated .... shall stand modified in the following manner –

....
....

(Here give details of the modification intended)

Statement

1. Name of the employee in full
2. Sex
3. Religion
4. Whether unmarried/married/widow/widower
5. Department/Branch/Section where employed
6. Post held with Ticket Number, or Serial Number, if any
7. Date of appointment
8. Address in full

Place .... Signature/Thumb-impression of the Employee
Date ....

Declaration by Witnesses

Modification of nomination signed/thumb-impressed before me.

Name in full and full address of witnesses   Signature of Witnesses
1. ....   1. ....
2. ....   2. ....

Place ....
Date ....

Certificate by the Employer

Certified that the above modifications have been recorded.

Employer's reference Number, if any   Signature of the employer/officer authorised
                                              Designation
Date ....   Name and address of the establishment or
                                              rubber stamp thereof

Acknowledgement by the Employee

Received the duplicate copy of the notice for modification in Form 'H' filed by me on ...., duly certified by the employer.

Date ....   Signature of the Employee

Note: Strike out the words not applicable.

Important points relating to "nomination" are given below:
(a) Nomination is required to be done within 30 days.
(b) Information relating to nomination is required to be submitted in Form 'F' in duplicate.
(c) An employee has a right to distribute the amount of gratuity payable to him under this Act among more than one nominee.
(d) Nomination is required to be done in favour of one or more members of the family of an employee in order to protect the interests of his family. If any nomination is made in favour of a person who is not a member of his family, such nomination is considered as void.
(e) However, if the employee has no family at the time of making nomination, nomination can be made in favour of any person or persons. But, if the employee acquires the family subsequently, the nomination already made becomes invalid and the concerned employee has to make a fresh nomination in favour of one or more members of his family within 90 days.
For this purpose, Form 'G' in duplicate is required to be submitted with necessary details.
(f) An employee has a right to modify his nomination at any time. For that purpose, he has to give a notice in writing to his employer by giving necessary details in Form 'H'.
(g) If a nominee predeceases the employee, then in such case, the interest of the deceased nominee is reverted to the employee. Thereafter, the employee has to make a fresh nomination in respect of such interest.
(h) Every nomination is required to be sent by an employee to his employer. The employer has to keep it safe in his custody.
(i) Nomination takes effect from the date of the receipt of the nomination by the employer.

3.14 Determination of the Amount of Gratuity

Provisions relating to application for gratuity [Section 7 (1)], determination of gratuity [Section 7 (2)], Payment of gratuity [Section 7 (3)], Payment of interest on the amount of gratuity [Section 7 (3-A)], dispute as to gratuity [Section 7 (4)], Powers of controlling authority [Section 7 (5)], appeal etc. have been made in the Payment of Gratuity Act of 1972. Section 7 is reproduced below for further information.

Section 7 – Determination of the Amount of Gratuity:

(1) A person who is eligible for payment of gratuity under this Act or any person authorised, in writing, to act on his behalf shall send a written application to the employer, within such time and in such form as may be prescribed for payment of such gratuity [Section 7 (1)].

(2) As soon as gratuity becomes payable, the employer shall, whether an application referred to in sub-section (1) has been made or not, determine the amount of gratuity and give notice in writing to the person to whom the gratuity is payable and also to the controlling authority specifying the amount of gratuity so determined [Section 7 (2)].

(3) The employer shall arrange to pay the amount of gratuity within thirty days from the date it becomes payable to the person to whom the gratuity is payable [Section 7 (3)].

(3-A) If the amount of gratuity payable under sub-section (3) is not paid by the employer within the period specified in sub-section (3), the employer shall pay, from the date on which the gratuity becomes payable to the date on which it is paid, simple interest at such rate, not exceeding the rate notified by the Central Government from time to time for repayment of long-term deposits, as that Government may, by notification specify [Section 7 (3-A)].

It is provided that no such interest shall be payable if the delay in the payment is due to the fault of the employee and the employer has obtained permission in writing from the controlling authority for the delayed payment on this ground [Proviso to Section 7 (3-A)].

(4) (a) If there is any dispute as to the amount of gratuity payable to an employee under this Act or as to the admissibility of any claim of, or in relation to, an employee for payment of gratuity, or as to the person entitled to receive the gratuity, the employer shall deposit with the controlling authority such amount as he admits to be payable by him as gratuity [Section 7 (4) (a)].

(b) Where there is a dispute with regard to any matter or matters specified in clause (a), the employer or employee or any other person raising the dispute may make an application to the controlling authority for deciding the dispute [Section 7 (4) (b)].

(c) The controlling authority shall, after due inquiry and after giving the parties to the dispute a reasonable opportunity of being heard, determine the matter or matters in dispute and if, as a result of such inquiry any amount is found to be payable to the employee, the controlling authority shall direct the employer to pay such amount or, as the case may be, such amount as reduced by the amount already deposited by the employer [Section 7 (4) (c)].

(d) The controlling authority shall pay the amount deposited, including the excess amount, if any, deposited by the employer, to the person entitled thereto [Section 7 (4) (d)].

(e) As soon as, may be after a deposit is made under clause (a), the controlling authority shall pay the amount of the deposit –
- (i) to the applicant where he is the employee; or
- (ii) where the applicant is not the employee, to the nominee or, as the case may be, the guardian of such nominee or heir of the employee if the controlling authority is satisfied that there is no dispute as to the right of the applicant to receive the amount of gratuity [Section 7 (4) (e)].

(5) For the purpose of conducting an inquiry under sub-section (4), the controlling authority shall have the same powers as are vested in a court, while trying a suit, under the Code of Civil Procedure, 1908 (5 of 1908), in respect of the following matters, namely –
- (a) enforcing the attendance of any person or examining him on oath;
- (b) requiring the discovery and production of documents;
- (c) receiving evidence on affidavits;
- (d) issuing commissions for the examination of witnesses [Section 7 (5)].

(6) An inquiry under this section shall be a judicial proceeding within the meaning of Sections 193 and 228, and for the purpose of Section 196, of the Indian Penal Code, 1860 (45 of 1860) [Section 7 (6)].

(7) Any person aggrieved by an order under sub-section (4), may, within sixty days from the date of the receipt of the order, prefer an appeal to the Appropriate Government or such other authority as may be specified by the Appropriate Government in this behalf [Section 7 (7)].

It is also provided that the Appropriate Government or the appellate authority, as the case may be, may, if it is satisfied that the appellant was prevented by sufficient cause from preferring the appeal within the said period of sixty days, and extend the said period by a further period of sixty days [Proviso 1 to Section 7 (7)].

It is further provided that no appeal by an employer shall be admitted unless at the time of preferring the appeal, the appellant either produces a certificate of the controlling authority to the effect that the appellant has deposited with him an amount equal to the amount of gratuity required to be deposited under sub-section (4), or deposits with the appellate authority such amount [Proviso 2 to Section 7 (7)].

(8) The Appropriate Government or the appellate authority, as the case may be, may, after giving the parties to the appeal a reasonable opportunity of being heard, confirm, modify or reverse the decision of the controlling authority [Section 7 (8)].

In the Payment of Gratuity (Central) Rules, 1972, Rule 7 dealing with application for gratuity, Rule 8 giving the information about notice for payment of gratuity, Rule 9 making clear the mode of payment of gratuity, Rule 10 dealing with application to controlling authority for direction, Rule 11 making clear the procedure for dealing with application for direction are incorporated. These rules and various forms relating to these rules are given below.

Rule 7: Application for Gratuity:

(1) An employee who is eligible for payment of gratuity under the Act, or any person authorised in writing, to act on his behalf, shall apply, ordinarily within thirty days from the date of the gratuity became payable, in Form 'I' to the employer.

Provided that where the date of superannuation or retirement of an employee is known, the employee may apply to the employer before thirty days of the date of superannuation or retirement.

(2) A nominee of an employee who is eligible for payment of gratuity under the second proviso to sub-section (1) of Section 4 shall apply, ordinarily within thirty days from the date the gratuity became payable to him, in Form 'J' to the employer:

Provided that an application on plain paper with relevant particulars shall also be accepted. The employer may obtain such other particulars as may be deemed necessary by him.

(3) A legal heir of an employee who is eligible for payment of gratuity under the second proviso to sub-section (1) of Section 4 shall apply, ordinarily within one year from the date the gratuity became payable to him in Form 'K' to the employer.

(4) Where gratuity becomes payable under the Act before the commencement of these rules, the periods of limitation specified in sub-rules (1), (2) and (3) shall be deemed to be operative from the date of such commencements.

(5) An application for payment of gratuity filed after the expiry of the periods specified in this rule shall also be entertained by the employer, if the applicant adduces sufficient cause for the delay in preferring his claim, and no claim for gratuity under the Act

shall be invalid merely because the claimant failed to present his application within the specified period. Any dispute in this regard shall be referred to the controlling authority for his decision.

(6) An application under this rule shall be presented to the employer either by personal service or by registered post with due acknowledgement.

Various forms required to be submitted under Rule 7:

(1) Application for Gratuity by an employee:

FORM 'I'

[*See* sub-rule (1) of Rule 7]

Application for Gratuity by an Employee

To,

    1.   (Give here name or description of the establishment with full address)

Sir/Gentlemen,

I beg to apply for payment of gratuity to which I am entitled to under sub-section (1) of Section 4 of the Payment of Gratuity Act, 1972 on account of my superannuation / retirement / resignation after completion of not less than five years of continuous service / total disablement due to accident / total disablement due to disease with effect from the .... Necessary particulars relating to my appointment are given in the statement below.

Statement

(1) Name in full
(2) Address in full
(3) Department / Branch / Section where last employed
(4) Post held with Ticket Number, or Serial Number, if any
(5) Date of appointment
(6) Date and cause of termination of service
(7) Total period of service
(8) Amount of wages last drawn
(9) Amount of gratuity claimed

    2.   I was rendered totally disabled as a result of –

        (Here give the details of the nature of disease or accident)

The evidences/witnesses in support of my total disablement are as follows:

        (Here give details)

    3.   Payment may please be made in cash/open or crossed bank cheque.

    4.   As the amount of gratuity payable is less than Rupees one thousand, I shall request you to arrange for payment of the sum due to me by Postal Money Order at the address mentioned above after deducting postal money order commission therefrom.

                              Yours faithfully,
                          Signature/Thumb-impression of the
                                      applicant employee

Place ....
Date ....

Notes: (1) Strike out the words not applicable
               (2) Strike out paragraph or paragraphs not applicable.

(2) Application for Gratuity by a nominee:

FORM 'J'

[*See* sub-rule (2) of Rule 7]

Application for Gratuity by a Nominee

To,

    1.   (Give here name or description of the establishment with full address)

Sir/Gentlemen,

I beg to apply for payment of gratuity to which I am entitled to under sub-section (1) of Section 4 of the Payment of Gratuity Act, 1972 as a nominee of late ....

(Name of the employee)

who was an employee of your .... establishment and died on the .... The gratuity is payable on account of the death of the aforesaid employee while in service / superannuation of the aforesaid employee on .... / retirement or resignation of the aforesaid employee on .... after completion of .... years of service / total disablement of the aforesaid employee due to accident or disease while in service with effect from.. . Necessary particulars relating to my claim are given in the statement below:

Statement

(1) Name of the applicant nominee
(2) Address in full of the applicant nominee
(3) Marital status of the applicant nominee (unmarried / married / widow / widower)
(4) Name in full of the employee
(5) Marital status of the employee
(6) Relationship of the nominee with the employee
(7) Total period of service of the employee
(8) Date of appointment of the employee
(9) Date and cause of termination of service of the employee
(10) Department / Branch / Section where the employee last worked
(11) Post last held by the employee with Ticket or Serial Number, if any
(12) Total wages last drawn by the employee.
(13) Date of death and evidence / witness as proof of death of the employee.
(14) Reference Number of recorded nomination if available
(15) Total gratuity payable to employee
(16) Share of gratuity claimed

    2.   I declare that the particulars mentioned in the above statement are true and correct to be the best of my knowledge and belief.

    3.   Payment may please be made in cash / crossed or open bank cheque.

    4.   As the amount payable is less than rupees one thousand, I shall request you to arrange for payment of the sum due to me by postal money order at the address mentioned above after deducting postal money order commission therefrom.

Yours faithfully,

Signature/Thumb-impression of
the applicant nominee

Place ....
Date ....

Notes: (1) Strike out the words not applicable
                (2) Strike out the paragraph or paragraphs not applicable.

(3) Application for Gratuity by a Legal Heir:

FORM 'K'

[*See* sub-rule (3) of Rule 7]

Application for Gratuity by Legal Heir

To,

    1.   (Give here the name or description of the establishment with full address)

Sir/Gentlemen,

I beg to apply for payment of gratuity to which I am entitled to under sub-section (1) of Section 4 of the Payment of Gratuity Act, 1972 as a legal heir of late ....

(Name of the employee) who was an employee of your .... establishment and died on the ...., without making any nomination. The gratuity is payable on account of the death of the aforesaid employee while in service / superannuation of the aforesaid employee on the .... retirement or resignation of the aforesaid employee on the .... after completion of .... years of service / total disablement of the aforesaid employee due to accident or disease while in service with effect from................ . Necessary particulars relating to my claim are given in the statement below:

Statement

(1) Name of the applicant legal heir
(2) Address in full of applicant legal heir
(3) Marital status of the applicant legal heir (unmarried / married / widow / widower)
(4) Name in full of the employee
(5) Relationship of the applicant with the employee
(6) Religion of both the applicant with the employee
(7) Date of appointment and total period of service of the employee
(8) Department / Branch / Section where the employee worked last
(9) Post last held by the employee with Ticket or Serial Number, if any
(10) Total wages last drawn by the employee
(11) Date and cause of termination of service of the employee (death or otherwise)
(12) Date of death of the employee and evidence / witness in support thereof
(13) Total gratuity payable to the employee
(14) Percentage of the gratuity claimed
(15) Basis of the claim and evidence / witness in support thereof

    2.   I declare that the particulars mentioned in the above statement are true and correct to be best of my knowledge and belief.

    3.   Payment may please be made in cash/open or crossed bank cheque.

    4.   As the amount payable is less than Rupees one thousand, I shall request you to arrange for payment of the sum due to me by postal money order at the address mentioned above, after deducting postal money order commission therefrom.

Yours faithfully,
Signature/Thumb-impression of the
applicant legal heir

Place ....
Date ....

Note: Strike out the words not applicable

Rule 8: Notice for Payment of Gratuity:

(1) Within fifteen days of the receipt of an application under Rule 7 for payment of gratuity, the employer shall –

    (i) if the claim is found admissible on verification, issue a notice in Form 'L' to the applicant employee, nominee or legal heir, as the case may be, specifying the amount of gratuity payable and fixing a date, not being later than the thirtieth day after the date of receipt of the application, for payment thereof, or

    (ii) if the claim for gratuity is not found admissible, issue a notice in Form 'M' to the applicant employee, nominee or legal heir, as the case may be, specifying the reasons why the claim for gratuity is not considered admissible.

In either case, a copy of the notice shall be endorsed to the controlling authority.

(2) In case payment of gratuity is due to be made in the employer's office, the date fixed for the purpose in the notice in Form 'L' under clause (i) of sub-rule (1) shall be re-fixed by the employer, if a written application in this behalf is made by the payee explaining why it is not possible for him to be present in person on the date specified.

(3) If the claimant for gratuity is a nominee or a legal heir, the employer may ask for such witness or evidence as may be deemed relevant for establishing his identity or maintainability of his claim as the case may be. In that case the time-limit specified for issuance of notices under sub-rule (1) shall be operative with effect from the date such witness or evidence, as the case may be, called for by the employer is furnished to the employer.

(4) A notice in Form 'L' or Form 'M' shall be served on the applicant either by personal service after taking receipt or by registered post with due acknowledgement.

(5) A notice under sub-section (2) of Section 7 shall be in Form 'L'.

(1) Form 'L' for notice for Payment of Gratuity:

FORM 'L'

[*See* clause (i) of sub-rule (1) of Rule 8]

Notice for Payment of Gratuity

To,

    1.   (Name and address of the applicant employee / nominee / legal heir)

You are hereby informed as required under clause (*i*) of sub-rule (1) of Rule 8 of the Payment of Gratuity (Central) Rules, 1972 that a sum of ₹ .... (₹ ....) is payable to you as gratuity / as your share of gratuity in terms of nomination made by .... on .... recorded in this .... as a legal heir of .... an employee of this .... establishment.

    2.   Please call at .... on .... (Here specify place) (date) at .... for collecting your payment in cash / open or crossed cheque.

    3.   Amount payable shall be sent to you by postal money order at the address given in your application after deducting the postal money order commission, as desired by you, by ....

Brief statement of calculation

    (1)   Total period of service of the employee concerned .... years .... months.
    (2)   Wages last drawn
    (3)   Proportion of the admissible gratuity payable in terms of nomination / as a legal heir
    (4)   Amount payable

Place ....   Signature of the Employer/authorised officer.
Date ....   Name or description of establishment or rubber stamp thereof

Copy to the Controlling Authority
Note: Strike out the words not applicable.

(2) Form 'M' for notice rejecting a claim for Payment of Gratuity:

FORM 'M'
[*See* clause (ii) of sub-rule (1) of Rule 8]
Notice Rejecting the Claim for Payment of Gratuity

To,
    (Name and address of the applicant employee/nominee/legal heir)

You are hereby informed as required under clause (ii) of sub-rule (1) of Rule 8 of the Payment of Gratuity (Central) Rules, 1972 that your claim for payment of gratuity as indicated on your application in Form .... under the said rules is not admissible for the reasons stated below:

Reasons
(Here specify the reasons)

Place .... Signature of the employee/authorised officer.
Date ....

                                  Name or description of establishment or rubber stamp thereof.

Copy to Controlling Authority
Note: Strike out the words not applicable

Rule 9: Mode of Payment of Gratuity:

The gratuity payable under the Act shall be paid in cash or, if so desired by the payee, in Demand Draft or bank cheque to the eligible employee, nominee or legal heir, as the case may be.

Provided that in case the eligible employee, nominee or legal heir, as the case may be, so desires and the amount of gratuity payable is less than rupees one thousand, payment may be made by postal money order after deducting the postal money order commission thereof from the amount payable.

Provided further that intimation about the details of payment shall also be given by the employer to the controlling authority of the area.

Provided further that in the case of nominee, or an heir, who is a minor, the controlling authority shall invest the gratuity amount deposited with him for the benefit of such a minor in terms of deposit with the State Bank of India or any of its subsidiaries or any Nationalised Bank.

Explanation: "Nationalised Bank" means a corresponding new bank specified in the First Schedule of the Banking Companies (Acquisition and Transfer of Undertakings) Act, 1950 (5 of 1970) or a corresponding new bank specified in the First Schedule of the Banking Companies (Acquisition and Transfer of Undertakings) Act, 1980 (40 of 1980).

Rule 10: Application to Controlling Authority for Direction:

(1) If an employer –
    (i) refuses to accept a nomination or to entertain an application sought to be filed under Rule 7, or
    (ii) issues a notice under sub-rule (1) of Rule 8 either specifying an amount of gratuity which is considered by the applicant less than what is payable or rejecting eligibility to payment of gratuity, or
    (iii) having received an application under Rule 7 fails to issue any notice as required under Rule 8 within the time specified therein,

The claimant employee, nominee or legal heir, as the case may be, may within ninety days of the occurrence of the cause for the application, apply, in Form 'N' to the controlling authority for issuing a direction under sub-section (4) of Section 7 with as many extra copies as are required for the opposite parties.

Provided that the controlling authority may accept any application under this sub-rule, on sufficient cause being shown by the applicant, after the expiry of the specified period.

(2) Application under sub-rule (1) and other documents relevant to such an application shall be presented in person to the controlling authority or shall be sent by registered post with due acknowledgement.

Form 'N' for Application for Direction:

FORM 'N'

[*See* sub-rule of Rule 10]

Application for Direction

Before the Controlling Authority under the Payment of Gratuity Act, 1972

Application ....   Date ....

BETWEEN

(Name in full of the applicant with full address)

AND

(Name in full of the employer concerned with full address)

The applicant is an employee of the above mentioned employer/a nominee of late ....,an employee of the above mentioned employer / a legal heir of late ...., an employee of the above mentioned employer, and is entitled to payment of gratuity under Section 4 of the Payment of Gratuity Act, 1972 on account of his own/ aforesaid employee's superannuation on .... /his own retirement/ aforesaid employee's resignation .... on .... after

(date)   (date)

completion of .... years of continuous service / his own / aforesaid .... employees' total disablement with effect from .... due to ....

(date)

accident / disease / death of aforesaid employee on ....

2. The applicant submitted an application under Rule of the Payment of Gratuity Act, 1972 on the .... but the above mentioned employer refused to entertain it/issued a notice dated the .... under the clause .... of sub-rule of rule .... offering an amount of gratuity which is less than my due / issued a notice dated the .... under clause .... of sub-rule ...., of rule .... rejecting my eligibility to payment of gratuity. The duplicate copy of the said notice is enclosed.

3. The applicant submits that there is a dispute on the matter (specify the dispute).

4. The applicant furnishes the necessary particulars in the annexure hereto and prays that the Controlling Authority may be pleased to determine the amount of gratuity payable to the petitioner and direct the above mentioned employer to pay the same to the petitioner.

5. The applicant declares that the particulars furnished in the annexure hereto are true and correct to the best of his knowledge and belief.

Date: Signature of the applicant/Thumb-impression
                                                                                    of the applicant

ANNEXURE

1. Name in full of applicant with full address   ..   ..   ..
2. Basis of claim:
    (Death/Superannuation/Retirement/Resignation/Disablement of employee)   ..   ..
3. Name and address of the employee in full   ..   ..   ..
4. Marital status of the employee (unmarried/married/widow/widower)   ..   ..   ..
5. Name and address of the employer (in full)   ..   ..   ..
6. Department/Branch/Section where the employer was last employed (if known)   ..   ..
7. Post held by the employee with Ticket or Serial Number if any (if known)   ..   ..
8. Date of appointment of the employee (if known)   ..   ..   ..
9. Date and cause of termination of service of the employee
    (superannuation/retirement/resignation/disablement/death)   ..   ..   ..
10. Total period of service by the employee   ..   ..   ..
11. Wages last drawn by the employee   ..   ..
12. If the employee is dead, date and cause thereof   ..   ..   ..
13. Evidence/witness in support of death of the employee   ..   ..
14. If a nominee, Number and date of recording of nomination with the employer   ..   ..
15. Evidence/witness in support of being a legal heir if a legal heir   ..   ..   ..
16. Total gratuity payable to employee (if known)   ..   ..   ..
17. Percentage of gratuity payable to the applicant as nominee/legal heir   ..   ..   ..
18. Amount of gratuity claimed by the applicant   ..   ..   ..

Place ....   Signature/Thumb-impression of the applicant
Date   ....

Note: Strike out the words not applicable.

11. Procedure for dealing with Application for Direction:

(1) On receipt of an application under Rule 10, the controlling authority shall, by issuing a notice in Form 'O', call upon the applicant as well as the employer to appear before him on a specified date, time and place, either by himself or through his authorised representative together with all relevant documents and witnesses, if any.

(2) Any person desiring to act on behalf of an employer or employee, nominee or legal heir, as the case may be, shall present to the controlling authority a letter of authority from the employer or the person concerned, as the case may be, on whose behalf he seeks to act together with a written statement explaining his interest in the matter and praying for permission so as to act. The controlling authority shall record thereon an order either according to his approval or specifying, in the case of refusal to grant the permission prayed for, the reasons for the refusal.

(3) A party appearing by an authorised representative shall be bound by the acts of the representative.

(4) After completion of hearing on the date fixed under sub-rule (1), or after such further evidence, examination of documents, witnesses, hearing and enquiry, as may be deemed necessary, the controlling authority shall record his finding as to whether any amount is payable to the applicant under the Act. A copy of the finding shall be given to each of the parties.

(5) If the employer concerned fails to appear on the specified date of hearing after due service of notice without sufficient cause, the controlling authority may proceed to hear and determine the application *ex parte*. If the applicant fails to appear on the specified date of hearing without sufficient cause, the controlling authority may dismiss the application.

Provided that an order under this sub-rule may, on good cause being shown within thirty days of the said order, be reviewed and the application re-heard after giving not less than fourteen days' notice to the opposite party of the date fixed for re-hearing of the application.

Form 'O' for Notice for appearance before the Controlling Authority:

FORM 'O'

[*See* sub-rule (1) of Rule 11]

Notice for Appearance before the Controlling Authority

From: The Controlling Authority under the Payment of Gratuity Act, 1972.

To ....

(Name and address of the employer/applicant)

Whereas Shri ...., an employee under you/a nominee(s)/legal heir(s) of Shri ...., an employee under the above-mentioned employer, has /have filed an application under sub-rule (1) of Rule 10 of the Payment of Gratuity (Central) Rules, 1972 alleging that –

[A copy of the said application is enclosed]

Now, therefore, you are hereby called upon to appear before me at .... (place) either personally or through a person duly authorised in this behalf for the purpose of answering all material questions relating to the application on the .... day of 20 ..... at .... 'o' clock in the forenoon/afternoon in support of/to answer the allegation; and as the day fixed for your appearance is appointed for final disposal of the application you must be prepared to produce on that day all the witnesses upon whose evidence, and the documents upon which you intend to rely in support of your allegation/defence.

Take notice that in default of your appearance on the day before-mentioned the application will be dismissed/heard and determined in your absence.

Given under my hand and seal, this .... day of .... 20 ....

Controlling Authority

Note: Strike out the words and paragraphs not applicable.

3.14.1 Direction of Payment of Gratuity

Rule 17 provides for the direction of payment of gratuity. It states that, "*if a finding is recorded under sub-rule (4) of Rule 11 that the applicant is entitled to payment of gratuity* under the Act, the controlling authority shall issue a notice to the employer concerned in Form 'R' specifying the amount payable and directing payment thereof to the applicant under intimation to the Controlling Authority within thirty days from the date of receipt of the notice by the employer. A copy of the notice shall be endorsed to the applicant employee, nominee or a legal heir, as the case may be".

Form 'R' for making clear the contents of Notice for Payment of Gratuity:

FORM 'R'

[See Rule 17]

Notice for Payment of Gratuity

To,

(Name and address of the employer)

Whereas Shri/Smt./Kumari .... of .... an employee

(address)

under you/a nominee(s) legal heir(s) of late .... an employee under you, filed an application under Section 7 of the Payment of Gratuity Act, 1972, before me.

And whereas the application was heard in your presence on .... and after the hearing. I have come to the finding that the said Shri/Smt./Kumari .... is entitled to a payment of ₹ .... as gratuity under the Payment of Gratuity Act, 1972.

Now, therefore, I hereby direct you to pay the said sum of ₹ .... to Shri/Smt/Kumari .... within thirty days of the receipt of this notice with an intimation thereof to me.

Given under my hand and seal, this .... day of .... 20 ....

Controlling Authority

Copy to

(Applicant under rule)

He is advised to contact the employer for collecting payment.

Note: The portion not applicable to be deleted.

3.14.2 Maintenance of Records of Cases by the Controlling Authority

Rule 16 of the Payment of Gratuity (Central) Rules, 1972 provides for maintaining the records of cases by the controlling authority. Rule 16 is reproduced below.

(1) The controlling authority shall record the particulars of each case under Section 7, in Form 'Q' and at the time of passing order shall sign and date the particulars so recorded.

(2) The controlling authority shall, while passing orders in each case, also record the findings on the merits of the case and file it together with the memorandum of evidence with the order sheet.

(3) Any record, other than a record of any order or direction, which is required by these rules to be signed by the controlling authority, may be signed on behalf of and under the direction of the controlling authority by any subordinate officer appointed in writing for this purpose by the controlling authority.

Form 'Q' shows the particulars of application under Section 7 as follows:

FORM 'Q'

[*See* sub-rule (1) of Rule 16]

Particulars of Application under Section 7

1. Serial Number.
2. Date of the application.
3. Name and address of the applicant.
4. Name and address of the employer.
5. Amount of gratuity claimed.
6. Dates of hearing.
7. Findings with date.
8. Amount awarded.
9. Cost, if any, awarded.
10. Date of notice issued for payment of gratuity.
11. Date of appeal, if any.
12. Decision of the appellate authority.
13. Date of issue of final notice for payment of gratuity.
14. Date of payment of gratuity by employer with mode of payment.
15. Date of receipt of application for recovery of gratuity.
16. Date of issue of Recovery Certificate.
17. Date of recovery.
18. Other remarks.
19. Signed.
20. Date.

3.15 Recovery of Gratuity

As gratuity is a compulsory payment according to the provisions of this Act, it must be paid to an employee on fulfilling the conditions laid down in the Act by his employer. If the amount of gratuity payable under this Act is not paid by the employer within the time limit prescribed for the payment, he must make an application to the controlling authority. On receiving the application by the aggrieved person, the controlling authority issues the certificate for that amount to the collector who recovers the same together with compound interest.

The provisions relating to the recovery of the amount of gratuity are made in Section 8 which are as follows:

"*If the amount of gratuity payable under this Act is not paid by the employer, within the prescribed time, to the person entitled thereto, the controlling authority shall, on an application made to it in this behalf by the aggrieved person, issue a certificate for that amount to the Collector, who shall recover the same, together with compound interest thereon at such rate as the Central Government may, by notification, specify from the date of expiry of the prescribed time, as arrears of land revenue and pay the same to the person entitled thereto*" [Section 8].

It is also provided that the controlling authority shall, before issuing a certificate under this section, give the employer a reasonable opportunity of showing cause against the issue of such certificate [Proviso 1 to Section 8].

It is further provided that the amount payable under this section shall, in no case exceed the amount of gratuity payable under this Act [Proviso 2 to Section 8].

3.15.1 Application for Recovery of Gratuity

"Where an employer fails to pay the gratuity due under the Act in accordance with the notice by the controlling authority under Rule 17 or Rule 18, as the case may be, the employee concerned, his nominee or legal heir, as the case may be, to whom the gratuity is payable, may apply to the controlling authority in duplicate in Form 'T' for recovery thereof under Section 8 of the Act" [Rule 19 of the Payment of Gratuity (Central) Rules, 1972.

Form 'T' is given below -

FORM 'T'
[*See* Rule 19]
Application for Recovery of Gratuity

1. Before the Controlling Authority under the Payment of Gratuity Act, 1972

Application No. ....   Date ....

BETWEEN
(Name in full of the applicant with address)
AND
(Name in full of the employer with full address)

The applicant is an employee of the above mentioned employer/a nominee of late ...., an employee of the above mentioned employer/a legal heir of late ...., an employee of the above mentioned employer, and you were pleased to direct the said employer in your notice dated the .... under Rule .... of Payment of Gratuity (Central) Rules, 1972 for payment of a sum of ₹ .... as gratuity payable under the Payment of Gratuity Act, 1972.

2. The application submits that the said employer failed to pay the said amount of gratuity to me as directed by you although I approached him for payment.

3. The applicant therefore prays that a certificate may be issued under Section .... of the said Act for recovery of the said sum of ₹ .... due to me as gratuity in terms of your direction.

Signature/Thumb-impression of the applicant

Place ....
Date ....

Note: Strike out the words not applicable.

Rule 18 referred to in Rule 19 pertains to appeal. Rule 18 is reproduced below.

Rule 18: Appeal

(1) The Memorandum of appeal under sub-section (7) of Section 7 of the Act be submitted to the appellate authority with a copy thereof to the opposite party and the controlling authority either through delivery in person or under registered post acknowledgement due.

(2) The Memorandum of appeal shall contain the facts of the case, the decision of the controlling authority, the grounds of appeal and the relief sought.

(3) There shall be appended to the Memorandum of appeal a certified copy of the finding of the controlling authority and direction for payment of gratuity.

(4) On receipt of the copy of Memorandum of appeal, the controlling authority shall forward records of the case to the appellate authority.

(5) Within 14 days of the receipt of the copy of the Memorandum of appeal, the opposite party shall submit his comments on each paragraph of the memorandum with additional plea, if any, to the appellate authority with a copy to the appellant.

(6) The appellate authority shall record its decision after giving the parties to the appeal a reasonable opportunity of being heard. A copy of the decision shall be given to the parties to the appeal and a copy thereof shall be sent to the controlling authority returning his records of the case.

(7) The controlling authority shall, on receipt of the decision of the appellate authority, make necessary entry in the records of the case maintained in Form 'Q' under sub-rule (1) of Rule 16.

(8) On receipt of the decision of the appellate authority, the controlling authority shall, if required under that decision, modify his direction for payment of gratuity and issue a notice to the employer concerned in Form 'S' specifying the modified amount payable and directing payment thereof to the applicant, under intimation to the controlling authority within fifteen days of the receipt of the notice by the employer. A copy of the notice shall be endorsed to the applicant employee, nominee or legal heir, as the case may be, and to the appellate authority.

Form 'S' makes clear the contents of notice for payment of gratuity as determined by the Appellate Authority.

FORM 'S'

[See sub-rule (5) of Rule 18]

Notice for Payment of Gratuity as Determined by Appellate Authority

To,

    (Name and address of the employer)

Whereas a notice was given to you on .... Form 'R' requiring you to make a payment of ₹ .... to Shri/Smt./Kumari .... as gratuity under the Payment of Gratuity Act, 1972.

Whereas you/the applicant went in appeal before the appellate authority, who has decided that an amount of ₹ .... is due to be paid to Shri/Smt./Kumari .... as Gratuity due under the Payment of Gratuity Act, 1972;

Now, therefore I hereby direct you to pay the said sum of ₹ .... to Shri/Smt./Kumari .... [within 15 days] of the receipt of this notice with an intimation thereof to me.

Given under my hand and seal, this .... day of .... 20...........

Controlling Authority

Copy to:
1. The applicant.
   He is advised to contact the employer for collecting payment.
2. The Appellate Authority.

Note: The portion not applicable to be deleted.

3.16 Protection of Gratuity

Section 13 of this Act, expressly provides for the protection of gratuity. It states that, *"no gratuity payable under this Act and no gratuity payable to an employee employed in any establishment, factory, mine, oilfield, plantation, port railway company or shop exempted under Section 5 shall be liable to attachment in execution of any decree or order of any civil, revenue or criminal court".*

However, gratuity payable to the heirs of an employee on his death is attachable.

3.17 Appointment and Powers of Inspectors

Section 7-A deals with the appointment of Inspectors while Section 7-B makes clear the powers of Inspectors appointed for the purposes of this Act.

3.17.1 Appointment of Inspectors

(1) The Appropriate Government may, by notification, appoint as many Inspectors, as it deems fit, for the purposes of this Act [Section 7-A (1)].

(2) The appropriate Government may, by general or special order, define the area to which the authority of an Inspector so appointed shall extend and where two or more Inspectors are appointed for the same area, also provide, by such order, for the distribution or allocation of work to be performed by them under this Act [Section 7-A (2)].

(3) Every Inspector shall be deemed to be a public servant within the meaning of Section 21 of the Indian Penal Code (45 of 1860) [Section 7-A (3)].

3.17.2 Powers of Inspectors

The powers of an Inspector appointed under this Act have been enumerated in Section 7-A. These powers are as under:

Subject to any rules made by the Appropriate Government in this behalf, an Inspector may, for the purpose of ascertaining whether any of the provisions of this Act or the conditions, if any, of any exemption granted thereunder, have been complied with, exercise all or any of the following powers, namely;

(a) to require an employer to furnish such information as he may consider necessary;

(b) to enter and inspect, at all reasonable hours, with such assistants (if any), being persons in the service of the Government or local or any public authority, as he thinks fit, any premises of or place in any factory, mine, oilfield, plantation, port, railway company, shop or other establishment to which this Act applies, for the purpose of examining any register, record or notice or other document required to be kept or exhibited under this Act or the rules made thereunder, or otherwise kept or exhibited in relation to the employment of any person or the payment of gratuity to the employees, and requires the production thereof for inspection;

(c) to examine with respect to any matter relevant to any of the purposes aforesaid, the employer or any person whom he finds in such premises or place and who, he has reasonable cause to believe, is an employee employed therein;

(d) to make copies of, or take extracts from, any register, record or notice, or other documents, as he may consider relevant, and where he has reason to believe that any offence under this Act has been committed by an employer, search and seize with such assistance as he may think fit, such register, record, notice or other document as he may consider relevant in respect of that offence;

(e) to exercise such other powers as may be prescribed [Section 7-B (1)].

Any person required to produce any register, record, notice or other document or to give any information by an Inspector under sub-section (1) shall be deemed to be legally bound to do so within the meaning of Sections 175 and 176 of the Indian Penal Code, (45 of 1860) Section 7-B (2)].

The provisions of the Code of Criminal Procedure, 1973 (2 of 1974) shall so far as may be, apply to any search or seizure under this section as they apply to any search or seizure made under the authority of a warrant issued under Section 94 of that Code [Section 7-B (3)].

3.18 Penalties

Provisions have been made in Section 9 of this Act for imposing penalties for false statement or false representation and also for contravention of the Act. The penalties for these offences are mentioned below:

(a) Penalty for false representation or false statement:

Whoever, for the purpose of avoiding any payment to be made by himself under this Act or of enabling any other person to avoid such payment, knowingly makes or causes to be made any false statement or false representation shall be punishable with imprisonment for a term which may extend to six months, or with fine which may extend to ten thousand rupees or with both [Section 9 (1)].

(b) Penalty for contravention of the Act:

An employer who contravenes, or makes default in complying with any of the provisions of this Act or any rule or order made thereunder shall be punishable with imprisonment for a term which shall not be less than three months but which may extend to one year, or with a fine which shall not be less than rupees ten thousand but which may extend to rupees twenty thousand, or with both [Section 9 (2)].

It is provided that where the offence relates to non-payment of any gratuity payable under this Act, the employer shall be punishable with imprisonment for a term which shall not be less than six months but which may extend to two years unless the court trying the offence, for reasons to be recorded by it in writing, is of opinion that a lesser term of imprisonment or the imposition of a fine would meet the ends of justice [Proviso to Section 9 (2)].

(c) Penalty for failure to pay insurance premium or contribution:

If an employer fails to pay insurance premium under Section 4-A (1) or any contribution to an approved gratuity fund under Section 4-A (2), such employer is held liable to pay the amount of gratuity due, along with the interest for delayed payment forthwith to the controlling authority. Whoever contravenes this provision is punishable with fine which may extend to ₹ Ten thousand and in the case of continuing offence with a further fine which may extend to ₹ One thousand for each day during which the offence continues [Section 4-A (6)].

3.19 Exemption of the Employer from Liability in Certain Cases

According to the provisions of Section 10, when an employer is charged with the offence punishable under this Act, such an employer is entitled to have any other person whom the employer charges as the actual offender brought before the Court at the time appointed for hearing the charge. However, the employer is entitled to do so only upon the complaint duly made by him and on giving to the complaint not less than three clear days' notice in writing of his intention to do so.

If the employer can prove to the satisfaction of the Court that he has observed due diligence to enforce the execution of this Act and the said other person committed the offence in question without that employer's knowledge, consent or connivance, then the other person shall be convicted of the offence and is held liable to the like punishment as if he were the employer. The employer then is discharged from any liability under this Act in respect of such offence.

Section 10 is reproduced below to be familiar with the provisions of this Act relating to exemption of employer from liability in certain cases.

"Where an employer is charged with an offence punishable under this Act, he shall be entitled upon complaint duly made by him and on giving to the complaint not less than three clear days' notice in writing of his intention to do so, to have any other person whom he charges as the actual offender brought before the court at the time appointed for hearing the charge; and if, after the commission of the offence has been proved, the employer proves to the satisfaction of the court –

    (a)   that he has observed due diligence to enforce the execution of this Act, and
    (b)   that the said other person committed the offence in question without his knowledge, consent or connivance,
that other person shall be convicted of the offence and shall be liable to the like punishment as if he were the employer and the employer shall be discharged from any liability under this Act in respect of such offence:

It is provided that in seeking to prove as aforesaid, the employer may be examined on oath and his evidence and that of any witness whom he calls in his support shall be subject to cross-examination on behalf of the person he charges as the actual offender and by the prosecutor [Proviso 1 to Section 10].

It is further provided that, if the person charged as the actual offender by the employer cannot be brought before the court at the time appointed for hearing the charge, the court shall adjourn the hearing from time to time for a period not exceeding three months and if by the end of the said period the person charged as the actual offender cannot still be brought before the court, the court shall proceed to hear the charge against the employer and shall, if the offence be proved, convict the employer [Proviso 2 to Section 10].

3.20 Cognizance of Offences [Section 11]

No court shall take cognizance of any offence punishable under this Act save on a complaint made by or under the authority of the appropriate Government [Section 11 (1)].

It is provided that where the amount of gratuity has not been paid, or recovered, within six months from the expiry of the prescribed time, the Appropriate Government shall authorise the controlling authority to make a complaint against the employer, whereupon the controlling authority shall, within fifteen days from the date of such authorisation, make such complaint to a Magistrate having jurisdiction to try the offence [Proviso to Section 11].

No court inferior to that of a Metropolitan Magistrate or a Judicial Magistrate of the first class shall try any offence punishable under this Act [Section 11 (2)].

3.21 Protection of Action Taken in Good Faith

No suit or other legal proceeding shall lie against the controlling authority or any other person in respect of anything which is in good faith done or intended to be done under this Act or any rule or order made thereunder [Section 12].

There is the provision relating to protection of gratuity in Section 13 of the Act and according to that section, *"No gratuity payable under this Act and no gratuity payable to an employee employed in any establishment, factory, mine, oil field, plantation, port, railway, company or shop exempted under Section 5 shall be liable to attachment in execution of any decree or order of any civil, revenue or criminal court"*.

3.22 Act to Override Other Enactments

The provisions of this Act or any rule made thereunder shall have an effect notwithstanding anything inconsistent therewith contained in any enactment other than this Act or in any instrument or contract having effect by virtue of any enactment other than this Act [Section 14].

3.23 Power to Make Rules

(1) The Appropriate Government may, by notification, make rules for the purpose of carrying out the provisions of this Act [Section 15 (1)].

(2) Every rule made by the Central Government under this Act shall be laid, as soon as may be after it is made, before each House of Parliament while it is in session, for a total period of thirty days which may be comprised in one session or in two or more successive sessions, and if, before the expiry of the session immediately following the session or the successive sessions aforesaid, both Houses agree in making any modification in the rule or both Houses agree that the rule should not be made, the rule shall, thereafter, have effect only in such modified form or be of no effect as the case may be, so, however, that any such modification or annulment shall be without prejudice to the validity of anything previously done under that rule [Section 15 (2)].

3.24 Display of Abstract of the Act and Rules

Rule 20 of the Payment of Gratuity (Central) Rules of 1972 states that, *"the employer shall display an abstract of the Act and the rule made thereunder as given in Form 'U' in English and in the language understood by the majority of the employees at a conspicuous place at or near the main entrance of the establishment"*.

Form 'U' is given below:

FORM 'U'
Abstract of the Act and Rules

1. **Extent of the Act:** The Act extends to the whole of India:

Provided that in so far as it relates to plantations or ports, it shall not extend to the State of Jammu and Kashmir [Section 1(2)].

2. **To whom the Act Applies:** Act applies to (a) every factory, mine, oilfield, plantation, port and railway company; (b) every shop or establishment within the meaning of any law for the time being in force in relation to shops and establishments in a State, in which ten or more persons are employed, or were employed, on any day of the preceding twelve months; and (c) such other establishments or class of establishments in which, ten or more employees are employed, or were employed, on any day of the preceding twelve months, as the Central Government may, by notification, specify in this behalf [Section 1(3)].

3. **Definitions:** (a) "Appropriate Government" means (i) in relation to an establishment –
    - (a) belonging to, or under the control of the Central Government,
    - (b) having branches in more than one State,
    - (c) of a factory belonging to, or under the control of, the Central Government.
    - (d) of a major port, mine, oilfield or railway company, the Central Government,

    (ii) in any other case, the State Government [Section 2(a)].

    (b) "Completed year of service" means continuous service for one year [Section 2(b)].

    (c) "Continuous Service" means uninterrupted service and includes service which is interrupted by sickness, accident, leave, lay-off, strike or a lock-out or cessation of work due to any fault of the employees concerned, whether such uninterrupted or interrupted service was rendered before or after the commencement of this Act.

    Explanation I: In the case of an employee who is not in uninterrupted service for one year, he shall be deemed to be in continuous service if he has been actually employed by an employer during the twelve months immediately preceding the year for not less than –
    - (i) 190 days, if employed below the ground in a mine, or
    - (ii) 240 days, in any other case, except when he is employed in a seasonal establishment.

    Explanation II: An employee of a seasonal establishment shall be deemed to be in continuous service if he has actually worked for not less than seventy five per cent of the number of days on which the establishment was in operation during the year [Section 2(d)].

    (d) "Controlling authority" means an authority appointed by an Appropriate Government under Section 3 [Section 2(d)].

    (e) "Family", in relation to an employee, shall be deemed to consist of –
    - (i) in the case of a male employee himself, his wife, his children, whether married or unmarried, his dependant parents and the widow and children, of his pre-deceased son, if any;
    - (ii) in the case of a female employee, herself, her husband, her children, whether married or unmarried, her dependent parents and the dependant parents of her husband and the widow and children of her pre-deceased son, if any

Provided that if a female employee by a notice in writing to the Controlling Authority, expresses her desire to exclude her husband from her family, the husband and his dependant parents shall no longer be deemed, for the purposes of this act be included in the family of such female employee unless the said notice is subsequently withdrawn by such female employee.

Explanation III: Where the personal law of an employee permits the adoption by him of a child, any child lawfully adopted by him shall be deemed to be included in his family, and where a child of an employee has been adopted by another person and such adoption is under the personal law of the person making such adoption, lawful, such child shall be deemed to be excluded from the family of the employee [Section 2(h)].

4. Nomination: (1) Each employee, who has completed one year of service, after the commencement of the Payment of Gratuity (Central) Rules, 1972 shall make within thirty days of completion of one year of service, a nomination [Section 6 (1)].

(2) If an employee has a family at the time of making a nomination, the nomination shall be made in favour of one or more members of his family and any nomination made by such employee in favour of a person who is not a member of his family shall be void [Section 6(3)].

(3) If at the time of making a nomination, the employee has no family, the nomination can be made in favour of any person or persons, but if the employee subsequently acquires a family, such nomination shall forthwith become invalid and the employee shall make within 90 days fresh nomination in favour of one or more members of his family [Section 6(4) read with Rule 6(3)].

(4) A nomination or a fresh nomination or a notice of modification of nomination shall be signed by the employee or, if illiterate, shall bear his thumb-impression in the presence of two witnesses, who shall also sign a declaration to that effect in the nomination, fresh nomination or notice of modification of nomination as the case may be [Rule 6(5)].

(5) A nomination may, subject to the provisions of sub-sections (3) and (4) of Section 6, be modified by an employee any time after giving to his employer a written notice of his intention to do so [Section 6(5)].

(6) A nomination or fresh nomination or notice of modification of nomination shall take effect from the date of receipt of the same by the employer [Rule 6 (6)].

5. Application for Gratuity: (1) An employee who is eligible for payment of gratuity under the Act, or any person authorised in writing, to act on his behalf, shall apply ordinarily within thirty days from the date gratuity becomes payable.

Provided that where the date of superannuation or retirement of an employee is known, the employee may apply to such employer before thirty days of the date of superannuation or retirement [Rule 7(1)].

(2) A nominee of an employee who is eligible for payment of gratuity shall apply, ordinarily within thirty days from the date the gratuity became payable to him, to the employer [Rule 7(2)].

(3) A legal heir of an employee who is eligible for payment of gratuity shall apply, ordinarily within one year from the date the gratuity became payable to him, to the employer [Rule 7(3)].

(4) An application for payment of gratuity filed after the expiry of the periods specified above shall also be entertained by the employer if the applicant adduces a sufficient cause for the delay [Rule 7(5)].

6. Payment of Gratuity: (1) Gratuity shall be payable to an employee on the termination of his employment after he has rendered continuous services for not less than five years –

    (a) on his superannuation, or

    (b) on his retirement or resignation, or

    (c) on his death or disablement due to accident or disease

Provided that the completion of continuous service of five years shall not be necessary where the termination of the employment of any employee is due to death or disablement.

Disablement means such disablement which incapacitates an employee for the work which he was capable of performing before the accident or disease resulting in such disablement [Section 4(1)].

(2) For every completed year of service or part thereof in excess of six months, the employer shall pay gratuity to an employee at the rate of fifteen days' wages based on the rate of wages last drawn by the employee concerned.

Provided that in the case of a piece-rated employee, daily wages shall be computed on the average of the total wages received by him for a period of three months immediately preceding the termination of his employment, and, for this purpose, the wages paid for any overtime work shall not be taken into account:

Provided further that in the case of an employee employed in a seasonal establishment, the employer shall pay the gratuity at the rate of seven days' wages for each season [Section 4(2)].

(3) The amount of gratuity payable to an employee shall not exceed ₹ 3,50,000.

7. Forfeiture of Gratuity: (1) The gratuity of an employee, whose services have been terminated for any act, wilful omission or negligence causing any damage or loss to, or destruction of property belonging to the employer, shall be forfeited to the extent of the damage or loss so caused.

(2) The gratuity payable to an employee shall wholly be forfeited –
  (a) if the services of such employee have been terminated for his riotous or disorderly conduct or of any other act of violence on his part, or
  (b) if the services of such employee have been terminated for any act which constitutes an offence involving moral turpitude, provided that such offence is committed by him in the course of his employment [Section 4(6)]

8. Notice of Opening, Change or Closure of the Establishment: (1) A notice shall be submitted by the employer to the controlling authority of the area within thirty days of any change in the name, address, employer or nature of business [Rule 3(2)].

(2) Where an employer intends to close down the business he shall submit a notice to the controlling authority of the area at least sixty days, before the intended closure [Rule 3(3)].

9. Application to Controlling Authority for direction: If an employer –
  (i) refuses to accept a nomination or to entertain an application for payment of gratuity, or
  (ii) issues a notice either specifying an amount of gratuity which is considered by the applicant less than what is payable or rejecting eligibility to payment of gratuity, or
  (iii) having received an application for payment of gratuity, fails to issue notice within fifteen days; the claimant employee, nominee, or legal heir, as the case may be, may within ninety days of the occurrence of the cause for the application, apply to the controlling authority for issuing a direction under sub-section (4) of Section 7 with as many extra copies as are the opposite party.

Provided that the controlling authority may accept any application on sufficient cause being shown by the applicant, after the expiry of the period of ninety days [Rule 10].

10. Appeal: Any person aggrieved by an order of the controlling authority may, within sixty days from the date of the receipt of the order, prefer an appeal to the Regional Labour Commissioner (Central) of the area, who has been appointed as the appellate authority by the Central Government.

Provided that the appellate authority may, if it is satisfied that the appellant was prevented by sufficient cause from preferring the appeal within the said period of sixty days, extend the said period by a further period of sixty days [Section 7(7)].

11. Machinery for Enforcement of the Act or Rules in Central Sphere: All Assistant Labour Commissioners (Central) have been appointed as Controlling Authorities and all the Regional Labour Commissioners (Central) as Appellate Authorities.

12. Powers of the Controlling Authority: The Controlling Authority for the purpose of conducting an inquiry as to the amount of gratuity payable to an employee or as to the admissibility of any claim of, or in relation to, an employee for payment of gratuity, or as to the person entitled to receive the gratuity, shall have the same powers as are vested in a court, under the Code of Civil Procedure, 1908, in respect of the following matters, namely –

    (a)   enforcing the attendance of any person or examining him on oath;

    (b)   requiring the discovery and production of documents;

    (c)   receiving evidence on affidavits; and

    (d)   issuing commissions for the examination of witnesses [Section 7(5)].

13. Recovery of Gratuity: If the amount of gratuity payable is not paid by the employer, within the prescribed name to the person entitled thereto, the controlling authority shall, on an application made to it in this behalf by the aggrieved person, issue a certificate for that amount to the Collector, who shall recover the same, together with compound interest thereon at the rate of nine per cent per annum, from the date of expiry of the prescribed time, as arrears of land revenue and pay the same to the person entitled thereto [Section 8].

14. Protection of Gratuity: No gratuity payable under the Payment of Gratuity Act and the rules made thereunder shall be liable to attachment in execution of any decree or order of any civil, revenue or criminal court [Section 13].

15. Penalties for Offences: (1) Whoever, for the purpose of avoiding any payment to be made by himself or of enabling any other persons to avoid such payment, knowingly makes or causes to be made any false statement or false representation, shall be punishable with imprisonment for a term which may extend to six months, or with fine which may extend to one thousand rupees, or with both [Section 9(1)].

(2) An employer who contravenes, or makes default in complying with, any of the provisions of in the Act or any rule or order made thereunder shall be punishable with imprisonment for a term which may extend to one year, or with fine which may extend to one thousand rupees, or with both;

Provided that if the offence relates to non-payment of any gratuity payable under the Payment of Gratuity Act, the employer shall be punishable with imprisonment for a term which shall not be less than three months unless the court trying the offence for reasons to be recorded by it in writing, is of opinion that a lesser term of imprisonment or the imposition of a fine would meet the ends of justice [Section 9(2)].

16. Display of Notice: The employer shall display conspicuously a notice at or near the entrance of the establishment in bold letters in English and in the language understood by the majority of the employees specifying the name of the officer with designation authorised by the employer to receive on his behalf notices under the Payment of Gratuity Act or the rules made thereunder [Rule 4].

17. Display of Abstract of the Act and Rules: The employer shall display an abstract of the Payment of Gratuity Act and the rules made thereunder in English and in the language understood by the majority of the employees at a conspicuous place at or near the main entrance of the establishment [Rule 20].

Points to Remember

- The Payment of Gratuity Act, 1972 is one of the Acts which provides social security. Under this Act, protection is provided to the workers against providential mishaps over which they have no control.

- Gratuity is one of the kinds of retirement benefits. It is received by an employee as reward for meritorious and long service.

- This Act is the Central Law.

- Act applies to (a) every factory, mine, oilfield, plantation, port and railway company; (b) every shop or establishment within the meaning of any law for the time being in force in relation to shops and establishments in a State, in which ten or more persons are employed, or were employed, on any day of the preceding twelve months; and (c) such other establishments or class of establishments in which, ten or more employees are employed, or were employed, on any day of the preceding twelve months, as the Central Government may, by notification, specify in this behalf.

- The gratuity is payable to an employee on the termination of his employment after he has rendered continuous service for not less than five years:

    (a) on his superannuation, or

    (b) on his retirement or resignation, or

    (c) on his death or disablement due to accident or disease subject to the provisions of this Act.

- The maximum amount of the gratuity payable under this Act is ₹ Ten lakhs.

- The Acts provides for nomination facility.

- Section 7 of the Act makes clear how the amount of gratuity is determined.

- The Act provides for the appointment of Inspectors for the purposes of this Act.

- Penalties are given in the Act for false statement, failure to pay contribution etc.

- There is the provision under Rule 20 of the Payment of Gratuity (Central) Rules of 1972 to display an abstract of the Act and the Rules made thereunder as given in Form 'U'.

Questions for Discussion

1. Explain the nature of gratuity payment and state the objects of the Payment of Gratuity Act of 1972.

2. Explain the scope and extent of the Payment of Gratuity Act of 1972.

3. How is the concept of continuous service defined in the Payment of Gratuity Act of 1972?

4. Explain the meaning of the concept of the Continuous service as used in the Payment of Gratuity Act.

5. Define the following as used in the Payment of Gratuity Act of 1972.
   (a) Appropriate Government
   (b) Employee and Employer
   (c) Controlling Authority
   (d) Wages

6. Who are the persons included in the family of a male and female according to the provisions of the Payment of Gratuity Act of 1972?

7. When is a gratuity payable? Explain various points relating to the payment of gratuity incorporated in Section 4 of the Act.

8. What are the provisions of the Payment of Gratuity Act of 1972 relating to the rate of the gratuity to be paid to the employees?

9. What are the circumstances in which gratuity becomes payable to an employee under the Payment of Gratuity Act of 1972?

10. When does an employee forfeit his right of gratuity?

11. Explain the provisions of the Payment of Gratuity Act, 1972 relating to compulsory insurance.

12. Describe the rules relating to the nomination by an employee under the Payment of Gratuity Act of 1972.

13. How is the amount of gratuity determined under the Payment of Gratuity Act, 1972?

14. Explain the mode of Payment of Gratuity under the Payment of Gratuity Act, 1972.

15. Explain the provisions of the Gratuity Act, 1972 relating to recovery of gratuity.

16. Describe the provisions as to the determination and recovery of the amount of gratuity under the Payment of Gratuity Act, 1972.

17. Who is the Controlling Authority under the Payment of Gratuity Act of 1972? Explain his powers and duties.

18. Can gratuity payable to an employee under the Payment of Gratuity Act of 1972 be attached in execution of any decree of a Court?

19. Explain the penalties for offences under the Payment of Gratuity Act, 1972.

20. Write notes on the following:
    (a) Objects of the Payment of Gratuity Act, 1972
    (b) Scope and extent of the Payment of Gratuity Act, 1972
    (c) Maximum amount of gratuity

(d) Provisions relating to better terms of gratuity

(e) Forfeiture of gratuity

(f) Power of the Appropriate Government to exempt an employee

(g) Compulsory insurance for payment of gratuity

(h) Provisions relating to nomination

(i) Determination of the amount of gratuity

(j) Appointment and powers of Inspectors

(k) Nature of penalties for various offences

(l) Exemption of the employer from liability in certain cases

(m) Salient Features and Provisions of the Payment of Gratuity Act, 1972.

(n) Eligibility for Gratuity.

21. Explain the nature of gratuity and state the salient features and provisions in the Payment of Gratuity Act of 1972.

Practical Problems

1. Mr. X is an employee of the renowned college. The Act of Payment of Gratuity, 1972 has been made applicable. Whether the gratuity payable to him on superannuation should include the period before take-over of that college for the purpose gratuity computed on the basis of the entire period of the service rendered by him?

   {**Hint:** Yes. He is entitled to gratuity computed on the basis of the entire period of service rendered by him [C. Sain V. the State of Haryana (1994) case}

2. On the date when Mr. X retired, the maximum amount of gratuity payable was provided at ₹ One Lakh. But later on in 2010 by an amendment ₹ Ten Lakhs has been provided as the maximum gratuity. Is this limit applicable to an employee who retired prior to the amendment came into effect?

   [**Hint:** No. The said limit of ₹ Ten Lakhs is not applicable. H. Chawdhary V. the controlling Authority under the Payment of Gratuity Act of 1972 [(1999) LIC 3422 (P and HHC)] Case]

3. Mr. A is the employer who makes default in complying with the provisions of this Act and the order made thereunder. What is the punishment for this offence?

[**Hint:** Mr. A is punishable with imprisonment for a term which shall not be less than three months but which may extend to one year, or with fine which shall not be less than ₹ Ten thousand but which may extend to ₹ Twenty thousand, or with both [Section 9 (2)].

4. Mr. X is the employee who's last drawn which included the basic salary and D.A. is ₹ 52,000 per month. He has completed thirty five years of service. Calculate the amount of gratuity payable to him.

[**Hint:** ₹ 10,50,000. But he is entitled to receive ₹ Ten Lakhs as gratuity which is the maximum].

5. The employees of XYZ Co. Ltd. claim that incentive bonus paid to them should be included in wages for the purposes of calculating gratuity payable to them. Can their claim be maintained?

[**Hint:** No. Wages do not include any bonus, commission etc. for the purposes of this Act according to Section 2 (5) of the Act. Kirloskar Brothers Ltd. V. Appellate Authority under the Payment of Gratuity Act (2003) III L.L.J. 1035 (M.P) case].

Chapter 4...

The Apprentices Act, 1961

Contents ...

- 4.1 Introduction
- 4.2 Basic Objective and Applicability of the Act
    - 4.2.1 The Scope and Application of the Act [Section 1]
- 4.3 Meaning and Definitions of 'Apprentice' and 'Apprenticeship Training' [Section 2 (aa) and Section 2 (aaa)]
- 4.4 Definitions of the Words, Terms etc. as given in Section 2 of the Act
- 4.5 Provisions of Section 3-A in respect of Training Places for the S.C. and the S.T. in Designated Trade
    - 4.5.1 Provisions of Section 3-B in respect of Reservation of Training Places for Other Backward Classes in Designated Trades
- 4.6 Contract of Apprenticeship and Novation of Contract of Apprenticeship [Section 4 and Section 5]
    - 4.6.1 Nature of Apprenticeship Contract
    - 4.6.2 Provisions of Section 4 of this Act Relating to Contract of Apprenticeship
    - 4.6.3 Novation of Contract of Apprenticeship
- 4.7 Termination of Apprenticeship Contract [Section 7]
- 4.8 Qualifications for being Engaged as an Apprentice [Section 3]
- 4.9 Period of "Apprenticeship Training" [Section 6]
- 4.10 Number of Apprentices for a Designated Trade [Section 8]
- 4.11 Provisions of Section 9 relating to "Practical and Basic Training of Apprentices" and the Provisions of Section 10 relating to "Related Instruction of Apprentices"
    - 4.11.1 Provisions relating to Practical and Basic Training
    - 4.11.2 Provisions of Section 10 relating to Related Instruction of Apprentices
- 4.12 Obligations of Employers and Apprentices
    - 4.12.1 Obligations of Employers under Section 11
    - 4.12.2 Obligation of Payment under Section 13
    - 4.12.3 Liability of an Employer for Compensation for Injury under Section 16
    - 4.12.4 Obligation of an Employer in Respect of Maintaining the Records and Furnishing the Returns under Section 19
    - 4.12.5 Obligation of Apprentices

4.13 Provisions of Section 14 of the Act relating to "Health, Safety and Welfare of Apprentices"

4.14 Provisions of Section 15 of the Act relating to "Hours of Work, Overtime, Leave and Holidays"

4.15 Settlement of Disputes [Section 20]

4.16 Holding of Test, Grant of Certificate to Apprentice and Conclusion of Training [Section 21]

4.17 Offer and Acceptance of Employment under Section 22 of the Act

4.18 The Authorities Appointed under the Act for the Administration of the Act

    4.18.1 Constitution of Councils

    4.18.2 Vacancies not to Invalidate Acts and Proceedings [Section 25]

    4.18.3 Appointments of the Central Apprenticeship Adviser and the State Apprenticeship Adviser [Section 26]

    4.18.4 Appointments of Deputy Advisers and Assistant Apprenticeship Advisers [Section 27]

    4.18.5 Powers of the Entry, Inspection etc. of the Apprenticeship Advisers under Section 29 of the Act

    4.18.6 Under Section 28 the Apprenticeship Advisers are the Public Servants

    4.18.7 Provisions of Section 34 relating to 'Delegation of Powers'

4.19 Offences and Penalties

    4.19.1 Nature of Offences and Penalties for those Offences in respect of any Employer or any Other Person [Section 30]

    4.19.2 Offences by Companies [Section 32]

4.20 Cognizance of Offences [Section 33]

4.21 Miscellaneous Provisions of the Act

    4.21.1 Provisions of Section 35 relating to Construction of References

    4.21.2 Protection of Action Takes in Good Faith

    4.21.3 Power to Make Rules [Section 37]

- Points to Remember
- Questions for Discussion
- Practical Problems

Learning Objectives...

After going through this chapter, you will be able to know :
- The objects, applications of the Act, and definitions as given in the Act
- Provisions of the Act relating to apprentices and their training
- Various Authorities under the Act
- Offences and Penalties for the offences under the Act

4.1 Introduction

Young citizens are considered as the wealth of the nation in the form of human resources. Hence, they must be properly educated and trained. The question of undertaking legislation for regulating the training of apprentices in the industrial sector was under the consideration of the Government for a long time.

The Expert Committee which went into the question recommended such legislation. Before the passing of the Apprentices Act of 1961, apprentices were governed by the only standing provisions contained in the Model Standing Orders framed under the Industrial Employment (Standing Orders) Act of 1946. With the development of industries in the public as well as private sectors, it felt necessary to make certain laws for the regulation and control of training and employment of apprentices. Therefore, the Apprentices Act of 1961 was passed. Under this Act, employers in specified industries to which this Act is applicable are obliged to train a certain number of apprentices for designated trades according to prescribed national standards. The definition of "Designated trade" is given in Section 2 (e) of the Act. Now let us consider various provisions of the Act.

4.2 Basic Objective and Applicability of the Act

The basic objective behind the enactment is to provide for the regulation and control of training and employment of apprentices and for various matters connected therewith.

The Act seeks to promote a conducive climate for training and imparting skills on the youths to prepare them to meet the growing needs of the fast expanding industries, trade as well as commerce to be gainfully employed therein.

Besides this, the Act also seeks to create such healthy conditions with the employers wherein apprentices may not be exploited and victimised. Thus, the Act is a security and welfare legislation.

The Government of India considered it necessary to utilise the facilities available for the training of apprentices and the development of their skills. Hence, to ensure their training and development in accordance with the programmes, standards, needs and so on made clear by the expert bodies, the Apprentices Act of 1961 was enacted.

The Act came into force on 1st March, 1962. This Act has been amended many times so far. By amending the Act in 1986, the scope of "Designated Trade" has been widened and the "National Council" was re-named. Thereafter, by inserting Section 7 (4) and increasing the penalty under Section 31, the Act was amended in 1997.

The Apprentices Rules have also been amended from time to time. By amending the Rules in 2013, the amount of payment of stipend to apprentices has been increased under Rule 11 of the Apprentices Rules of 1992 w.e.f. 27-09-2013.

4.2.1 The Scope and Application of the Act [Section 1]

The Act extends to the whole of India [Section 1 (2)]. It applies to any area or to any industry in any area if the Central Government of India by notification in the official Gazette specifies that area or that industry to which it shall apply.

The provisions of Section 1 (4) make it clear that the provisions of this Act shall not apply to:

(i) any area or to any industry in any area unless the Central Government by notification in the Official Gazette specifies that area or industry as an area or industry to which the said provisions shall apply with effect from such date as may be provided in the notification;

(ii) any such special apprentice scheme for imparting training to apprentices as may be notified by the Central Government in the Official Gazette.

It may be noted that the provision has been made in the Act for the reservation of training places in every designated trade by the employer for the Scheduled Castes and Scheduled Tribes.

This Act does not apply to the contracts of personal service entered on behalf of minors. Such contracts do not stand on the same footing as a contract of apprentice or contract of marriage of a minor.

4.3 Meaning and Definitions of "Apprentice" and "Apprenticeship Training" [Section 2 (aa) and Section 2 (aaa)]

The word 'Apprentice' is derived from the French word *'Apprendre'*. *Apprendre* means to learn. The meaning of 'Apprentice' as given in the Oxford Dictionary is "*a learner of craft who is bound by legal agreement to serve an employer for a period of years, with a view to learn some handicraft, trade etc. in which the employer is reciprocally bound to instruct him*". Thus, in simple words, an apprentice is one who is learning a trade, a craft etc. while apprenticeship means a state of being an apprentice.

According to Section 2 (aa), "*Apprentice means a person who is undergoing apprenticeship training in pursuance of a contract of apprenticeship.*" While, "apprenticeship training" means a course of training in any industry or establishment undergone in pursuance of a contract of apprenticeship and under prescribed terms and conditions which may be different for different categories of apprentices [Section 2 (aaa)].

From the definitions of an apprentice and apprenticeship training, the following important points become clear.

1. It is inherent in the word 'apprentice', there is no element of employment as such in a trade or in industry wherein he takes training.

2. It implies that there is only adequate provision for training to enable the trainee after completion of his course of training to be suitably employed as a regular worker.

3. The important object or purpose in respect of apprenticeship is to impart on the part of the employer and to accept on the part of the other concerned person learning under certain agreed terms as per the contract of apprenticeship [E.S.I. Corporation V. Tata Engg. and Co. AIR 1976 SC 66].

4. Certain amount of payment can be made during the apprenticeship by whatever name it is called [E.S.I. Corporation V. Tata Engg. and Co. AIR 1976 SC 66].

5. An apprentice has to obey his master or employer in all his lawful commands. He has to take care of the property of his employer and also to endeavour to learn his trade. He has also to perform all the conditions of the contract of apprenticeship not contrary to law.

6. Apprentices under this Act are mere trainees and are not employees or workers. They are not employed for wages. Thus, the difference between an apprentice and a worker is that an apprentice is a person who is engaged for learning a trade or craft and he is paid a stipend during the apprenticeship period while a worker is a person who is employed for doing the work entrusted to him for which he is appointed and he is paid wages.

7. There is no compulsion on the employers to employ the apprentices after the period of apprenticeship is over.

4.4 Definitions of the Words, Terms etc. as given in Section 2 of the Act

Definitions of certain words, terms etc. are stated in Section 2 of the Act. We have already considered the definitions of 'Apprentice' and 'Apprenticeship Training'. The other remaining definitions of the terms, words etc. which are stated in Section 2 of the Act are as follows.

1. **"All India Council"** means the All India Council of Technical Education established by the resolution of the Government of India in the former Ministry of Education No. F. 16-10/44-E-III, dt. 30-11-1945; [Section 2 (a)].

2. **"Apprenticeship Adviser"** means the Central Apprenticeship Adviser appointed under sub-section (1) of Section 26 or the State Apprenticeship Adviser appointed under sub-section (2) of that Section; [Section 2 (b)]. Provisions relating to the appointment of Apprenticeship Advisers, Deputy and Assistant Apprenticeship Advisers, their status, powers etc. are given in Sections 26, 27, 28 and 29 of the Act.

3. **"Apprenticeship Council"** means the Central Apprenticeship Council or the State Apprenticeship Council established under sub-section (1) of Section 24; [Section 2 (c)]. The constitution of the Central Apprenticeship Council and the State Apprenticeship Council is given in Section 24 of the Act.

4. **"Appropriate Government"** means :
   1. **In relation to –**
      (a) the Central Apprenticeship Council, or (aa) the Regional Boards, or (aaa) the practical training of graduate or technical apprenticeship or of technician (vocational) apprentices, or;
      (b) any establishment of any railway, major port, mine or oilfield, or;
      (c) any establishment owned, controlled or managed by –
         (i) the Central Government or a department of the Central Government;
         (ii) a company in which not less than fifty-one per cent of the share capital is held by the Central Government or partly by that Government and partly by one or more State Governments;
         (iii) a corporation (including a co-operative society) established by or under a Central Act, which is owned, controlled or managed by the Central Government, [Section 2 (d) (1)].
   2. **In relation to –**
      (a) a State Apprenticeship Council, or;
      (b) any establishment other than an establishment specified in sub-clause (1) of this clause the State Government [Section 2 (d) (2)].

5. **"Board or State Council of Technical Education"** means the Board or State Council of Technical Education established by the State Government; [Section 2 (dd)]. The Board or State Council of Technical Education is one of the Authorities appointed under Section 23 for the administration of the Act.

6. **"Designated trade"** means any trade or occupation or any subject field in engineering or technology or any vocational course which the Central Government, after consultation with the Central Apprenticeship Council, may, by notification in the Official Gazette, specify as a designated trade for the purposes of the Act [Section 2 (e)].

The above mentioned definition of 'Designated Trade' implies that unless the Central Government issues a notification specifying the trade, occupation or subject field of the corporation, company etc. as 'designated trade' for the purposes of this Act, the trade, occupation or subject field of that concern, corporation, company etc is not designated trade and the provisions of this Act are not applicable [Patel P. K. S. and others V Gujarat State Land Development Corporation Ltd. and others (1993) 1 LLJ 916 (Guj)].

In exercising the powers conferred by sub-section e of Section 2 of this Act and after consulting the Central Apprenticeship Council, the Central Government has specified certain subject fields for vocational courses as designated trade for the purposes of this Act.

These fields include banking, accountancy and auditing, marketing, salesmanship, office secretary-ship, stenography, dairying, poultry farming, health care, child-care and nutrition, food preservation, crop-cultivation, sericulture, apiculture, floriculture, plant protection, mechanical servicing, textile designing etc.

7. **"Employer"** means any person who employs one or more other persons to do any work in an establishment for remuneration and includes any person entrusted with the supervision and control of employees in such establishment; [Section 2 (f)].

8. **"Establishment"** includes any pace where any industry is carried on and where an establishment consists of different departments or has branches, whether situated in the same place or at different places, all such departments or branches shall be treated as part of that establishment [Section 2 (9)].

9. **"Establishment in private sector"** means an establishment which is not an establishment in the public sector; [Section 2 (h)].

10. **"Establishment in public sector"** means an establishment owned, controlled or managed by –
    (i) the Government or a department of the Government;
    (ii) a Government company as defined in Section 617 of the Companies Act, 1956 (1 of 1956);
    (iii) a corporation (including a co-operative society) established by or under a Central, Provincial or State Act, which is owned, controlled or managed by the Government;
    (iv) a local authority; [Section 2 (i)].

11. **"Graduate or technician apprentice"** means an apprentice who holds, or is undergoing training in order that he may hold a degree or diploma in engineering or technology or equivalent qualification granted by any institution recognised by the Government and undergoes apprenticeship training in any such subject field in engineering or technology as may be prescribed; [Section 2 (j)].

12. **"Industry"** means any industry or business in which any trade, occupation or subject field in engineering or technology or any vocational course may be specified as a designated trade; [Section 2 (k)].

13. **"National Council"** means the National Council for Training in Vocational Trades established by the resolution of the Government of India in the Ministry of Labour (Directorate General of Resettlement and Employment) No. TR/E.P.-24-56, dated 21-8-1956 and re-named as the National Council for Vocational Training by the resolution of the Government of India in the Ministry of Labour (Directorate General of Employment and Training) No. DGET./12/21/80-TC, dated 30-9-1981 [Section 2 (l)].

14. **"Prescribed"** means prescribed by the rules made under this Act; [Section 2 (m)].

15. **"Regional Board"** means any Board of Apprenticeship Training registered under the Societies Registration Act, 1860 (21 of 1860), at Bombay, Calcutta, Madras or Kanpur; [Section 2 (mm)].

16. **"State"** includes a Union Territory [Section 2 (n)].

17. **"State Council"** means a State Council for Training in Vocational Trades established by the State Government; [Section 2(o)].

18. **"State Government"** in relation to a Union Territory, means the Administrator thereof; [Section 2 (p)].

19. **"Technician (vocational) apprentice"** means an apprentice who holds or is undergoing training in order that he may hold a certificate in a vocational course involving two years of study after the completion of the secondary stage of school education recognized by the All-India Council and undergoes apprenticeship training in any such subject field in any vocational course as may be prescribed; [Section 2 (pp)].

20. **"Trade apprentice"** means an apprentice who undergoes apprenticeship training in any such trade or occupation as may be prescribed; [Section 2 (q)].

21. **"Worker"** means any person who is employed for wages in any kind of work and who gets his wages directly from the employer but shall not include an apprentice referred to in clause (aa); [Section 2 (r)].

4.5 Provisions of Section 3-A in respect of Training Places for the S.C. and the S.T. in Designated Trade

1. In every designated trade, training places shall be reserved by the employer for the Scheduled Castes and the Scheduled Tribes and where there is more than one designated trade in an establishment, such training places shall be reserved also on the basis of the total number of apprentices in all the designated trades in such establishment [Section 3-A (1)].

2. The number of training places to be reserved for the Scheduled Castes and the Scheduled Tribes under sub-section (1) shall be such as may be prescribed, having regard to the population of the Scheduled Castes and the Scheduled Tribes in the State concerned [Section 3-A (2)].

In this section, the expressions "Scheduled Castes" and "Scheduled Tribes" shall have the meanings as in clauses (24) and (25) of article 366 of the Constitution [Explanation to Sections 3-A].

4.5.1 Provisions of Section 3-B in respect of Reservation of Training Places for Other Backward Classes in Designated Trades

Section 3-B provides for the reservation of training places for other backward classes in designated trades. These provisions are as under –

1. In every designated trade, training places shall be reserved by the employer for the Other Backward Classes and where there is more than one designated trade in an establishment, such training places shall be reserved also on the basis of the total number of apprentices in all the designated trades in such establishment [Section 3-B (1)].

2. The number of training places to be reserved for the Other Backward Classes under sub-section (1) shall be such as may be prescribed, having regard to the population of the Other Backward Classes in the State concerned [Section 3-B (2)]. Thus, in this Act, the provisions have been made in respect of the reservation of training places not only for S.C. and S.T., but also for other backward classes in designated trades.

4.6 Contract of Apprenticeship and Novation of Contract of Apprenticeship [Section 4 and Section 5]

Provisions relating to contract of apprenticeship in respect of minor apprentices, registration of the contract, terms and conditions in contract of apprenticeship training etc. have been made in Section 4 of the Act while Section 5 deals with Novation of contracts of apprenticeship. Now let us consider various aspects relating to these topics.

4.6.1 Nature of Apprenticeship Contract

The essence of a contract of apprenticeship between the employer or master on the one hand and an apprentice on the other hand is that the employer or master should teach and guide and the apprentice should learn and serve accordingly.

It is this contract to teach to guide and to learn that distinguishes it from an ordinary contract of hiring and service. Therefore, its nature is different from other contracts. Apprentices are mere trainees and not employees or workers and are not employed for wages. Moreover, the employer is not bound to employ the apprentices after the period of their apprenticeship is over.

4.6.2 Provisions of Section 4 of this Act relating to 'Contract of Apprenticeship'

1. No person shall be engaged as an apprentice to undergo apprenticeship training in a designated trade unless such person or, if he is minor, his guardian has entered into a contract of apprenticeship with the employer [Section 4 (1)].

2. The apprenticeship training shall be deemed to have commenced on the date on which the contract of apprenticeship has been entered into under sub-section (1) [Section 4 (2)].

3. Every contract of apprenticeship may contain such terms and conditions as may be agreed to by the parties to the contract [Section 4 (3)]. It is provided that no such term or condition shall be inconsistent with any provision of this Act or any rule made thereunder [Proviso to Section 4 (3)].

4. Every contract of apprenticeship entered into under sub-section (1) shall be sent by the employer within such period as may be prescribed to the Apprenticeship Adviser for registration [Section 4 (4)].

5. The Apprenticeship Adviser shall not register a contract of apprenticeship unless he is satisfied that the person described as an apprentice in the contract is qualified under this Act for being engaged as an apprentice to undergo apprenticeship training in the designated trade specified in the contract [Section 4 (5)].

6. Where the Central Government, after consulting the Central Apprenticeship Council, makes any rule varying the terms and conditions of apprenticeship training of any category of apprentices undergoing such training, then, the terms and conditions of every contract of apprenticeship relating to that category of apprentices and subsisting immediately before the making of such rule be deemed to have been modified accordingly [Section 4 (6)].

From these provisions mentioned above, we come to know the following important points relating to "Contract of Apprenticeship".

(a) Registration of Contract of Apprenticeship: For the purpose of engaging any person as an apprentice to undergo apprenticeship training in a designated trade; the following two conditions are required to be satisfied.

(i) A contract of apprenticeship must be entered into between the apprentice, or with his guardian if he is a minor and the employer; and

(ii) That contract must be submitted to the Apprenticeship Adviser appointed under Section 26 of this Act by the employer for registration. The Apprenticeship Adviser shall not register the contract unless he is satisfied that the person described as an apprentice in the contract is qualified under this Act for being engaged as an apprentice to undergo the apprenticeship training in the designated trade specified in the contract submitted to him.

In this context of registration of contract of apprenticeship, it may be noted that non-registration of the contract of apprenticeship is not void and illegal. The non-registration of the contract does not change the character of the apprentice and the apprentices do not acquire the status of workman. In U.P. State Electricity Board V Shiv Mohan Singh and others case [2005 I L.L.J. 117 (S.C.)], it was held that the term "shall" mentioned in Section 4 (4) of this Act is merely directory and not mandatory.

(b) Apprentices engaged under this Act as per the Contract of Apprenticeship are Merely Trainees and not Workers: A person was engaged as an apprentice. He claimed that there was no valid and legal contract of apprenticeship for the reason that the contract made in the first instance was cancelled and the second contract was antedated. He contended that his services could be terminated only after the notice and payment of retrenchment compensation under the Industrial Dispute Act. It was held in that case i.e. Raj Kumar Srivastava V. U.P. State [1996 – I L.L.J. 1054 (A11)] case that he himself applied for engagement as the apprentice under the Apprentices Act of 1961 and also signed both the contracts under the provisions of that Act. As Section 18 of the Act makes it clear that every apprentice undergoing the training shall be a trainee not a worker. Hence, the person engaged as an apprentice was rightly held not to be a workman.

(c) Commencement of Apprenticeship Training: The training of apprenticeship is deemed to have commenced on the date on which the contract of apprenticeship is entered into [Section 4 (2)]

(d) Minor as an Apprentice: A contract of apprenticeship in respect of a minor falls in the category of necessary services as it is for the benefit of a minor. A minor can enter into a contract of apprenticeship [Section 4 (1)] if he satisfies the conditions laid down in the Act which are as follows.

  (i) He has attained the age of fourteen years.
  (ii) He satisfies the prescribed standards of education and physical fitness as per the provisions of the Act.
  (iii) His guardian has entered into a contract of apprenticeship with the employer.

(e) Terms and Conditions in the Contract of Apprenticeship Training: The contract of apprenticeship may contain such terms and conditions as may be agreed by the parties to the contract. However, such terms and conditions must be consistent with the provisions of the Act and the Rules made thereunder.

(f) Modification of Terms and Conditions: The terms and conditions of a contract of apprenticeship can be modified subject to the provisions of Section 4 (6) of the Act.

4.6.3 Novation of 'Contract of Apprenticeship'

Sometimes, it becomes difficult for some reason to fulfil the obligations under the contract and a new contract is entered into in the place of old existing contract subject to the provisions of the Act. The provisions relating to Novation of contracts of apprenticeship have been made in Section 5 of the Act. But before studying the provisions relating to "Novation of Contracts of Apprenticeship", let us understand the meaning of 'Novation of contract'.

4.6.3.1 Meaning of 'Novation of Contract'

When a promisee agrees to accept performance of a contract from a third party, an original or old contract is considered to be null and void along with all rights and obligations of the old contract. It is technically known as novation. Thus, in other words, novation of contract means a substitution of a new contract in the place of the old existing contract. Novation discharges the original contract. New contract can be entered into between the same parties or between different parties but the consideration of the old contract must be mutually discharged.

E.g. X borrows ₹ 50,000 from Y under a contract. Thereafter, X, Y and M agree that Y shall hence forth accept M as his debtor and M shall accept Y as his creditor for the payment of X's debt of ₹ 50,000. As a result of this new contract, old debt of X to Y has come to an end and a new debt from M to Y has been contracted. Here one important thing must be noted that novation should take place before the expiry of the time or the performance of the original contract.

4.6.3.2 Provisions of Section 5 of the Act relating to "Novation of Contracts of Apprenticeship"

It is stated in Section 5 of the Act that, *"Where an employer with whom a contract of apprenticeship has been entered into, is for any reason, unable to fulfil his obligations under the contract and with the approval of the Apprenticeship Adviser it is agreed between the employer, the apprentice or his guardian and any other employer that the apprentice shall be engaged as an apprentice under the other employer for the unexpired portion of the period of apprenticeship training, the agreement, on registration with the Apprenticeship Adviser, shall be deemed to be the contract of apprenticeship between the apprentice or his guardian and other employer, and on and from the date of such registration, the contract of apprenticeship with the first employer shall terminate and no obligation under that contract shall be enforceable at the instance of any party to the contract against the other party thereto."*

From the provisions of Section 5, we come to know the following requirements so far as the novation of a contract of apprenticeship is concerned.

(a) For any reason, the employer with whom the contract of apprenticeship has been entered into is unable to fulfil his obligations under the contract.

(b) With the approval of the Apprenticeship Adviser, it is agreed between the employer, the apprentice or the guardian if the apprentice is minor and any other employer that the apprentice shall be engaged as an apprentice under the other employer for the unexpired portion of the period of apprenticeship training.

(c) Such agreement must be approved by the Apprenticeship Adviser, and

(d) The agreement is registered with the Apprenticeship Adviser.

When the agreement is registered with the Apprenticeship Adviser, it is deemed to be the contract of apprenticeship between the apprentice or if he is minor, with his guardian and the other employer. Further on, and from the date of such registration of the contract of apprenticeship, the contract of apprenticeship with the first employer is terminated and no obligation under the contract is enforceable at the instance of any party to the contract against the other party thereto.

4.7 Termination of Apprenticeship Contract [Section 7]

The provisions of Section 7 make clear as to when the contract of apprenticeship is terminated and also the procedure in respect of the termination of apprenticeship contract. These provisions are given below.

1. The contract of apprenticeship shall terminate on the expiry of the period of apprenticeship training [Section 7 (1)].

2. Either party to a contract of apprenticeship may make an application to the Apprenticeship Adviser for the termination of the contract, and when such application is made, shall send by post a copy thereof to the other party to the contract [Section 7 (2)].

3. After considering the contents of the application and the objections, if any, filed by the other party, the Apprenticeship Adviser may, by order in writing, terminate the contract, if he is satisfied that the parties to the contract or any of them have or has failed to carry out the terms and conditions of the contract and it is desirable in the interests of the parties or any of them to terminate the same [Section 7 (3)].

It is provided that where a contract is terminated:

(a) for failure on the part of the employer to carry out the terms and conditions of the contract, the employer shall pay to the apprentice such compensation as may be prescribed;

(b) for such failure on the part of the apprentice, the apprentice or his guardian shall refund to the employer as cost of training such amount as may be determined by the Apprenticeship Adviser [Proviso to Section 7 (3)].

4. Notwithstanding anything contained in any other provision of this Act, where a contract of apprenticeship has been terminated by the Apprenticeship Adviser before the expiry of the period of apprenticeship training and a new contract of apprenticeship is being entered into with a new employer, the Apprenticeship Adviser may, if he is satisfied that the contract of apprenticeship with the previous

employer could not be completed because of any lapse on the part of the previous employer, permit the period of apprenticeship training already undergone by the apprentice with his previous employer to be included in the period apprenticeship training to be undertaken with the new employer [Section 7 (4)]. Thus, the contract of apprenticeship is terminated –

(i) on the expiry of the period of apprenticeship training, and

(ii) by the order in writing terminating the contract by the Apprenticeship Adviser.

The procedure that is followed in this respect is as follows.

Any of the parties to a contract of apprenticeship can make an application for the termination of the contract to the Apprenticeship Adviser. When any such application is received, the Apprenticeship Adviser sends its copy by post to the other concerned party to the contract. After considering the contents of the application and objections, if any, filed by that other concerned party, the Apprenticeship Adviser takes the action to terminate the contract. But before doing so, the Adviser must be satisfied that –

(i) the parties to the contract or any one of them have or has failed to carry out the terms and conditions of the contract, and

(ii) it is desirable in the interests of the parties or any of them to terminate the contract of apprenticeship.

It is further provided that,

(i) when an apprenticeship contract is terminated because of the failure on the part of the employer to carry out the terms and conditions of the contract, the employer is required to pay to the concerned apprentice such compensation as may be prescribed, and

(ii) when an apprenticeship contract is terminated for failure on the part of the apprentice to carry out the terms and conditions of the contract, the apprentice or if he is a minor, his guardian has to refund to the employer as the cost of training such amount as may be determined by the Apprenticeship Adviser.

When an apprenticeship contract is terminated on its novation, an apprentice under one employer is transferred to some other employer for the remaining term of the apprenticeship contract [Section 5].

4.8 Qualifications for being Engaged as an Apprentice [Section 3]

A person shall not be qualified for being engaged as an apprentice to undergo apprenticeship training in any designated trade, unless he –

(a) is not less than fourteen years of age, and

(b) satisfies such standards of education and physical fitness as may be prescribed [Section 3].

It is also provided that different standards may be prescribed in relation to apprenticeship training in different designated trades and for different categories of apprentices [Proviso to Section 3].

Thus, it becomes clear from these provisions of Section 3 that the age of an apprentice undergoing apprenticeship training in any designated trade must be at least 14 years of age and above and he must satisfy the standards of education and physical fitness as prescribed for the apprenticeship training.

Further, it is also provided that different standards may be prescribed by the Central Government in relation to apprenticeship training in different designated trades and for different categories of apprentices. In pursuance of the power given to the Central Government under Section 37 (1) to make Rules, it is laid down in the Apprenticeship Rules of 1962 that a person shall be eligible for being engaged as –

(i) a trade apprentice, if he satisfies the minimum educational qualifications as specified in Schedule I to the said Rules of 1962.

(ii) a graduate or technician or technician vocational apprentice, if he satisfies one of the minimum qualifications specified in Schedule I-A to the Apprenticeship Rules of 1962, [Rule 3], and

(iii) an apprentice if he satisfies the minimum standards of physical fitness specified in Schedule II to the said Rules of 1962 [Rule 4]. Rules 3 and 4 of the Apprenticeship Rules of 1962 are given below for your information.

Rule 3: Standard of Education

1. A person shall be eligible for being engaged as trade apprentice if he satisfies the minimum educational qualifications as specified in Schedule I.
2. A person shall be eligible for being engaged as a graduate or technician or technician (vocational) apprentice if he satisfies one of the minimum educational qualifications specified in Schedule I-A:

Provided that –

(a) no Engineering Graduate or Diploma holder or Vocational Certificate holder who had training or job experience for a period of one year or more, after the attainment of these qualifications shall be eligible for being engaged as an apprentice under the Act;

(b) no Sandwich Course Student shall be eligible for being engaged as an apprentice under the Act after passing the final examination of the technical institution wherein such student is undergoing the course, unless so approved by the Regional Central Apprenticeship Advisers;

(c) a person who has been a Graduate or Technician or Technician (Vocational) apprentice under the Act and in whose case the contract of apprenticeship was terminated for any reason whatsoever shall not be eligible for being engaged as an apprentice again under the Act without the prior approval of the Apprenticeship Adviser.

Rule 4: Standard Physical Fitness

1. A person shall be eligible for being engaged as an apprentice if he satisfies the minimum standards of physical fitness specified in Schedule II.

Provided that a person who has undergone institutional training in a school or other institution recognised by or affiliated to the National Council or the All India Council or a Statutory University or a State Board of Technical Education and has passed the examination or tests conducted by these bodies, or is undergoing institutional training in a school or institution so recognised or affiliated in order that he may acquire a degree or diploma in engineering or technology or certificate in vocational course or equivalent qualification shall, if he has already undergone medical examination in accordance with the rules for the admission to the school or institution, be deemed to have complied with the provisions of this rule.

The provisions in respect of every designated trade, training places are reserved for Scheduled Castes, Schedule Tribes and Other Backward Classes in Sections 3-A and 3-B. These provisions have already been considered.

4.9 Period of "Apprenticeship Training" [Section 6]

The provisions relating to the period of apprenticeship training for trade apprentices, graduate technician apprentices etc. have been made in Section 6 of the Act which are as follows.

The period of apprenticeship training, which shall be specified in the contract of apprenticeship, shall be as follows:

1. in the case of trade apprentices who, having undergone institutional training in a school or other institution recognised by the National Council, have passed the trade tests or examinations conducted by that Council or by an institution recognised by that Council the period of apprenticeship training shall be such as may be determined by that Council or by an institution recognised by that Council [Section 6 (a)].

2. in the case of trade apprentices who, having undergone institutional training in a school or other institution affiliated to or recognised by a Board or State Council of Technical Education or any other authority which the Central Government may, by notification in the Official Gazette specify in this behalf, have passed the trade tests or examinations conducted by that Board or State Council or authority, the period of apprenticeship training shall be such as may be prescribed [Section 6 (aa)].

3. in the case of other trade apprentices, the period of apprenticeship training shall be such as may be prescribed [Section 6 (b)].

4. In the case of graduate or technician apprentices, technician (vocational) apprentices, the period of apprenticeship training shall be such as may be prescribed [Section 6 (c)].

4.10 Number of Apprentices for a Designated Trade [Section 8]

The Central Government is empowered under Section 8 to determine for each designated trade the ratio of trade apprentices to the workers other than unskilled workers in that trade. In determining this ratio; which factors are to be considered are made clear in Section 8 (2) of this Act. The provisions of Section 8 are given below.

1. "The Central Government shall after consulting the Central Apprenticeship Council, by order notified in the Official Gazette, determine for each designated trade the ratio of trade apprentices to workers other than unskilled workers in that trade [Section 8 (1)].

    It is provided that nothing contained in this sub-section shall be deemed to prevent any employer from engaging a number of trade apprentices in excess of the ratio determined under this sub-section [Provisio to Section 8 (1)].

2. In determining the ratio under sub-section (1), the Central Government shall have regard to the facilities available for apprenticeship training under this Act in the designated trade concerned as well as to the facilities that may have to be made available by an employer for the training a graduate or technician apprentices technician (vocational) apprentices, if any, in pursuance of any notice issued to him under sub-section (3A) by the Central Apprenticeship Adviser or such other person as is referred to in that sub-section [Section 8 (2)].

3. The Apprenticeship Adviser may, by notice in writing, require an employer to engage such number of trade apprentices within the ratio determined by the Central Government for any designated trade in his establishment, to undergo apprenticeship training in that trade and the employer shall comply with such requisition [Section 8 (3)].

It is provided, that in making any requisition under this sub-section, the Apprenticeship Adviser shall have regard to the facilities actually available in the establishment concerned [Proviso 1 to Section 8 (3)].

It is provided further that the Apprenticeship Adviser may, on a representation made to him by an employer and keeping in view the more realistic employment potential, training facilities and other relevant factors, permit him to engage such number of apprentices for a designated trade as is lesser than the number arrived at by the ratio for that trade, not being lesser than fifty per cent of the number so arrived, subject to the condition that the employer shall engage apprentices in other trades in excess in number equivalent to such shortfall [Proviso 2 to Section 8 (3)].

(4) The Central Apprenticeship Adviser or any other person not below the rank of an Assistant Apprenticeship Adviser authorised by the Central Apprenticeship Adviser in writing in this behalf shall, having regard to –

   (i) the number of marginal persons (including technical and supervisory persons) employed in a designated trade;

(ii) the number of management trainees engaged in the establishment;

(iii) the totality of the training facilities available in a designated trade; and

(iv) such other factors as he may consider fit in the circumstances of the case, by notice in writing, require an employer to impart training to such number of graduate or technician apprentices [technician (vocational) apprentices], in such trade in his establishment as may be specified in such notice and the employer shall comply with such requisition [Section 8 (3-A)].

In this sub-section the expression "management trainee" means a person who is engaged by an employer for undergoing a course of training in the establishment of the employer (not being apprenticeship training under this Act) subject to the condition that on successful completion of such training, such person shall be employed by the employer on a regular basis [Explanation to Section 8 (3-A)].

(5) Several employers may join together for the purpose of providing practical training to the apprentices under them by moving them between their respective establishments [Section 8 (4)].

(6) Where, having regard to the public interest, a number of apprentices in excess of the ratio determined by the Central Government [or in excess of the number specified in a notice issued under sub-section (3A)] should, in the opinion of the appropriate Government be trained, the appropriate Government may require employers to train the additional number of apprentices [Section 8 (5)].

(7) Every employer to whom such requisition as aforesaid is made shall comply with the requisition if the Government concerned makes available such additional facilities and such additional financial assistance as are considered necessary by the Apprenticeship Adviser for the training of the additional number of apprentices [Section 8 (6)].

(8) Any employer not satisfied with the decision of the Apprenticeship Adviser under sub-section (6), may make a reference to the Central Apprenticeship Council and such reference shall be decided by a Committee thereof appointed by that Council for the purpose and the decision of that Committee shall be final [Section 8 (7)].

In order to attract the provisions of this Act, it is necessary that a person claiming to be an apprentice is undergoing apprenticeship training in a designated trade in an establishment as defined in this Act. In M.P. Electricity Board V. B. K. Pandey Case [(1991) I L.L.J. 323 (M.P.)], it was held that the Board has not been notified as designated trade by the Central Government in the Official Gazette and hence the concerned respondents (defendants in the suit) are not apprentices.

4.11 Provisions of Section 9 relating to "Practical and Basic Training of Apprentices" and the Provisions of Section 10 relating to "Related Instruction of Apprentices"

Every apprentice undergoing apprenticeship training in a designated trade in an establishment is a trainee and not a worker [Section 18]. Therefore, there is an obligation imposed on the employers to provide practical and basic training to every apprentice engaged by the employers under Section 9 of this Act. Provisions have been made in Section 10 of this Act to give a course of related appropriate instruction to trade apprentices and technical (vocational) apprentices. Now let us consider these provisions.

4.11.1 Provisions relating to Practical and Basic Training

1. Every employer shall make suitable arrangements in his workshop for imparting a course of practical training to every apprentice engaged by him in accordance with the programme approved by the Apprenticeship Adviser [Section 9 (1)].

2. The Central Apprenticeship Adviser or any other person not below the rank of an Assistant Apprenticeship Adviser authorised by the Central Apprenticeship Adviser in writing in this behalf shall be given all reasonable facilities for access to each such apprentice with a view to test his work and to ensure that the practical training is being imparted in accordance with the approved programme [Section 9 (2)].

    It is provided that the State Apprenticeship Adviser or any other person not below the rank of an Assistant Apprenticeship Adviser authorised by the State Apprenticeship Adviser in writing in this behalf shall also be given such facilities in respect of apprentices undergoing training in establishments in relation to which the appropriate Government is the State Government [Proviso to Section 9 (2)].

3. Such of the trade apprentices who have not undergone institutional training in a school or other institution recognised by the National Council or any other institution affiliated to or recognised by the Board or State Council of Technical Education or any other authority which the Central Government may, by notification in the Official Gazette, specify in this behalf, shall, before admission in the workshop for practical training, undergo a course of basic training [Section 9 (3)].

4. Where an employer employs in his establishment five hundred or more workers, the basic training shall be imparted to the trade apprentices either in separate parts of the workshop building or in a separate building which shall be set up by the employer himself, but the appropriate Government may grant loans to the employer on easy terms and repayable by easy installments to meet the cost of the land, construction and equipment for such separate building [Section 9 (4)].

Where an employer has more than one factory at different places and each of them having less than Five Hundred workers, but the total strength of the workers of all the factories belonging to him exceeds Five Hundred workers, all the factories are treated as one unit for the purposes of the applicability of this Act [Shaw Wallace and Company, Ltd. Madras V. Director of Employment and Training, Madras (1977) 51 F.J.R. 208].

5. Notwithstanding anything contained in sub-section (4), if the number of apprentices to be trained at any time in any establishment in which five hundred or more workers are employed, is less than twelve the employer in relation to such establishment may depute all of any such apprentices to any Basic Training Centre or Industrial Training Institute for basic training in any designated trade, in either case, run by the Government [Section 9 (4-A)].

6. Where an employer deputes any apprentice under sub-section (4A), such employer shall pay to the Government the expenses incurred by the Government on such training, at such rate as may be specified by the Central Government [Section 9 (4-B)].

7. Where an employer employs in his establishment less than five hundred workers, the basic training shall be imparted to the trade apprentices in training institutes set up by the Government [Section 9 (5)].

8. In any such training institute, which shall be located within the premises of the most suitable establishment in the locality or at any other convenient place the trade apprentices engaged by two or more employers may be imparted basic training [Section 9 (6)].

9. In the case of an apprentice other than graduate or technician apprentice [technician (vocational) apprentices] the syllabus of, and the equipment to be utilised for, practical training including basic training shall be such as may be approved by the Central Government in consultation with the Central Apprenticeship Council [Section 9 (7)].

10. In the case of graduate or technician apprentices technician (vocational) apprentices the programme of apprenticeship training and the facilities required for such training in any subject field in engineering o technology or vocational course shall be such as may be approved by the Central Government in consultation with the Central Apprenticeship council [Section 9 (7-A)].

11. (a) Recurring costs (including the cost of stipends) incurred by an employer in connection with basic training, imparted to trade apprentices other than those referred to in clauses (a) and (aa) of Section 6 shall be borne –

(i) If such employer employs two hundred and fifty workers or more, by the employer;

(ii) If such employer employs less than two hundred and fifty workers by the employer; and the Government in equal shares up to such limit as may be laid down by the Central Government and beyond that limit, by the employer alone; and,

(b) Recurring costs (including the costs of stipends), if any, incurred by an employer in connection with practical training, including basic training imparted to trade apprentices referred to in clauses (a) and (aa) of Section 6 shall, in every case, be borne by the employer;

(c) Recurring costs (excluding the cost of stipends) incurred by an employer in connection with the practical training imparted to graduate or technician apprentices technician (vocational) apprentices shall be borne by the employer and the cost of stipends shall be borne by the Central Government and the employer in equal shares up to such limit as may be laid down by the Central Government and beyond that limit, by the employer alone [Section 9 (8)].

4.11.2 Provisions of Section 10 relating to 'Related Instruction of Apprentices'

1. A trade apprentice who is undergoing practical training in an establishment shall, during the period of practical training, be given a course of related instruction (which shall be appropriate to the trade) approved by the Central Government in consultation with the Central Apprenticeship Council, with a view to giving the trade apprentice such theoretical knowledge as he needs in order to become fully qualified as a skilled craftsman [Section 10 (1)].

2. Related instruction shall be imparted at the cost of the employer and the employer shall, when so required, afford all facilities for imparting such instruction [Section 10 (2)].

3. Any time spent by a trade apprentice in attending classes on related instruction shall be treated as part of his paid period of work [Section 10 (3)].

4. In the case of trade apprentices who, after having undergone a course of institutional training, have passed the trade tests conducted by the National Council or have passed the trade tests and examinations conducted by a Board or State Council of Technical Education or any other authority which the Central Government may, by notification in the Official Gazette, specify in this behalf, the related instruction may be given on such reduced or modified scale as may be prescribed [Section 10 (4)].

5. Where any person has, during his course in a technical institution, become a graduate or technician apprentice, technician (vocational) apprentice and during his apprenticeship training he has to receive related instruction, then, the employer shall release such person from practical training to receive the related instruction in such institution, for such period as may be specified by the Central Apprenticeship Adviser or by any other person not below the rank of an Assistant Apprenticeship Adviser authorised by the Central Apprenticeship Adviser in writing in this behalf [Section 10 (5)].

4.12 Obligations of Employers and Apprentices

There are certain obligations of employers in relation to the apprentices undergoing training under this Act. These obligations can be studied under the following heads.

(a) Obligations to provide training to the apprentices [Section 11].

(b) Obligation to make payment under Section 13.

(c) Liability of an employer for compensation for injury under Section 16.

(d) Obligation to maintain records and to furnish returns under Section 19.

4.12.1 Obligations of Employers under Section 11

Without prejudice to the other provisions of this Act, every employer shall have the following obligations in relation to an apprentice, namely –

1. to provide the apprentice with the training in his trade in accordance with the provisions of this Act, and the rules made there under [Section 11 (a)].

2. if the employer is not himself qualified in the trade, to ensure that a person who possesses the prescribed qualifications is placed in charge of the training of the apprentice [Section 11 (b)].

3. to provide adequate instructional staff, possessing such qualifications as may be prescribed, for imparting practical and theoretical training and facilities for trade test of apprentices [Section 11 (bb)].

4. to carry out his obligations under the contract of apprenticeship [Section 11 (c)].

4.12.2 Obligation of Payment under Section 13

Section 11 makes it obligatory on the employer to provide training for the apprentices while Section 13 provides for the remuneration. The provisions of Section 13 are as under.

1. The employer shall pay to every apprentice during the period of apprenticeship training such stipend at a rate not less than the prescribed minimum rate, or the rate which was being paid by the employer on 1st January, 1970, to the category of apprentices under which such apprentices falls, whichever is higher as may be specified in the contract of apprenticeship and the stipend so specified shall be paid at such intervals and subject to such conditions as may be prescribed [Section 13 (1)].

2. An apprentice shall not be paid by his employer on the basis of piece work nor shall he be required to take part in any output bonus or other incentive scheme [Section 13 (2)]. Rule 11 of the Apprentices Rules of 1992 lays down the minimum rates of stipend payable to an apprentice. The Rule 11 of the Apprentices Rules of 1992 is as under.

Payment of stipend to apprentices –

1. The minimum rate of stipend payable to trade apprentices shall be as follows, namely:

    (a) During the first year of training — ₹ 2100 per month.
    (b) During the second year of training — ₹ 2400 per month.
    (c) During the third year of training — ₹ 2800 per month.
    (d) During the fourth year of training — ₹ 3100 per month.

   It is also provided that in the case of trade apprentices referred to in clause (a) of Section 6 of the Act, the period of training already undergone by them in a school or other institution recognised by the National Council, shall be taken into account for the purpose of determining the rate of stipend payable. These rates have been made effective from 27th September, 2013.

2. The minimum rates of stipend payable to graduate, technician and technician (vocational) apprentices shall be as follows, namely:

    (a) Graduate Apprentices — ₹ 3560 per month.
    (b) Sandwich Course (Students from Degree Institutions) — ₹ 2530 per month.
    (c) Technician Apprentices — ₹ 2530 per month.
    (d) Sandwich course (Students from Diploma Institutions) — ₹ 2070 per month.
    (e) Technician (Vocational) Apprentices — ₹ 1970 per month.

   The above mentioned rates of stipend have been made effective from 23rd March, 2011.

3. The stipend for a particular month shall be paid by the tenth day of the following month.

4. No deduction shall be made from the stipend for the period during which an apprentice remains on casual leave or medical leave. Stipend shall, however, not be paid for the period for which an apprentice remains on extraordinary leave.

5. Notwithstanding anything contained in this rule, where an establishment has a system of deferred payment whereby only a portion of the stipend is paid to the apprentice every month and the balance is paid to the apprentice on the completion of training, such establishment shall be free to continue such system provided that the minimum amount paid to the apprentices every month shall not

be less than the monthly stipend prescribed under these rules and no deduction is made from the said accumulated amount on any account. Establishments which do not already have such a system shall be free to institute a system on the same conditions.

6. The continuance of payment of stipend to an apprentice shall be subject to the work and conduct of the apprentice being satisfactory.

7. Where the work and conduct of the apprentice is not satisfactory, the employer shall report the matter to the Apprenticeship Adviser and with his consent may stop the continuance of payment of stipend to the apprentices. Provided that the stipend of an apprentice shall not be stopped without intimating him the grounds thereof and giving him an opportunity of representing against the action proposed.

8. On report being made by the employer under sub-rule (7), the Apprenticeship Adviser shall give his decision thereon within 30 days of the receipt of the report and where the Apprenticeship Adviser does not communicate to the employer refusal to consent to the stopping of the payment of stipend within the period of thirty days, it shall be deemed that he has consented to the stopping of the stipend.

4.12.3 Liability of an Employer for Compensation for Injury under Section 16

If personal injury is caused to an apprentice, by accident arising out of and in the course of his training as an apprentice, his employer shall be liable to pay compensation which shall be determined and paid, so far as may be, in accordance with the provisions of the Workmen's Compensation Act, 1923 (8 of 1923), subject to the modifications specified in the Schedule.

4.12.4 Obligation of an Employer in Respect of Maintaining the Records and Furnishing the Returns under Section 19

1. Every employer shall maintain records of the progress of training of each apprentice undergoing apprenticeship training in his establishment in such form as may be prescribed [Section 19 (1)].

2. Every such employer shall also furnish such information and return in such form, to such authorities and at such intervals as may be prescribed [Section 19 (2)].

   The Rule 14 of the Apprentices Rules of 1992 pertains to 'Record and Returns' which is reproduced below.

(i) Establishments referred to in items (b) and (c) of sub-clause (1) of clause (d) of Section 2 of the Act shall submit in respect of trade apprentices returns and other information as hereinafter provided to the respective Regional Director.

(ii) Establishments referred to in item (b) of sub-clause (2) of clause (d) of Section 2 of the Act shall submit in respect of trade apprentices returns and other information as herein under provided to the respective State Apprenticeship Adviser.

3. Contracts of Apprenticeship Training in Format-1 as specified in Schedule-III shall be forwarded along with a forwarding letter in Format 1A as specified in Schedule III, by the establishment to the Regional Director or State Apprenticeship Adviser, as the case may be, as per following schedule:

For the apprentices engaged from 16th January to 15th April : 30th April.
For the apprentices engaged from 16th April to 15th July : 31st July.
For the apprentices engaged from 16th July to 15th October : 31st October.
For the apprentices engaged from 16th October to 15th January : 31st January.

4. Work diary in Format-2, as specified in Schedule-III shall be maintained by each trade apprentice and countersigned by his supervisor once a week.

5. Every employer shall maintain a register of attendance of the trade apprentices undergoing apprenticeship training in his establishment and action taken for irregular and unauthorised absence shall be recorded in the said register at the end of each month.

6. (a) Application forms of regular trade apprentices for appearing at All India Trade Test in Format-3 as specified in Schedule-III shall be forwarded with a forwarding letter in Format-3A as specified in Schedule-III by the establishment to the Regional Director or State Apprenticeship Adviser, as they case may be, as per following schedule:

(i) For All India Trade Test to be held in April/May: 31st December of previous year.

(ii) For All India Trade Test to be held in October/November: 30th June.

(b) Having scrutinised the application forms of such trade apprentices, the Regional director or State Apprenticeship Adviser, as the case may be, shall return the application forms to the employer with remarks whether or not the apprentice is allowed to appear in the All India Trade Test. If allowed it should be subject to fulfillment of eligibility criteria and if disallowed the reasons therefore should be recorded in the application form. The programme of the All India Trade Test and name of the trade testing centers for each apprentice should also be sent along with the application forms of such apprentices.

(c) After receiving the information under clause (b), the employer shall furnish eligibility certificate in respect of the eligible trade apprentices in Format-4 as specified in Schedule-III along with the application forms of such apprentices to the trade testing centers, fifteen days prior to the commencement of the All India Trade Test.

7. At the end of each half year, every establishment shall in respect of trade apprentices receiving training in the establishment submit a report in Form Apprenticeship-1 in Schedule-III to the concerned Apprenticeship Adviser as per the following schedule:

   For half year ending June : By 15th July.

   For half year ending December : By 15th January.

8. At the end of each half year, every Regional Director shall in respect of trade apprentices in the establishments referred to in items (b) and (c) of sub-clause (1) of clause (d) of Section 2 of the Act submit returns in forms ATS-1 & ATS-2 in Schedule-III to the Directorate General of Employment Training as per the following schedule:

   For half year ending June : By 31st July.

   For half year ending December : By 31st January.

9. At the end of each half year, every State Apprenticeship Adviser shall in respect of trade apprentices in the establishments referred to in items (b) of sub-clause (2) of clause (d) of Section 2 of the Act submit returns in forms ATS-1 & ATS-3 in Schedule-III to the Directorate General of Employment Training as per the following schedule:

   For half year ending June : By 31st July.

   For half year ending December : By 31st January.

10. On a Graduate or Technician or Technician (Vocational) apprentice joining an establishment, the employer shall prepare index cards in Form Apprenticeship-2 set out in Schedule-III with complete bio-data and retain one card with himself and forward within ten days from the date of the engagement of the apprentice, one card to each of the following authorities, namely:

    (a) The Central Apprenticeship Adviser,

    (b) The Director, Regional Board of Apprenticeship Training concerned; and

    (c) In the case of Sandwich course student, the Technical Institution concerned.

11. Every employer shall maintain a record of the work done and the studies undertaken by the graduate, technician and technician (Vocational) apprentices engaged in his establishment, for each quarter and at the end of each quarter shall send a report in Form Apprenticeship-3 set out in Schedule-III to the Director, Regional Board of Apprenticeship Training concerned.

4.12.5 Obligations of Apprentices

From the provisions of Sections 12, 13, and 17, we come to know the obligations of the apprentices which are as follows.

(i) Obligations of Trade Apprentices under Section 12 (1) of the Act: Every trade apprentice undergoing apprenticeship training shall have the following obligations, namely –

- (a) to learn his trade conscientiously and diligently and endeavour to qualify himself as a skilled craftsman before the expiry of the period of training;
- (b) to attend the practical and instructional classes regularly;
- (c) to carry out all lawful orders of his employer and superiors in the establishments;
- (d) to carry out his obligations under the contract of apprenticeship.

(ii) Obligations of Graduate or Technician Apprentices under Section 12 (2): Every graduate or technician apprentice technician (vocational) apprentice undergoing apprenticeship training shall have the following obligations, namely –

- (a) to learn his subject field in engineering or technology or vocational course conscientiously and diligently at his place of training;
- (b) to attend the practical and instructional classes regularly;
- (c) to carry out all lawful orders of his employer and superiors in the establishments; and
- (d) to carry out his obligations under the contract of apprenticeship which shall include the maintenance of such records of his work as may be prescribed.

(iii) Payment of Apprentices [Section 13 (2)]: An apprentice is not entitled to receive from his employer any payment on the basis of piece-work or take part in any output bonus or any other incentive scheme.

(iv) Obligations in respect of Conduct and Discipline [Section 17]: In all matters of conduct and discipline, the apprentice shall be governed by the rules and regulations applicable to employees of the corresponding category in the establishment in which the apprentice is undergoing training.

(v) Obligation is respect of Maintaining Record of Work by Apprentices under Rule 10 of the Apprentices Rules of 1992: Every graduate or technician or technician (vocational) apprentice shall maintain a daily record of the work done by him relating to the apprenticeship training in the form of a workshop or laboratory notebook.

4.13 Provisions of Section 14 of the Act relating to "Health, Safety and Welfare of Apprentices"

It is stated in Section 14 of the Act, *"Where any apprentices are undergoing training in a factory, the provisions of Chapters III, IV and V of the Factories Act, 1948 (63 of 1948), shall apply in relation to the health, safety and welfare of the apprentices as if they were workers within the meaning of that Act and when any apprentices are undergoing training in a mine, the provisions of Chapter V of the Mines Act, 1952 (35 of 1952), shall apply in relation to the health and safety of the apprentices as if they were persons employed in the mine."*

4.14 Provisions of Section 15 of the Act relating to "Hours of Work, Overtime, Leave and Holidays"

1. The weekly and daily hours of work of an apprentice while undergoing practical training in a workshop shall be such as may be prescribed [Section 15 (1)].

2. No apprentice shall be required or allowed to work overtime except with the approval of the Apprenticeship Adviser who shall not grant such approval unless he is satisfied that such overtime is in the interest of the training of the apprentice or in the public interest. [Section 15 (2)].

3. An apprentice shall be entitled to such leave as may be prescribed and to such holidays as are observed in the establishment in which he is undergoing training [Section 15 (3)].

   Rule 12 of the Apprentices Rule of 1992 throws light on the hours of work while an apprentice is undergoing the practical training. It is stated in Rule 12 that, "(1) The weekly hours of work of a trade apprentice while undergoing practical training shall be as follows, namely :

   (a) The total number of hours per week shall be 42 to 48 hours (including the time spent on related instruction).

   (b) Trade apprentices undergoing basic training shall ordinarily work for 42 hours per week including the time spent on related instruction.

   (c) Trade apprentices during the second year of apprenticeship shall work for 42 to 48 hours per week including the time spent on related instruction.

   (d) Trade apprentices during the third and subsequent years of apprenticeship shall work for the same number of hours per week as the workers in the trade in the establishment in which the trade apprentice is undergoing apprenticeship training.

(2) No trade apprentice shall be engaged on such training between the hours of 10 : 00 p.m. to 6 : 00 a.m. except with the prior approval of the Apprenticeship Adviser who shall give his approval if he is satisfied that it is in the interest of the training of the trade apprentice or in public interest.

(3) Graduate, technician and technician (vocational) apprentices shall work according to the normal hours of work of the department in the establishment to which they are attached for training."

Rule 13 is related to 'Grant of Leave to Apprentices' in respect of casual leave, medical leave, extraordinary leave etc. This Rule 13 of the Apprentices Rules of 1992 is reproduced below.

1. In establishments where proper leave rules do not exist or the total leave of different types, admissible to their workers is less than thirty-seven days in a year, the apprentice shall be entitled to the following kinds of leave and subject to the conditions specified under each kind of leave.

(a) Casual Leave:
 (i) Casual leave shall be admissible for a maximum period of twelve days in a year.
 (ii) Any holiday intervening during the period of casual leave shall not be counted for the purpose of the limit of twelve days.
 (iii) Casual leave not utilized during any year shall stand lapsed at the end of the year.
 (iv) Casual leave shall not be combined with medical leave. If casual leave is preceded or followed by medical leave, the entire leave taken shall be treated either as medical or casual leave, provided that it shall not be allowed to exceed the maximum period prescribed in respect of medical or casual leave, as the case may be.
 (v) Except in case of extreme urgency, applications for such leave shall be made to the appropriate authority and sanction obtained prior to availing of leave.

(b) Medical Leave:
 (i) Medical leave up to fifteen days for each year of training may be granted to the apprentice who is unable to attend duty owing to illness. The unused leave shall be allowed to accumulate up to a maximum of forty days.
 (ii) Any holiday intervening during the period of medical leave shall be treated as medical leave and accounted for in the limits prescribed under clause (i) above.
 (iii) The employer may call upon the apprentice to produce a medical certificate from a registered medical practitioner in support of his medical leave. A medical certificate shall, however, be necessary if the leave exceeds six days.
 (iv) It shall be open to the employer to arrange a special medical examination of an apprentice if he has reason to believe that the apprentice is not really ill or the illness is not of such a nature as to prevent attendance.

(v) A female apprentice with one surviving child may be granted maternity leave for a period of 90 days from the date of its commencement without payment of stipend and the apprenticeship training period shall be extended accordingly. The monthly stipend shall be paid to the apprentice during such extended period.

(c) Extraordinary Leave:

1. Extraordinary leave up to a maximum of ten days or more in a year may be granted to the apprentice, after he has exhausted the entire casual and medical leave, if the employer is satisfied with the genuineness of the grounds, on which the leave is applied for.

2. In establishments where proper leave rules exist for workers, the leave to apprentices shall be granted by the employers in accordance with those rules provided that in the case of trade apprentices grant of such leave shall be subject to the following conditions, namely -

(a) that every apprentice engaged in an establishment which works for five days in a week (with a total of 45 hours per week) shall put in a minimum attendance of 200 days in a year out of which one-sixth, namely, 33 days shall be devoted to related instructions and 167 days to practical training.

(b) that every apprentice engaged in an establishment which works for five and half days or six days in a week shall put in a minimum attendance of 240 days in a year, out of which one-sixth, namely 40 days, shall be devoted to related instruments and 200 days to practical training;

(c) an apprentice who for any reason is not able to undergo training for the period specified in clause (a) or clause (b), shall be given an opportunity to make up for the shortfall in the following year and shall be eligible to take the test conducted by the National Council -

(i) If he is engaged in an establishment referred to in clause (a) only if he has completed the period of training and has put in a minimum attendance of 600 days or 800 days accordingly as the period of training is three years or four years.

(ii) if he is engaged in an establishment referred to in clause (b) only if he has completed the period of training and has put in a minimum attendance of 720 days or 900 days accordingly as the period of training is three years or four years.

3. If the trade apprentice is not able to put in the minimum period of attendance specified in clause (c) of the proviso to sub-rule (2) during the period of training for circumstances beyond his control and the employer is satisfied with the grounds for shortfall in attendance and certifies that the apprentice has otherwise completed the full apprenticeship course, he shall be considered as having completed the full period of training and shall be eligible to take the test conducted by the National Council.

4. If a trade apprentice is not able to put in the minimum period of apprenticeship specified in clause (c) of the proviso in sub-rule (2) during the period of training and has not completed the full apprenticeship course, he shall not be considered as having completed the full period of training and the employer shall, under sub-rule (2) of Rule 7, extend his period of training until he completes the full apprenticeship course and the next test is held.

4.15 Settlement of Disputes [Section 20]

According to Section 18, apprentices are trainees and not workers. It is stated in Section 18 that : *(a) every apprentice undergoing apprenticeship training in a designated trade in an establishment shall be a trainee and not a worker, and (b) the provisions of any law with respect to labour shall not apply to or in relation to such apprentice,"* From this point of view, provisions relating to the settlement of disputes have been made in Section 20 which are as follows.

1. Any disagreement or dispute between an employer and an apprentice arising out of the contract to apprenticeship shall be referred to the Apprenticeship Adviser for decision [Section 20 (1)].

2. Any person aggrieved by the decision of the Apprenticeship Adviser under sub-section (1) may, within thirty days from the date of communication to him of such decision, prefer an appeal against the decision to the Apprenticeship Council and such appeal shall be heard and determined by a Committee of that Council appointed for the purpose [Section 20 (2)].

3. The decision of the Committee under sub-section (2) and subject only to such decision, the decision of the Apprenticeship Adviser under sub-section (1) shall be final [Section 20 (3)].

An apprentice was appointed and he served for 240 days. He claimed that since he worked for more than 240 days, his removal from service should be treated as retrenchment and his removal violates Section 25-F of the Industrial Disputes Act of 1947. It was contented by the employer that the respondent was only an apprentice and hence not entitled to the protection of Section 25 of the I.D. Act, 1947. It was held that the apprentice was not a worker and the Section 25-F of the I.D. Act would have no application [The National Small Industries V. Lakshminarayan case 2007 I L.L.J. 571 (S.C.)].

4.16 Holding of Test, Grant of Certificate to Apprentices and Conclusion of Training [Section 21]

When the test should be held and the certificate of proficiency in the trade to be granted to an apprentice is made clear in the provisions of Section 21 of the Act. It is stated in Section 21 of the Act that,

"(1) Every trade apprentice who has completed the period of training shall appear for a test to be conducted by the National Council to determine his proficiency in the designated trade in which he has undergone his apprenticeship training [Section 21 (1)].

(2) Every trade apprentice who passes the test referred to in sub-section (1) shall be granted a certificate of proficiency in the trade by the National Council [Section 21 (2)].

(3) The progress in apprenticeship training of every graduate or technician apprentice technician (vocational) apprentice shall be assessed by the employer from time to time [Section 21 (3)].

(4) Every graduate or technician apprentice or technician (vocational) apprentice who completes his apprenticeship training to the satisfaction of the concerned Regional Board, shall be granted a certificate of proficiency by that Board [Section 21 (4)].

4.17 Offer and Acceptance of Employment under Section 22 of the Act

According to Section 22 of the Act, the employer is not bound to offer or to provide any employment to any apprentice who completes the period of training in his establishment. It is also not obligatory on any apprentice to accept the employment under the employer. The provisions relating to offer and acceptance of employment under Section 22 are as follows.

1. It shall not be obligatory on the part of the employer to offer any employment to any apprentice who has completed the period of his apprenticeship training in his establishment, nor shall it be obligatory on the part of the apprentice to accept an employment under the Section 22 (1).

2. Notwithstanding anything in sub-section (1), where there is a condition in a contract of apprenticeship that the apprentice shall, after the successful completion of the apprenticeship training, serve the employer, the employer shall, on such completion, be bound to offer suitable employment to the apprentice, and the apprentice shall be bound to serve the employer in that capacity for such period and on such remuneration as may be specified in the contract [Section 22 (2)].

It is provided that where such period on remuneration is not, in the opinion of the Apprenticeship Adviser, reasonable, he may revise such period of remuneration so as to make it reasonable and the period of remuneration so revised shall be deemed to be the period or remuneration agreed to between the apprentice and the employer [Proviso to Section 22 (2)].

Provisions of Section 22 (2) make it clear that an apprentice after the completion of his training has to serve the employer if there is any such condition in the contract of apprenticeship for the remuneration as per the provisions.

4.18 The Authorities Appointed under the act for the Administration of the Act

For the purpose of the administration of this Act, provisions have been made to appoint certain authorities in Section 23 of this Act. It is stated in Section 23 of this Act that –

1. In addition to the Government, there shall be the following authorities under this Act, namely –

    (i) The National Council,

    (ii) The Central Apprenticeship Council,

    (iii) The State Council,

    (iv) The State Apprenticeship Council,

    (v) The All India Council,

    (vi) The Regional Boards,

    (vii) The Boards or State Council of Technical Education

    (viii) The Central Apprenticeship Adviser, and

    (ix) The state Apprenticeship Adviser [Section 23 (1)].

2. Every State Council shall be affiliated to the National Council and every State Apprenticeship Council shall be affiliated to the Central Apprenticeship Council [Section 23 (2)]. It is further stated in Section 23 (2-A) that, every Board or State Council of Technical Education and every regional board shall be affiliated to the Central Apprenticeship Council.

3. Each of the authorities specified in sub-section (1) shall, in relation to apprenticeship training under this Act, perform such functions as are assigned to it by or under this Act or by the Government [Section 23 (3)]. It is also provided that the State Council also performs such functions as are assigned to it by the National Council and the State Apprenticeship Council and the Board or State Council of Technical Education shall also perform such functions as are assigned to it by the Central Apprenticeship Council [Proviso to Section 23 (3)].

4.18.1 Constitution of Councils

1. The Central Government shall, by Notification in the Official Gazette, establish the Central Apprenticeship Council and the State Government shall, by Notification in the Official Gazette, establish the State Apprenticeship Council [Section 24 (1)].

2. The Central Apprenticeship Council shall consist of a Chairman and a Vice-Chairman and such number of other members as the Central Government may think expedient, to be appointed by that Government by notification in the Official Gazette from among the following categories of persons, namely –

(a) representatives of employers in establishment in the public and private sectors;
(b) representatives of the Central Government and of the State Government;
(c) persons having special knowledge and experience on matters relating to industry, labour and technical education, and
(d) representatives of the All India Council and of the Regional Boards [Section 24 (2)].

3. The number of persons to be appointed as members of the Central Apprenticeship Council from each of the categories specified in sub-section (2), the term of office of, the procedure to be followed in the discharge of their functions by, and the manner of filling vacancies among, the members of the Council shall be such as may be prescribed [Section 24 (3)].

4. The State Apprenticeship Council shall consist of a Chairman and A Vice-Chairman and such number of other members as the State Government may think expedient, to be appointed by the Government by notification in the Official Gazette, from among the following categories of persons, namely –
(a) representatives of employers in establishments in the public and private sectors;
(b) representatives of the Central Government and of the State Government;
(c) person having special knowledge and experience on matters relating to industry, labour and technical education, and
(d) representatives of the Board or of the State Council of Technical Education [Section 24 (4)].

5. The number of persons to be appointed as members of the State Apprenticeship Council from each of the categories specified in sub-section (4), the term of office of, the procedure to be followed in the discharge of their functions by, and the manner of filling vacancies among, the members of the Council shall be such as the State Government may, by notification in the Official Gazette, determine [Section 24 (5)].

6. The fees and allowances, if any, to be paid to the Chairman and the Vice-Chairman and the other members of the Central Apprenticeship Council, shall be such as may be determined by the Central Government and the fees and allowances, if any, to be paid to the Chairman and the Vice-Chairman and the other members of the State Apprenticeship Council shall be such as may be determined by the State Government [Section 24 (6)].

We can note the following important points considering the provisions of Sections 23 and 24 of this Act.
(a) The Central Government is one of the authorities to administer this Act and it has established the National Council for Vocational Training i.e. National Council.
(b) The Central Government has established the Central Apprenticeship Council. It consists of a chairman, a vice-chairman, and such number of other members as the Central Government may think expedient to be appointed. The Central Government appoints from among the categories of persons by notification in the Official Gazette as mentioned in Section 24 (2).

(c) All the authorities specified in Section 23 (1) have to perform all such functions as are assigned to them in relation to apprenticeship training under this Act and as are asked by the Central Government. The State Council has also to perform all such functions as are assigned to it by the National Council and the State Council of Technical Education. The Board or State Council of Technical Education has to perform all such functions as are assigned to it by the Central Apprenticeship Council [Section 23 (3)].

(d) The State Government has established State Apprenticeship Council. Every such state council is affiliated to the Central Apprenticeship Council. It performs many functions including the functions assigned to it by the Central Apprenticeship Council. The State Apprenticeship Council consists of a chairman, vice-chairman and members as per the provisions of Section 24 (4).

(e) The fees and allowances, if any, to be paid to the chairman, vice-chairman, and other members of the Central Apprenticeship Council and the State Apprenticeship Council are determined by the Central Government and the State Government respectively [Section 24 (6)].

4.18.2 Vacancies not to Invalidate acts and Proceedings [Section 25]

It is clearly stated in Section 25 of this Act that *"No act done or proceeding taken by the National Council, the Central Apprenticeship Council, the State Council or the State Apprenticeship Council under this Act shall be questioned on the ground merely of the existence of any vacancy in , or defect in the constitution of such Council."*

4.18.3 Appointments of the Central Apprenticeship Adviser and the State Apprenticeship Adviser [Section 26]

It is stated in Section 26 that,

"(1) The Central Government shall, by notification in the Official Gazette, appoint a suitable person as the Central Apprenticeship Adviser [Section 26 (1)].

(2) The State Government shall, by notification in the Official Gazette, appoint a suitable person as the State Apprenticeship Adviser [Section 26 (2)].

(3) The Central Apprenticeship Adviser shall be the Secretary to the Central Apprenticeship Council and the State Apprenticeship Adviser shall be the Secretary to the State Apprenticeship Council [Section 26 (3)]."

4.18.4 Appointments of Deputy Advisers and Assistant Apprenticeship Advisers [Section 27]

1. The Government may appoint suitable persons as Additional, Joint, Regional, Deputy and Assistant Apprenticeship Advisers to assist the Apprenticeship Adviser, in the performance of his functions [Section 27 (1)].

2. Every Additional, Joint, Regional, Deputy and Assistant Apprenticeship Advisers shall, subject to control of the Apprenticeship Advisor, perform such functions as may be assigned to him by the Apprenticeship Adviser [Section 27 (2)].

4.18.5 Powers of the Entry, Inspection etc. of the Apprenticeship Advisers under Section 29 of the Act

1. Subject to any rules made in this behalf, the Central Apprenticeship Adviser, or such other person, not below the rank of an Assistant Apprenticeship Adviser, as may be authorised by the Central Apprenticeship Adviser in writing in this behalf may –

(a) with such assistants, if any, as he thinks fit, enter, inspect and examine any establishment or part thereof at any reasonable time;

(b) examine any apprentice employed therein or require the production of any register, record or other documents maintained in pursuance of this Act and take on the spot or otherwise statements of any person which he may consider necessary for carrying out the purposes of this Act;

(c) make such examination and inquiry as he thinks fit in order to ascertain whether the provisions of this Act and the rules laid thereunder are being observed in the establishment;

(d) exercise such other powers as may be prescribed [Section 29 (1)]. It is also provided that a State Apprenticeship Adviser or such other person, not below the rank of an Assistant Apprenticeship Adviser, as may be authorised by the State Apprenticeship Adviser in writing in this behalf may also exercise any of the powers specified in clauses (a), (b), (c), or (d) of this sub-section in relation to establishments for which the appropriate Government is the State Government [Proviso to Section 29 (1)].

2. Notwithstanding anything in sub-section (1), no person shall be compelled under this section to answer any question or make any statement which may tend directly or indirectly to incriminate him [Section 29 (2)]. To incriminate means to indicate as involved in wrong doing.

4.18.6 Under Section 28 the Apprenticeship Advisers are the Public Servants

"Every Apprenticeship Adviser and every Additional, Joint, Regional, Deputy or Assistant Apprenticeship Adviser appointed under this Act, shall be deemed to be a public servant within the meaning of Section 21 of the Indian Penal code (45 of 1860)."

4.18.7 Provisions of Section 34 relating to 'Delegation of Powers'

By notification in the Official Gazette, the Appropriate Government may direct that any power exercisable by it under this Act, or the rules made there under shall, in relation to such matters and subject to such conditions, if any, as may be specified in the direction, be exercisable also –

(a) where the appropriate Government is the Central Government, by such officer or authority subordinate to the Central Government or by the State Government or by such officer or authority subordinate to the State Government, as may be specified in the notification; and
(b) where the appropriate Government is the State Government, by such officer or authority subordinate to the State Government, as may be specified in the notification." [Section 34]

4.19 Offences and Penalties

Provisions relating to offences and penalties in respect to the employers or any other persons so far as engaging the unqualified person as an apprentice, failing to carry out the terms and conditions of the contract of apprenticeship etc. have been made in Section 30, while offences in respect of companies have been made clear in Section 32. It is also mentioned in Section 31 how much fine should be imposed where no specific penalty is provided. It is stated in Section 31 that *"if any employer or any other person contravenes any provision of this Act for which no punishment is provided in Section 30, he shall be punishable will fine which shall not be less than one thousand rupees, but may extend to three thousand rupees."*

4.19.1 Nature of Offences and Penalties for those Offences in respect of any Employer or any Other Person [Section 30]

1. **If any employer –**
    (a) engages as an apprentice a person who is not qualified for being so engaged, or
    (b) fails to carry out the terms and conditions of a contract of apprenticeship, or
    (c) contravenes the provisions of this Act relating to the number of apprentices which he is required to engage under those provisions, he shall be punishable with imprisonment for a term which may extend to six months or with fine or with both [Section 30 (1)].

2. **If any employer or any other person –**
    (a) required to furnish any information or return –
        (i) refuses or neglects to furnish such information or return, or
        (ii) furnishes or causes to be furnished any information or return which is false and which he either knows or believes to be false or does not believe to be true, or
        (iii) refuses to answer, or gives a false answer to any question necessary for obtaining any information required to be furnished by him, or
    (b) refuses or wilfully neglect to afford the Central or the State Apprenticeship Adviser or such other person, not below the rank of an Assistant Apprenticeship Adviser, as may be authorised by the Central or the State Apprenticeship Adviser in writing in this behalf any reasonable facility for making any entry, inspection, examination or inquiry authorised by or under this Act, or

(c) requires an apprentice to work overtime without the approval of the Apprenticeship Adviser, or
(d) employs an apprentice on any work which is not connected with his training, or
(e) makes payment to an apprentice on the basis of piece-work, or
(f) requires an apprentice to take part in any output bonus or incentive scheme, he shall be punishable with imprisonment for a term which may extend to six months or with fine or with both []Section 30 (2).

4.19.2 Offences by Companies [Section 32]

1. If the person committing an offence under this Act is a company, every person who, at the time the offence was committed was in charge of, and was responsible to, the company for the conduct of business of the company, as well as the company, shall be deemed to be guilty of the offence and shall be liable to be proceeded against and punished accordingly [Section 32 (1)].

It is also provided that nothing contained in this sub-section shall render any such person liable to such punishment provided in this Act if he proves that the offence was committed without his knowledge or that he exercise all due diligence to prevent the commission of such offence [Proviso to Section 32 (1)].

2. Notwithstanding anything contained in sub-section (1), where an offence under this Act has been committed by a company and it is proved that the offence has been committed with the consent or connivance of, or is attributable to any negligence on the part of, any director, manager, secretary, or other officer of the company, such director, manager, secretary, or other officer shall also be deemed to be guilty of that offence and shall be liable to be proceeded against and punished accordingly [Section 32 (2)]. In the explanation to Section 32, it is stated that, *"For the purposes of this Section –*

(a) *"company" means a body corporate and includes a firm or other association of individuals; and*
(b) *"director" in relation to a firm means a partner in the firm."*

4.20 Cognizance of Offences [Section 33]

It is stated in Section 33 that, "No court shall take cognizance of any offence under this Act or the rules made thereunder except on a complaint thereof in writing made by the Apprenticeship Adviser or the officer of the rank of Deputy Apprenticeship Adviser and above within six months from the date on which the offence is alleged to have been committed."

4.21 Miscellaneous Provisions of the Act

4.21.1 Provisions of Section 35 relating to "Construction of References"

1. Any reference in this Act or in the rules made thereunder to the Apprenticeship Council shall, unless the context otherwise requires, means in relation to apprenticeship training in a designated trade in an establishment in relation to which the Central Government is the appropriate Government, the Central Apprenticeship Council and in

relation to apprenticeship training in a designated trade in an establishment in relation to which the State Government is the appropriate Government, the State Apprenticeship Council [Section 35 (1)].

2. Any reference in this Act or in the rules made thereunder to the Apprenticeship Adviser shall, unless the context otherwise requires –

   (a) means in relation to apprenticeship training in a designated trade in an establishment in relation to which the Central Government is the appropriate Government, the Central Apprenticeship Adviser and in relation to apprenticeship training in a designated trade in an establishment in relation to which the State Government is the appropriate Government, the State Apprenticeship Adviser;

   (b) deemed to include an Additional, a Joint, a Regional, a Deputy or an Assistant Apprenticeship Adviser performing the functions of the Apprenticeship Adviser assigned to him under sub-section (2) of Section 27 [Section 35 (2)].

4.21.2 Protection of Action Taken in Good Faith

"No suit, prosecution or other legal proceeding shall lie against any person for anything which is in good faith done or intended to be done under this Act." [Section 36]

4.21.3 Power to Make Rules [Section 37]

1. The Central Government may, after consulting the Central Apprenticeship Council, by notification in the Official Gazette, make rules for carrying out the purposes of this Act [Section 37 (1)].

2. Rules made under this Act may provide that a contravention of any such rule shall be punishable with fine which may extend to fifty rupees [Section 37 (2)].

3. Every rule made under this section shall be laid as soon as may be after it is made before each House of Parliament while it is in session for a total period or thirty days which may be comprised in one session or in two or more successive sessions, and if before the expiry of the session immediately following the session or the successive sessions aforesaid both Houses agree in making any modification in the rules or both Houses agree that the rule should not be made, the rule shall thereafter have effect only in such modified form or be of no effect, as the case may be; so however that any such modification or annulment shall be without prejudice to the validity of anything previously done under that rule [Section 37 (3)].

Points to Remember

- The basic objective of this Act is to regulate the training of apprentices and the control the training of apprentices.
- A person who is engaged to undergo a course of apprenticeship training under an employer in pursuance of a contract of apprenticeship is called an apprentice.

- An apprentice is not a worker and is paid stipend.
- A person is not qualified for being engaged as an apprentice unless he is not less than fourteen years of age.
- There are provisions relating to obligations of an employer and of an apprentice.
- The employer is required to pay a stipend to every apprentice during the apprenticeship training period.
- There are certain authorities appointed to administer the Act under Section 23 of the Act.
- The Act extends to the whole of India and is applicable to any area or any industry in the area if the Central Government specifies that area or industry to which it shall apply by notifications in the Official Gazette.
- There are provisions in Section 30 relating to offences and penalties for those offences.

Questions for Discussion

1. Define and explain the following terms.
   (a) Apprentice and Apprenticeship training
   (b) Designated trade
   (c) Appropriate Government
   (d) Employer
   (e) Establishments in private and public sector
   (f) Technical (vocational) apprentice
2. Explain the objects and applicability of the Act.
3. What are the qualifications for being engaged as an apprentice? Is an apprentice a worker under this Act?
4. What are the terms and conditions contained in a contract of apprenticeship? Must such a contract be registered?
5. What can be the number of apprentices in a designated trade?
6. Explain the provisions of the Act relating to a contract of apprenticeship and novation of a contract of apprenticeship.
7. Explain the obligations of employers and apprentices under a contract of apprenticeship.
8. When is a contract of apprenticeship terminated?
9. What are the provisions of the Act relating to work, overtime, leave, and holidays of an apprentice?

10. Explain the provisions of the Act relating to practical and basic training of apprentices and related instruction of apprentices.
11. What are the authorities under this Act? State their functions.
12. Explain the provisions of the Act as regards the penalties for various offences.
13. When does a contract of apprenticeship terminate?
14. Write short notes on the following.
    (a) The Authorities under the Act
    (b) Period of apprenticeship training
    (c) Novation of contract of apprenticeship
    (d) Offer and acceptance of employment
    (e) Settlement of disputes
    (f) Protection of action in good faith
    (g) Offences and penalties under the Act

Practical Problems

1. In what way can the conflict between the provision of Section 2 (5) of the Industrial Disputes Act according to which an apprentice is a workman and Section 18 of the Apprentices Act which says that an apprentice is not a worker be resolved?

   [**Hint:** The conflict can be resolved by applying the principle of harmonious construction so that each provision may operate without encroaching on the field of other. If a person is appointed as an apprentice under the Apprentices Act would not be a workman under Section 2 (5) of the I.D. Act. But a person designated as an apprentice but is not governed by the apprentices Act would be a workman under Section 2 (5) of the I.D. Act.]

2. Mr. X was appointed as an apprentice under the Apprenticeship Act in designated trade on 26-04-2012 and his service was terminated on 01-05-2014. Mr. X claimed that as he served for more than 240 days, his removal from service should be treated as retrenchment and his removal violated Section 25-F of the I.D. Act. Could he get protection under Section 25-F of the I.D. Act?

   [**Hint:** No. The services of Mr. X were not regularised and was not brought on the rolls of permanent employment. Hence Mr. X was not a workman but only apprentice.]

3. XYZ Co. has five factories at different places and each of them has less than 500 workers employed. However, the total strength of the workers of all the five

factories is about 1200. Can all these five factories be treated as one unit for the purpose of the applicability of this Act?

[**Hint:** Yes. Refer Section 9 (4) of the Act.]

4. Mr. X completed necessary apprenticeship training in the ABC company. Thereafter, he was called for interview but was not selected. Could the ABC company be compelled to appoint Mr. X?

[**Hint:** No. Refer Section 22 (1) of the Act.]

5. Mr. X completed the initial period of apprenticeship. This period was extended by three months. But his performance was bad during the extended period and hence, he was terminated. Could he claim for automatic confirmation and compensation?

[**Hint:** No. Refer Sections 7 and 22. No automatic confirmation on the completion of initial training period and no entitlement for any compensation].

www.ingramcontent.com/pod-product-compliance
Lightning Source LLC
Chambersburg PA
CBHW082232180426
43200CB00037B/2853